POSTCARD HISTORY SERIES

Hamilton

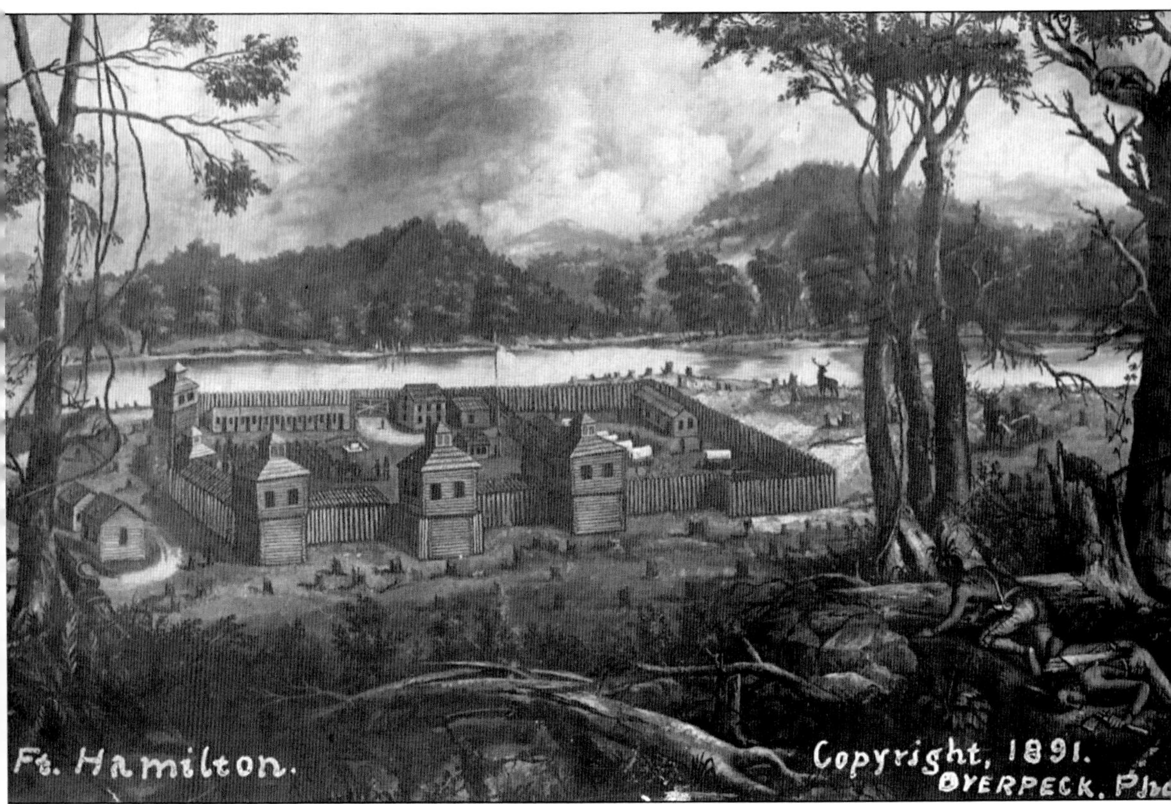

After the Indian attack in 1791 at Dunlap's Station, located near present-day Ross and Bevis, Ohio, the government ordered an amassing of troops at Fort Washington under the lead of Gen. Arthur St. Clair for an expedition up the Great Miami River to combat perceived Indian atrocities. The Army began its march in early September 1791, and by the 16th of that month, they had reached a spot alongside the river that was determined to be a prime location for the construction of a base of operations for upcoming fighting. Plans and construction began the next day, and Fort Hamilton, named after Secretary of the Treasury Alexander Hamilton, was born.

FRONT COVER: This is a view of the north side of High Street decorated for the 80th annual State of Ohio Odd Fellows Convention, held in Hamilton from June 18 to June 21, 1912 (see page 14 for additional information).

BACK COVER: This scene was captured outside the Duersch Cycle Company sometime in 1913, showing off the latest Merkel and Yale models of motorized cycles in front of the North Third Street business (see page 115 for additional information).

Postcard History Series

Hamilton

Brian Smith

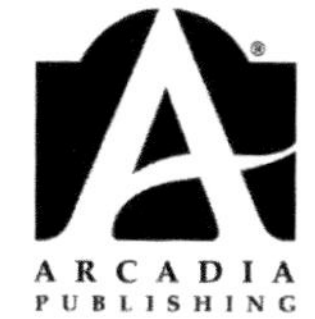

ARCADIA PUBLISHING

ISBN 978-1-4671-1502-5

Published by Arcadia Publishing
Charleston, South Carolina

Printed in the United States of America

Library of Congress Control Number: 2015942536

For all general information contact Arcadia Publishing at:
Telephone 843-853-2070
Fax 843-853-0044
E-mail sales@arcadiapublishing.com
For customer service and orders:
Toll-Free 1-888-313-2665

Visit us on the Internet at www.arcadiapublishing.com

Dedicated to the memory of Kenneth Smith,
who taught me the value of learning.

Contents

Acknowledgments

Creating this historical look back at the city of Hamilton was truly a labor of love. I wish to thank all of my friends and colleagues who gave their support and kind words during the past several months. Your friendship and interest means a great deal. Many thanks go out to Kathy Creighton, executive director of the Butler County Historical Society (BCHS) for allowing me to sort through the albums of cards on hand in the society's archives. Her time and assistance made my job all the easier. I would also like to express my appreciation of the entire BCHS family, from staff and volunteers to trustees. Your commitment to preserving our local history is not only admirable, but crucial, and I am proud and privileged to be a part of it. In addition, I express my thanks to fellow author and BCHS member Rich Piland for his thoughtful advice on navigating the publishing process. Speaking of the publishing process, I would be greatly remiss if I did not take the time to extend my gratitude to Sarah Gottlieb and Betsy Poore, as well as the entire Arcadia Publishing team, in making this volume a reality. I appreciate your dedication, time, and efforts.

Numerous local historians, past and present, have paved the way and provided inspiration for this work, including Jim Blount, Alta Harvey Heiser, Esther Benzing, George Crout, Stephen Cone, George Cummins, and many others. I encourage the reader to follow their examples. Get involved in preserving our past—it will make our future better.

Most importantly, I want to thank my family. Your constant excitement about the project and heartfelt encouragement have made this endeavor a rich and memorable experience and one that I will treasure the rest of my days. Thank you so much for being there and sharing it with me.

Unless otherwise noted, all postcards appear courtesy of the author's collection.

Introduction

The front-page headlines of publisher Homer Gard's *Butler County Democrat* for May 19, 1898, blared out in large letters, "Cuban Waters Will Soon Witness the Greatest Naval Battle of History—Spain's Fleet is to be Crushed." Numerous columns were dedicated to reporting on the war with Spain, both in Cuba and in the Philippines. Elsewhere in the paper, the Cincinnati and Hamilton Street Railway Company announced its offices would be located in the Lohmann Building in downtown Hamilton and that the interurban trip from Hamilton to Fountain Square in Cincinnati would take an hour and 20 minutes. The Detroit and Cleveland Navigation Company's Coast Line advertised summer cruises from Toledo or Cleveland to Mackinac Island for $24 per week, and Krebs & Company, located on Third and High Streets, advertised men's spring and summer suits from $7.50 to $12.50 during their war sale. A story that did not make the news that Thursday, yet would prove to have a profound effect on American society, was that Congress had approved a new special rate for mailed cards, dropping the price from 2¢ to 1¢. The 1898 Congressional act also specified that the words "Private Mailing Card" appear on the address side of the card. Private citizens could now send printed cards at the same reduced rate as businesses. The postcard, as most know it, was essentially born, and soon the country would be wild over collecting the images found on them.

The private mailing card of 1898 had an older cousin, known as the government-issued postal card of 1873. This simple card had a 1¢ stamp illustration in the upper right corner, while the opposite side of the card was blank. The cards were initially to be used for commercial and business posts; however, countless individuals used the cards to send personal messages. When spotted by postal personnel, such cards were returned to the sender citing misuse of the card for personal messages. A new development in 1893 added to the growing postal card dilemma. At the World's Columbian Exposition in Chicago, numerous publishers added printed images and views of the event onto the postal cards and sold them as souvenirs. These cards are considered the forefathers to the postcard of the early 20th century, but at the time, they added to the public confusion concerning the use of government postal cards in non-business uses. The confusion was costly and time-consuming. The general public and the postal service demanded a fix to the situation, and in 1898 Congress obliged with the private mailing card. By 1901, the postmaster ordered the private mailing card text be altered to simply "postcard."

From 1902 to 1907, a sender's written message was required to be on the image side of a picture postcard. In order to accommodate this writing, most cards of this era had a white margin along the bottom or sides of the card, which reduced the overall image size. The back side of the card was used entirely for the address, but in March 1907, the address side of cards was split, allowing for a larger message to be written on the back of the card. Images could now be enlarged to cover the entire front of the card, and the divided-back era began.

The first decade and a half of the 20th century is considered to be the golden age of postcards. Several factors led to the interest of postcards in the United States. Cost was certainly a factor. During this time, a letter cost 3¢ to mail, but a postcard cost only 1¢ and did not need an envelope. The creation of Rural Free Delivery (RFD) opened up large new expanses of postal customers and created an ease for folks outside of large cities to receive and send mail. The Eastman Kodak Company also added to the postcard craze. In 1902, Kodak created a special paper for the printing of postcards and in 1903, the company introduced the No. 3A Folding Pocket Camera, which utilized postcard-sized film and allowed the general public to take photographs and then have those images printed onto postcard backs. Kodak went a step further in 1907 and introduced the real-photo postcard developing service, which let customers make a postcard out of any photograph taken from any model camera. By 1910, thanks to inexpensive quality equipment and simple developing methods, both professionals and amateurs were turning out real-photo postcards for commercial, civic, and informational purposes as well as personal use. Prominent Hamilton photographers of this era, including C. Stanford Jacobi, Lucian C. Overpeck, Edward W. Seegmueller, C.M. Young, and others, regularly photographed local scenes, events, and landmarks for postcard sales. The 1913 flood is a prime example of such an event. After the water receded, C.S. Jacobi reportedly published and sold 15 different books and collections of his flood images in addition to estimated sales of 13,000–15,000 postcards.

Postcards became a sign of civic pride and advertisement. Publishing houses, including the Rotograph Company of New York, Curt Teich & Company of Chicago, and the Kraemer Art Company of Cincinnati, sent photographers throughout Southwest Ohio and beyond to capture images of any and every small village, large city, and midsize town in between. Hamilton architects such as Max Reutti, George W. Barkman, and Frederick G. Mueller had their structures and designs splashed on the fronts of cards sold locally at drugstores and stationery shops. Large national retailers, including S.H. Knox and Company, and even small local store owners like Frank M. Heck actually published their own series of cards. Consequently, images of Hamilton's industrial might, its religious, civic, and educational edifices, and its quaint tree-lined residential streets were mailed across the nation and around the globe.

By 1915, the postcard phenomenon had reached its peak, but it was not to last. Due to Germany's advanced lithographic processes and techniques, many of the top postcard publishers had their images printed in Berlin and other German cities. World War I forced the end of this business practice, and US publishers were forced to scale back on quality, ushering in the white border era (1915–1930) Between the war and the inclusion of a telephone in many American households, the golden age came to a close. Though real-photo cards continued to thrive, the printing of cards went through another phase during the 1930s and 1940s. Printed images during this time more closely resembled artistic sketches and were printed using colorful inks on paper with a linen-like texture. This now highly nostalgic style was popular through the 1950s. The linen era was eventually replaced by the Photochrome card—color photographic images printed on glossy paper—beginning in the late 1940s and extending to the present day. Currently, postcards have nearly come full circle back to their beginnings as an intended tool for commercial use. Businesses now send out the vast majority of mailed postcards; however, the postcard does still exist and is still sent from picturesque vacation destinations.

The majority of cards contained in this volume come from the aforementioned golden age of postcards, but examples from all eras and of all styles are included. These cards present a distinct look at how Hamilton has changed throughout the decades. They demonstrate how the city saw itself at select moments in time, as well as how it was perceived by the rest of the country and the world.

One

Downtown

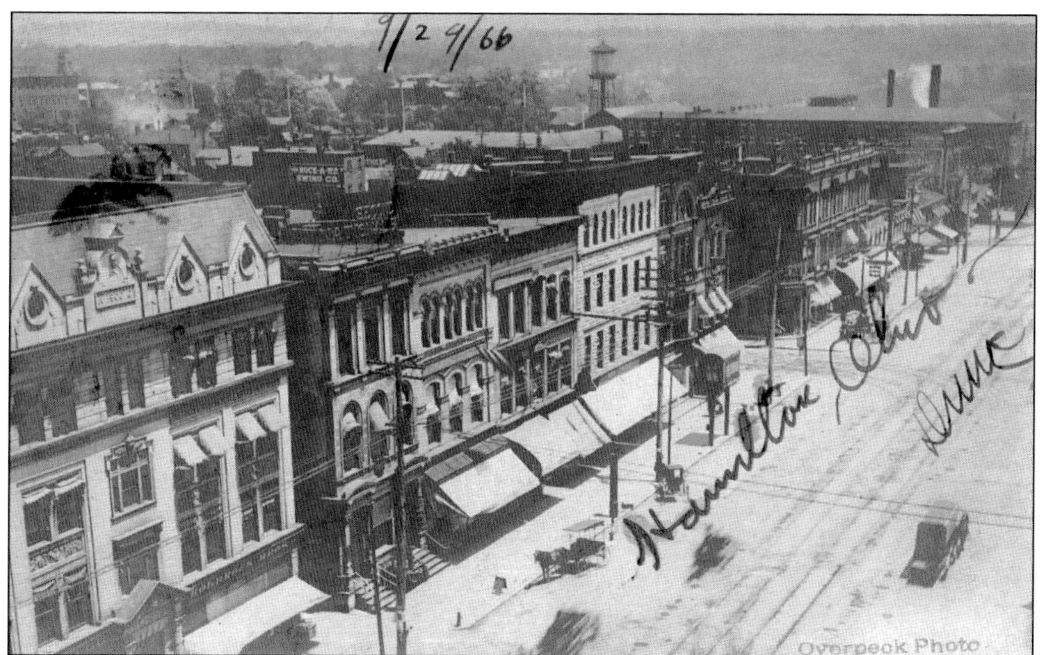

This is a real-photo postcard taken in 1905 from the roof of the Rentschler Building, viewing High Street to the east. The Mehrum Building (left), built in 1900, went through a major restoration and renovation project in 2014 and 2015. The buildings on the block that still remained in 2012, from the Mehrum Building east to the corner of Third Street, were also renovated as the Mercantile Buildings, part of an ongoing community push for downtown revitalization. Numerous renovation and reuse projects are springing up throughout the downtown area, including retail, restaurants, professional services, living spaces, commercial, and public spaces.

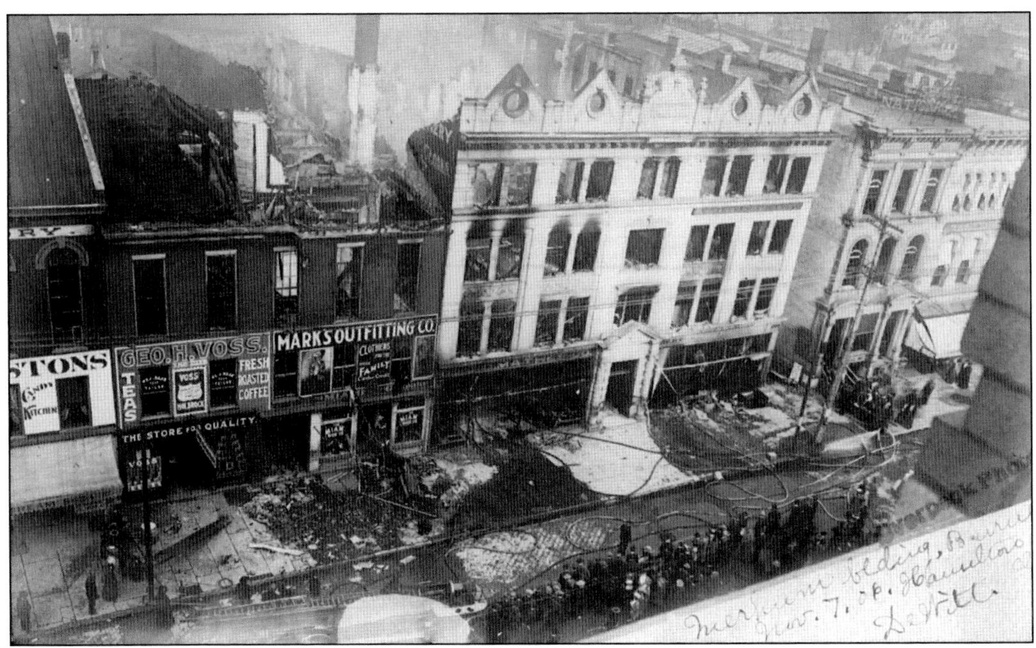

Shortly before 1:00 a.m. on Wednesday, November 7, 1906, a tremendous inferno gutted the Mehrum Building, leaving only its front facade intact. It is believed the blaze began in the millinery department of the C.D. Mathes Dry Goods Company. Fire companies No. 1 through No. 3 were initially called to battle the fire, but after fire chief William C. Dowty witnessed the scene, he immediately called in companies No. 4 and No. 5 as well, and all available hoses were laid out for use. The Mary Millikin Building to the west was heavily damaged, but the Second National Bank Building to the east fared far better. The total cost of the blaze topped over $400,000 for all structures involved. By 3:00 p.m. the following afternoon, the fire had been reduced to smoldering ruins. Miraculously, no loss of life occurred in the largest fire to ever hit the downtown business district.

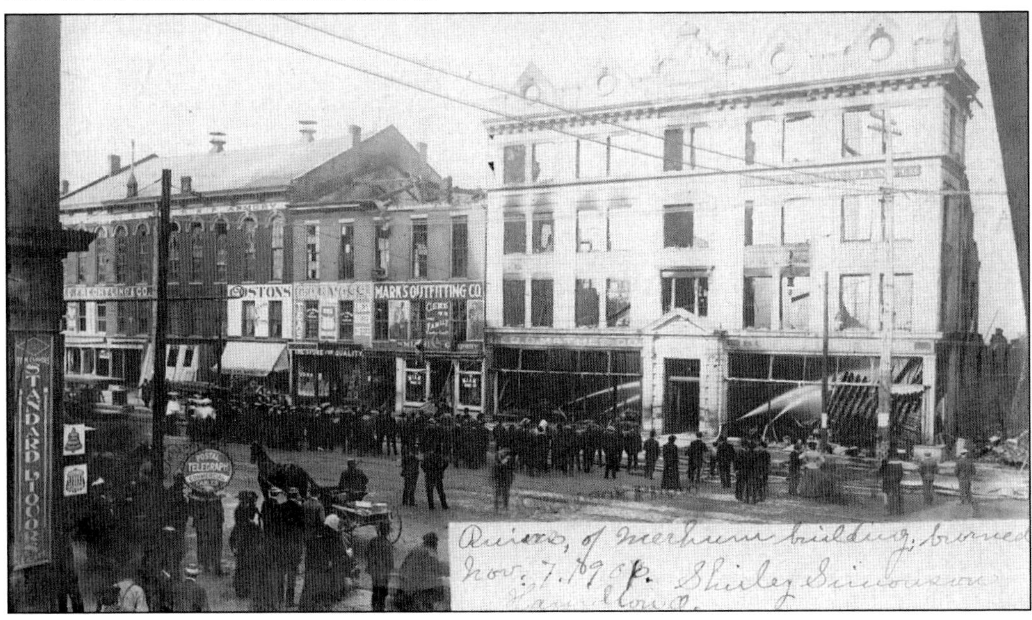

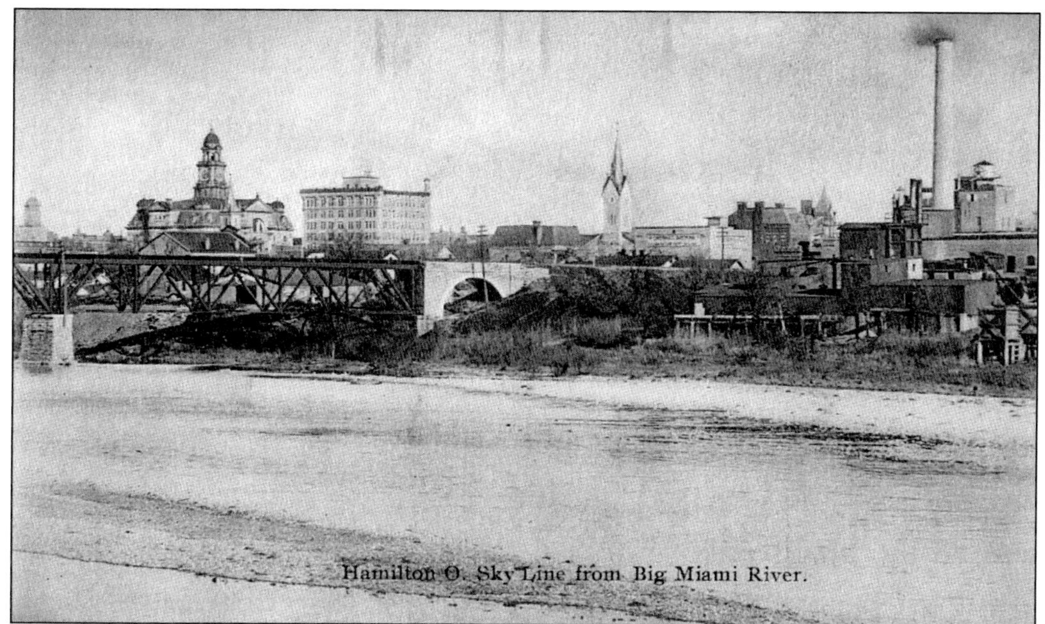

Pictured here around 1910 is the Hamilton skyline from the west across the Great Miami River. The courthouse and the Rentschler Building (left), and Zion Lutheran Church (center) still occupy their respective places, but the larger buildings (right), including the Cincinnati Brewing Company, the old Central High School, and the large stack and impressive facilities of the George Rupp & Company meat-packing plant have disappeared.

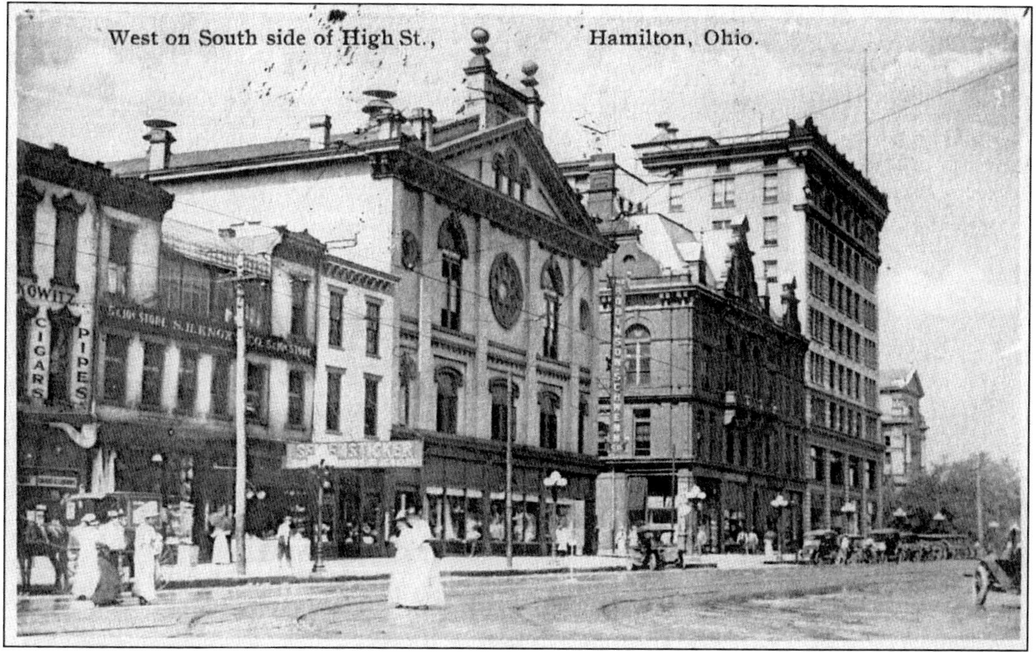

Originally constructed in 1866 as the Dixon Opera House, by the time this card was sent in 1919, the Robinson Schwenn Company had operated a department store at 221 High Street (center) for 12 years. The S.H. Knox & Company Five and Dime (left) is now the home of Ryan's Tavern, and the building adjacent to the Rentschler Building (right) is the old Masonic building.

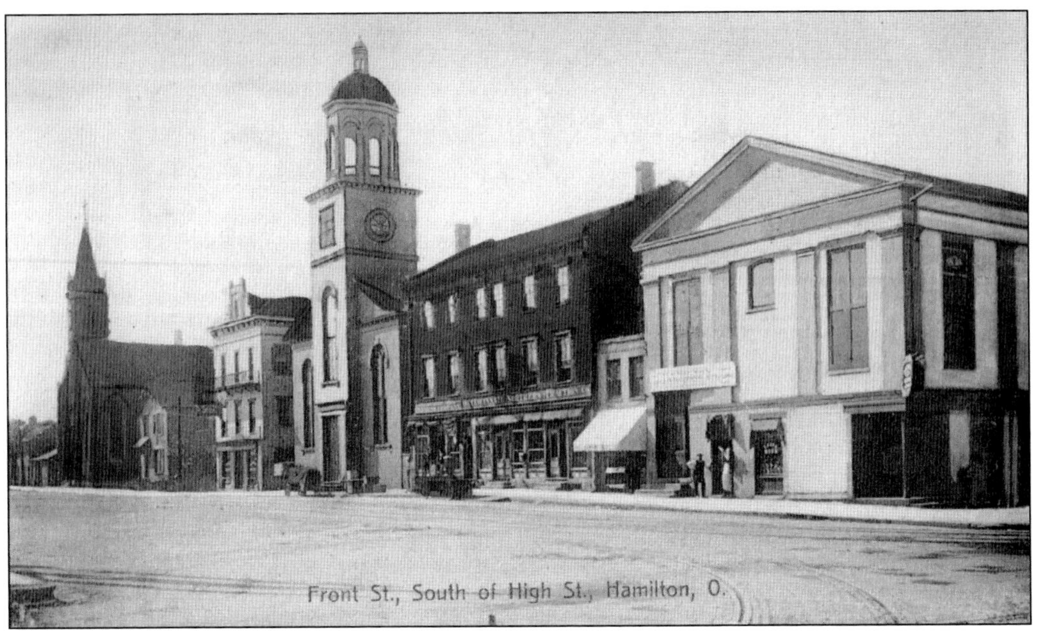

Around 1908, the southwest corner of Front and High Streets was a hub of activity. Businesses included, from right to left, George Kogroe's lunch counter, Joe Kopp's saloon, the Hamilton Tailoring Company, the Cincinnati Northern Traction station, the Southern Ohio Express Company, the First Presbyterian Church, and the Farmer's Hotel. One block south, St. Mary Catholic Church (left) stands in its original design, complete with bell tower.

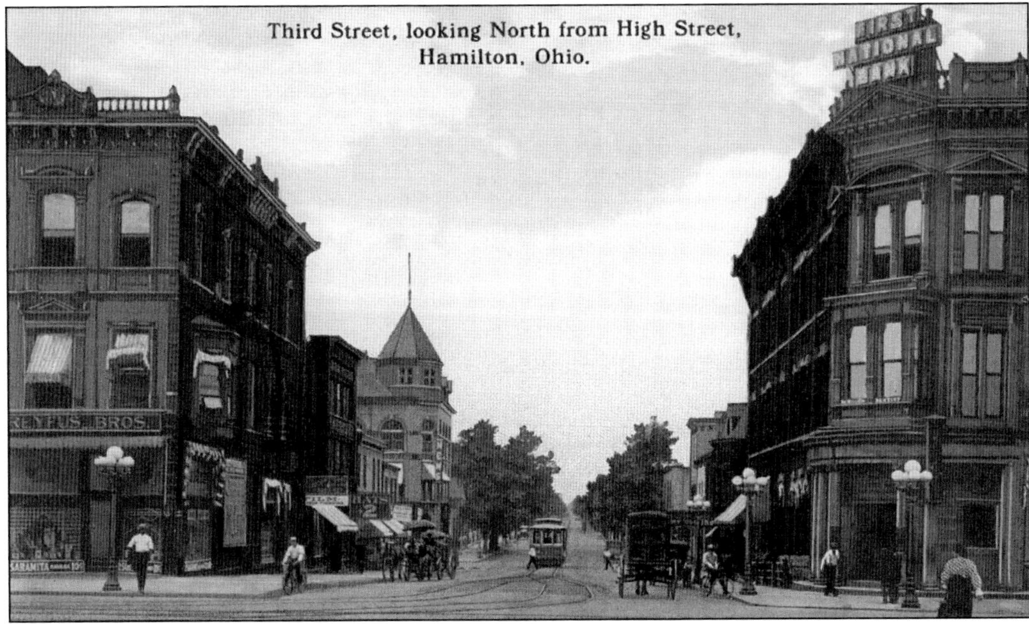

Downtown business was thriving in 1910 Hamilton. In the first block of North Third Street alone there were two confectioners, a tobacconist, a dentist, a restaurant, a fancy goods store, a grocer, a haberdasher, a bicycle store, a manicurist, a doctor, a notions store, a pawnbroker, two tailors, a toy store, a bank, a photography supply store, and a telegraph office. The spired building (center) is the Republican News Building.

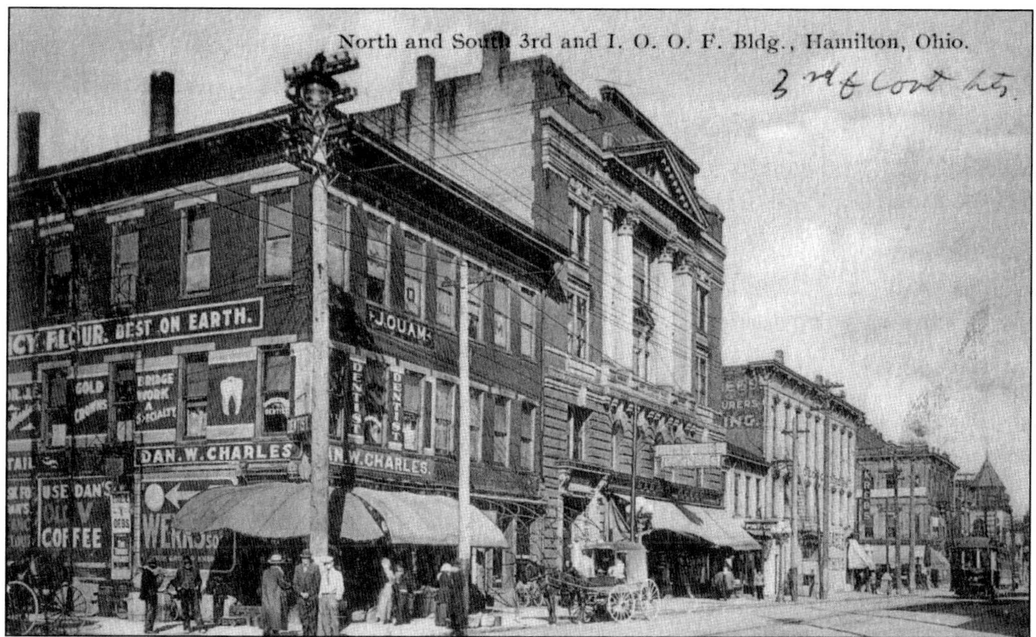

This is a busy view of the west side of South Third Street at Court Street. The Odd Fellows Temple sits prominently on the block. Who needs billboards when one can advertise on the building? The corner building housed Dan Charles's grocery on the first floor, dentist James Rothenbush's offices on the second floor, and the Junior Order of United American Mechanics lodge on the third floor.

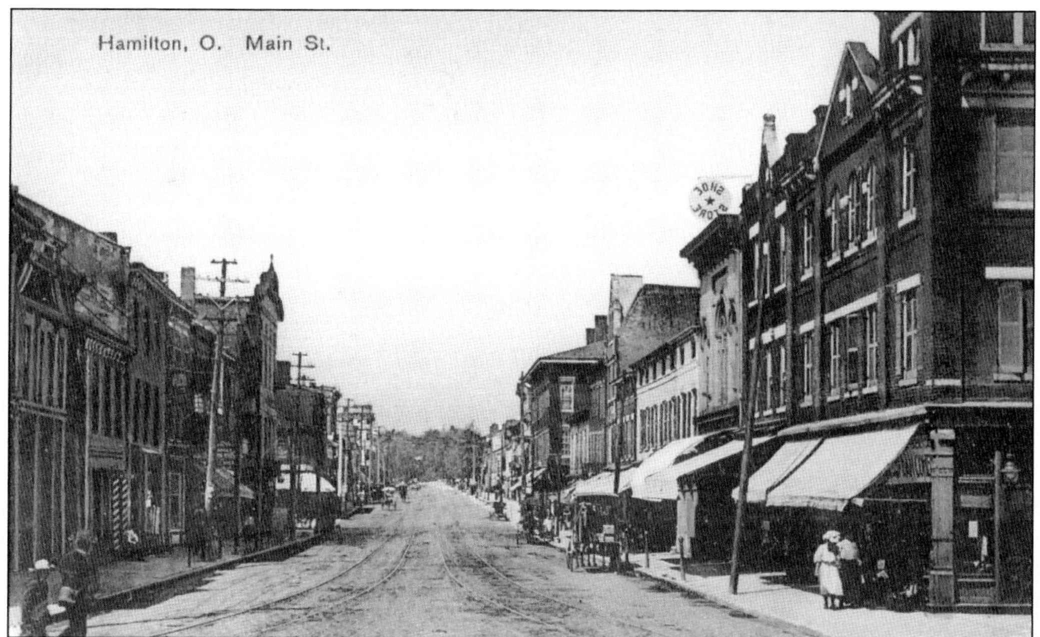

Pictured here is Main Street looking west from B Street in Rossville around 1908. The Main Street business district has a distinct small-town neighborhood look and feel to it, even though it is only a short walk across the bridge from downtown. Rumple Hall (right) housed Beeler Drug Store from 1867 to 1941.

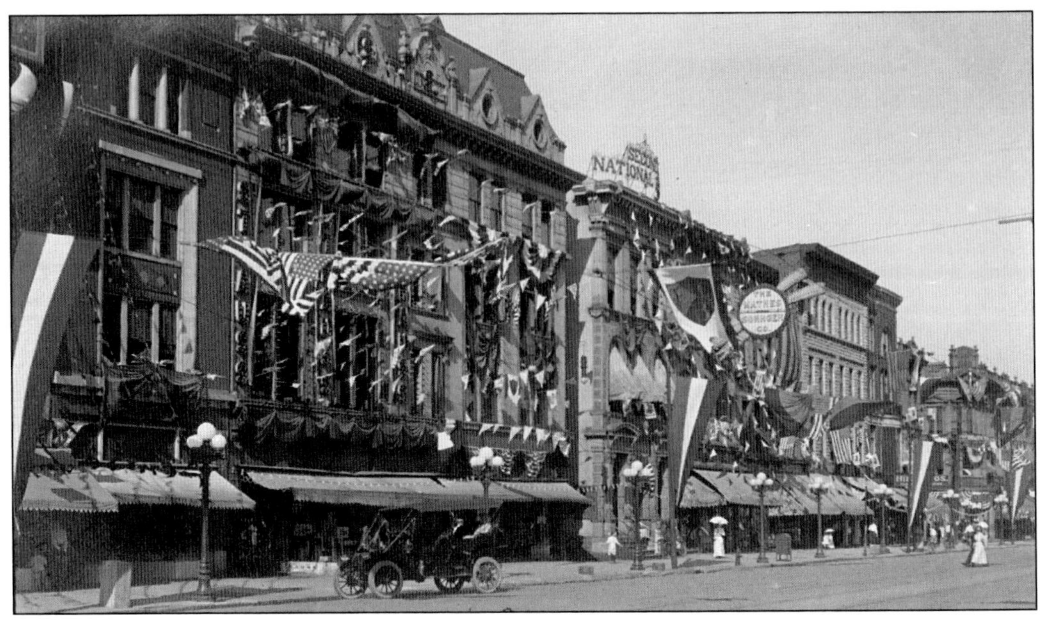

Window trimmer Coy E. Burnett was charged with devising the decoration plan for the 1912 Odd Fellows State Convention held in Hamilton. All businesses on High Street from Fourth Street west to the river, on Second and Third Streets from Dayton Street to Ludlow Street, and on Main Street west to D Street were asked to decorate and contribute monies to assist in covering the cost of materials. The High and Main Street Bridge was also heavily bunted. By the looks of things in these two views of High Street, it is safe to assume that Burnett had no trouble getting community support. A massive storm three days before the opening parade caused significant damage to the decorations, forcing a last-minute barrage of repairs and replacements. (Both, courtesy of BCHS.)

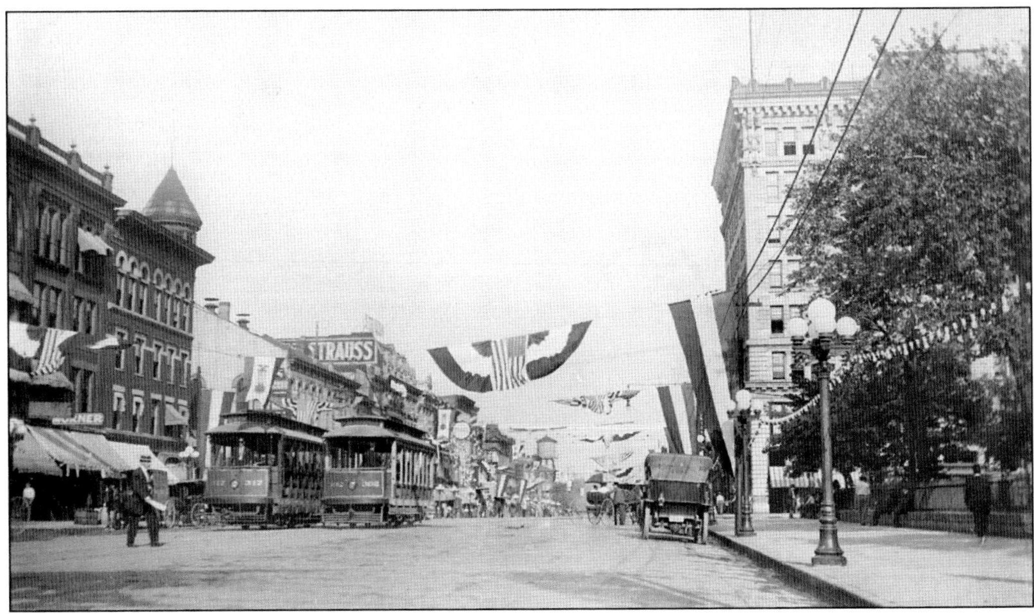

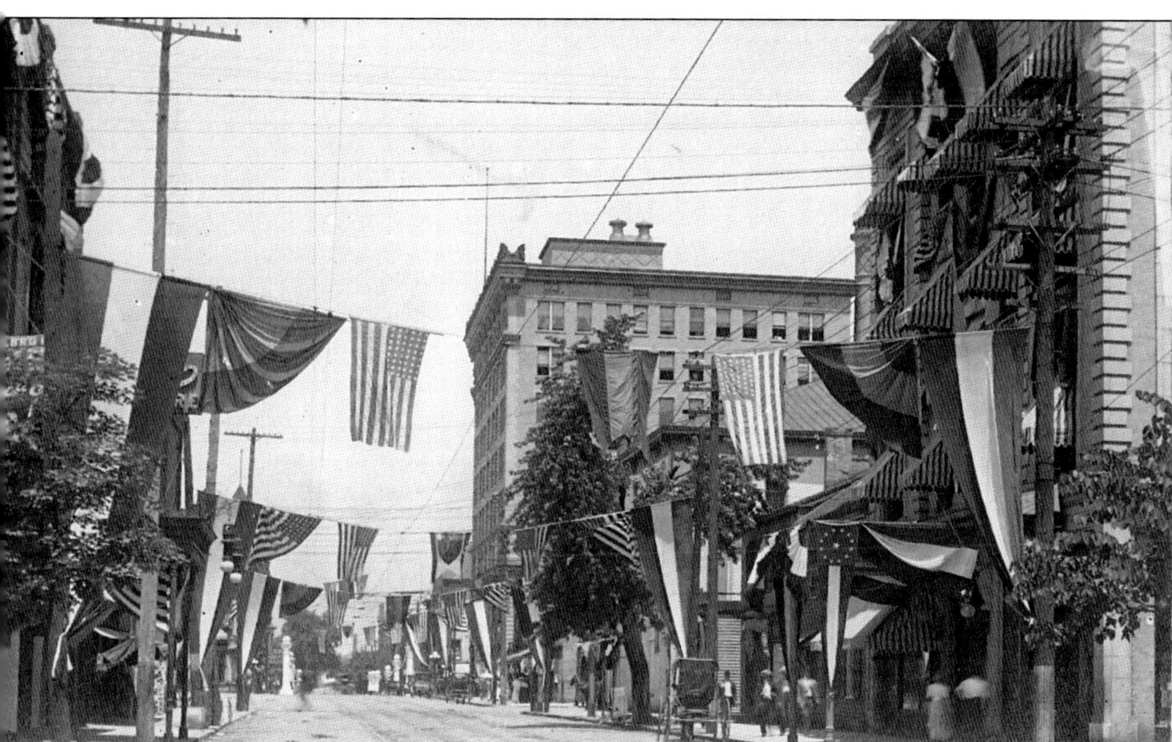

South Second Street is all decorated for the 1912 Odd Fellows State Convention. This view looking north gives an idea of how the side streets were almost literally overrun with banners and flags during the affair. The Hotel Connor (right) was a convenient place for conventioneers to stay, while the Smith Theater across the street provided ample entertainment when convention events were not in session. (Courtesy of BCHS.)

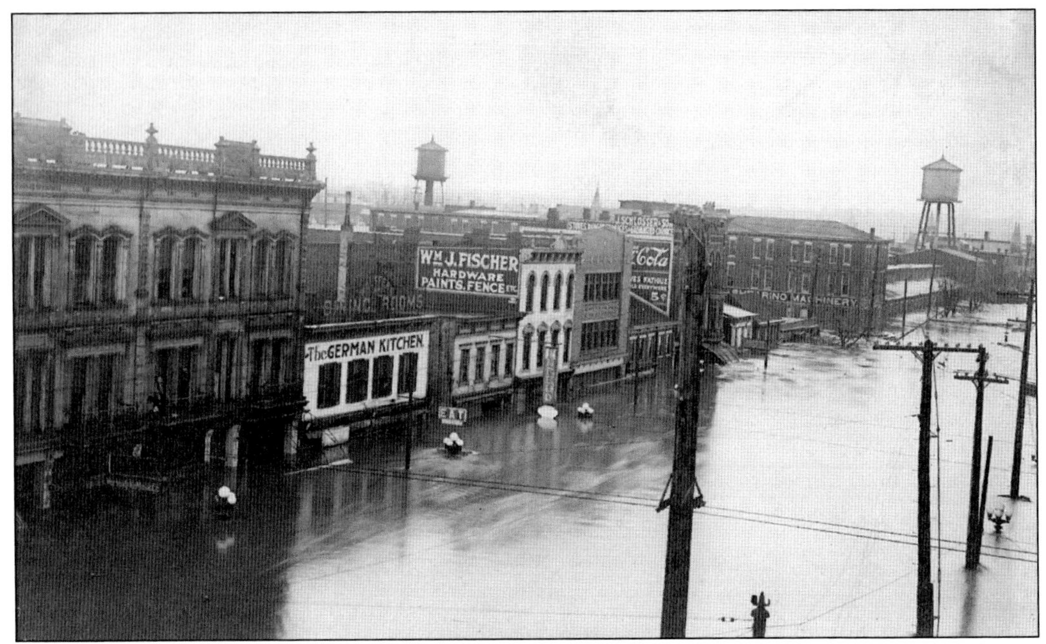

This is a view of High Street to the east during the 1913 flood. The floodwaters have just about peaked. Notice that the street lamps are nearly covered, and there is very little current around them. The Long & Alstatter works (right) stand at the corner of Fourth and High Streets.

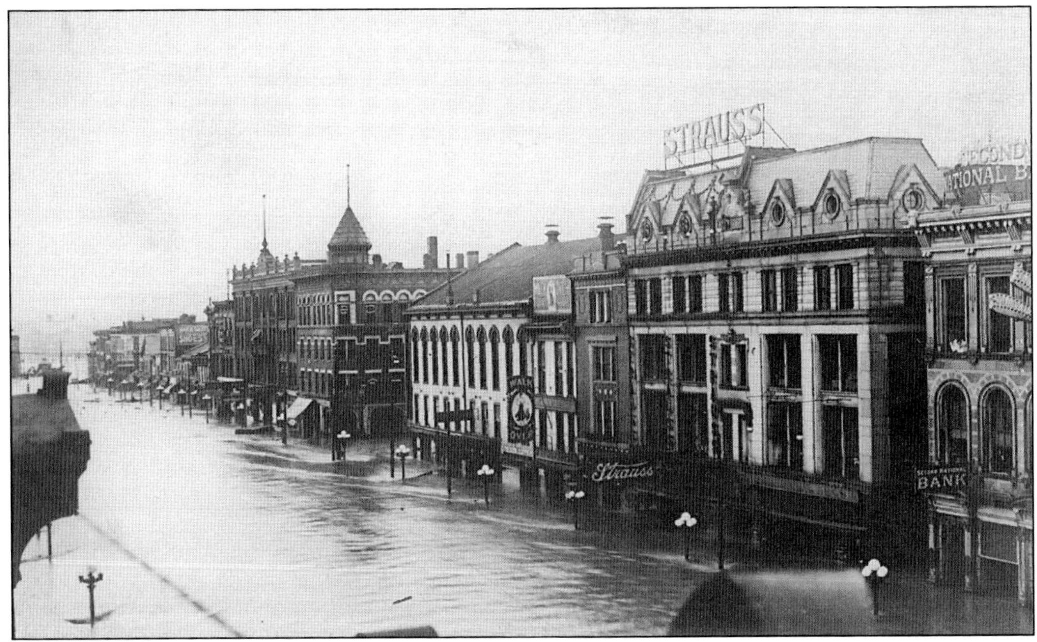

This view of High Street, looking west, was taken later in the day than the view above. Notice the water is much lower on the lamps, and the currents around them indicate the water is receding back toward the river. The spired building (left) on the northwest corner of Second and High Streets is the Miami Valley Bank Building.

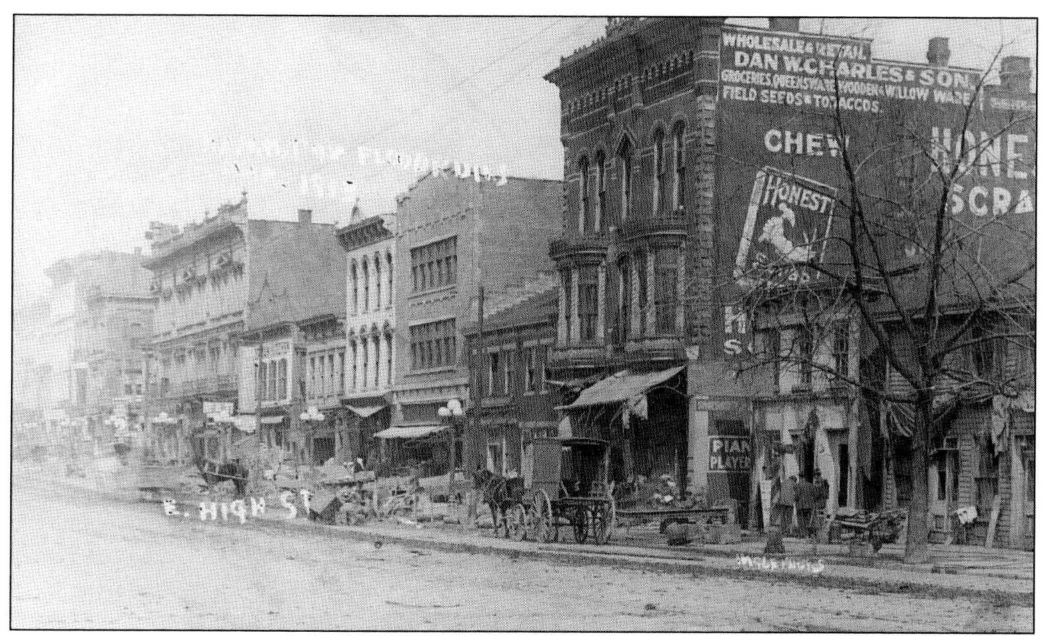

The long and arduous task of cleanup had begun by the time these images were taken a few days after the Great Miami was back within its banks. Local merchants stacked damaged and destroyed goods, materials, and furniture in front of their vacant storefront windows. The Imfeld Music store (below, center) has quite a pile of chairs, discarded stringed and brass musical instruments, drums, Victrolas and phonographs, display cases, and even a player piano filling the sidewalk and waiting to be carted away to the garbage heap. Inside, inches of thick brown mud had to be scraped and shoveled out so the drying process could begin.

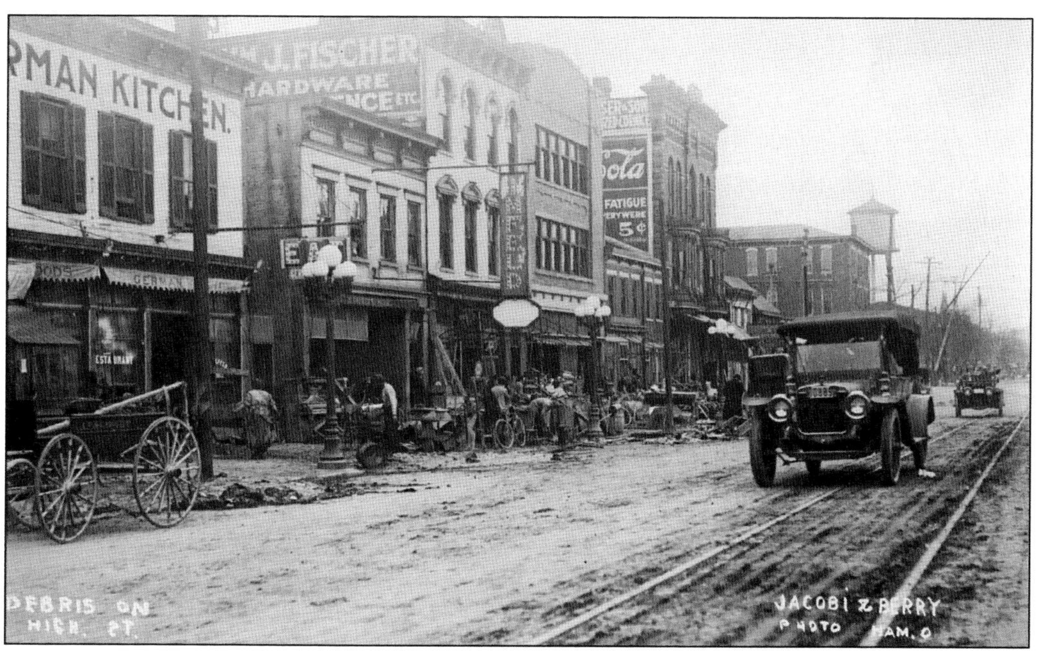

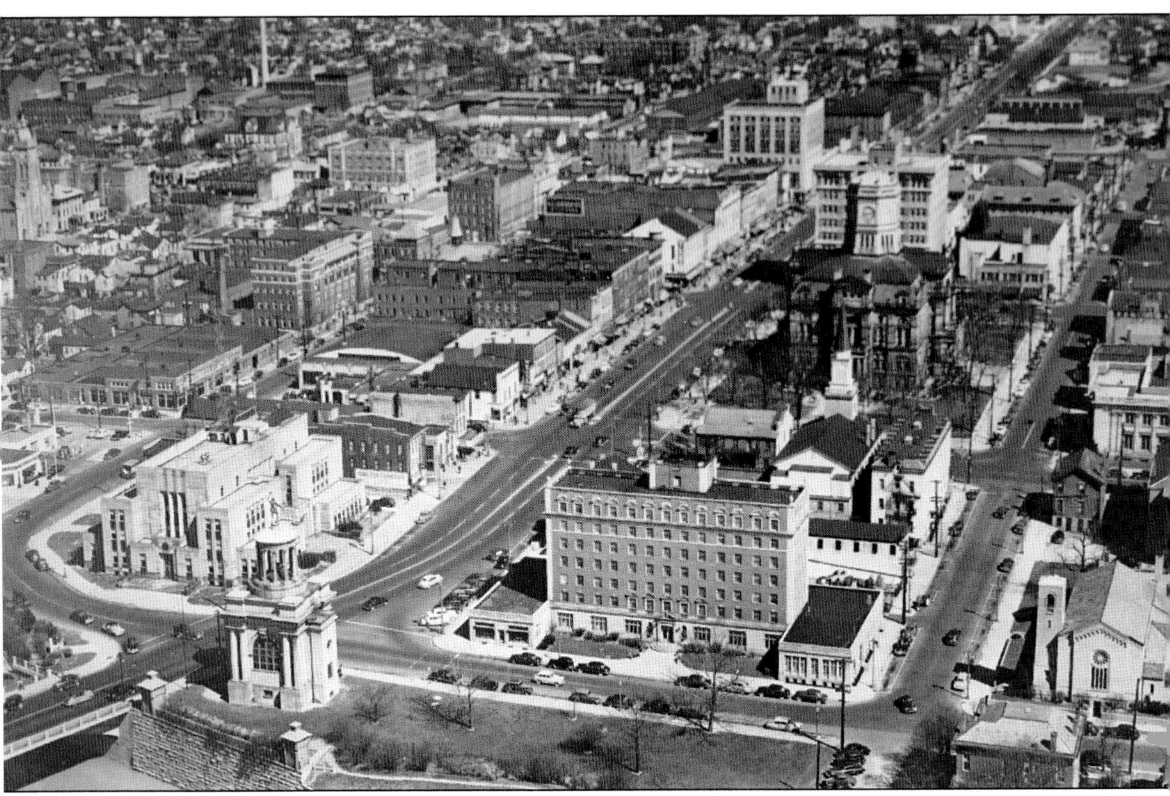

An interesting aerial view, looking east, captures a bustling and vibrant downtown Hamilton during the early 1950s. Numerous landmarks such as the old municipal building (lower left) and the Anthony Wayne Hotel (lower center) are enjoying new and revitalized uses, but many of the old structures have disappeared.

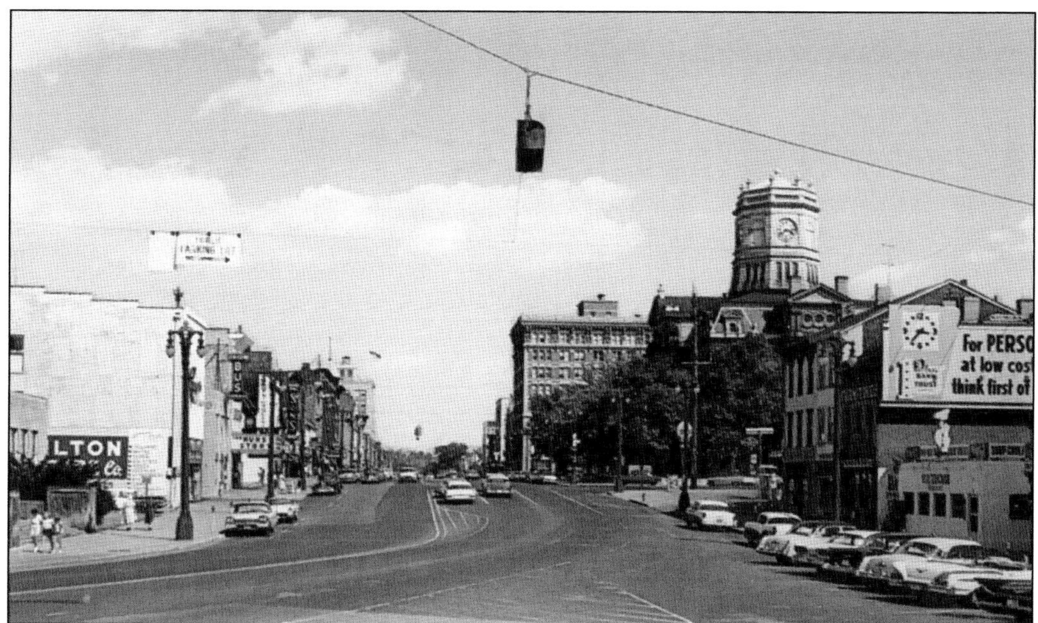

This view of High Street looking east is from 1959. The diner and buildings west of the courthouse (right) are now a parking lot, and the Union Bus Terminal and the newly remodeled Court Theater (right) were razed, with Lentil Park now occupying the northwest corner of Front and High Streets. In 1976, a new Butler County Administration Building was added on the opposite corner to the east.

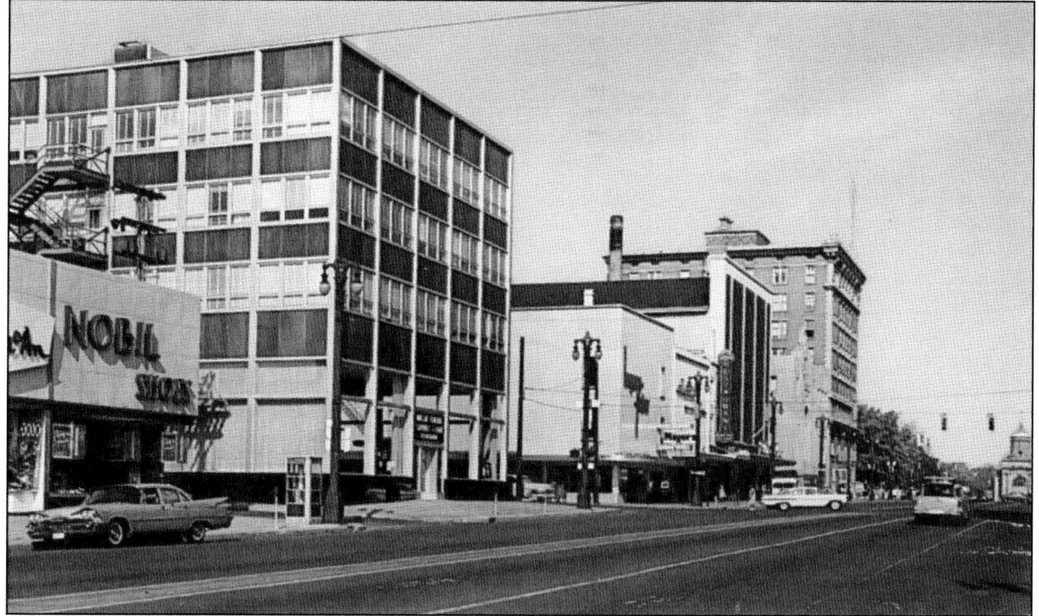

In the 1950s, the city wanted to display a modern style and personality. Metal facades began to pop up all over downtown to cover up the old and tired look of the previous century. Now, 60 years later, the vision is to rediscover the architectural heritage of Hamilton. Numerous downtown buildings are getting a new life along with an "old" look as their midcentury covers are removed, revealing their true character underneath.

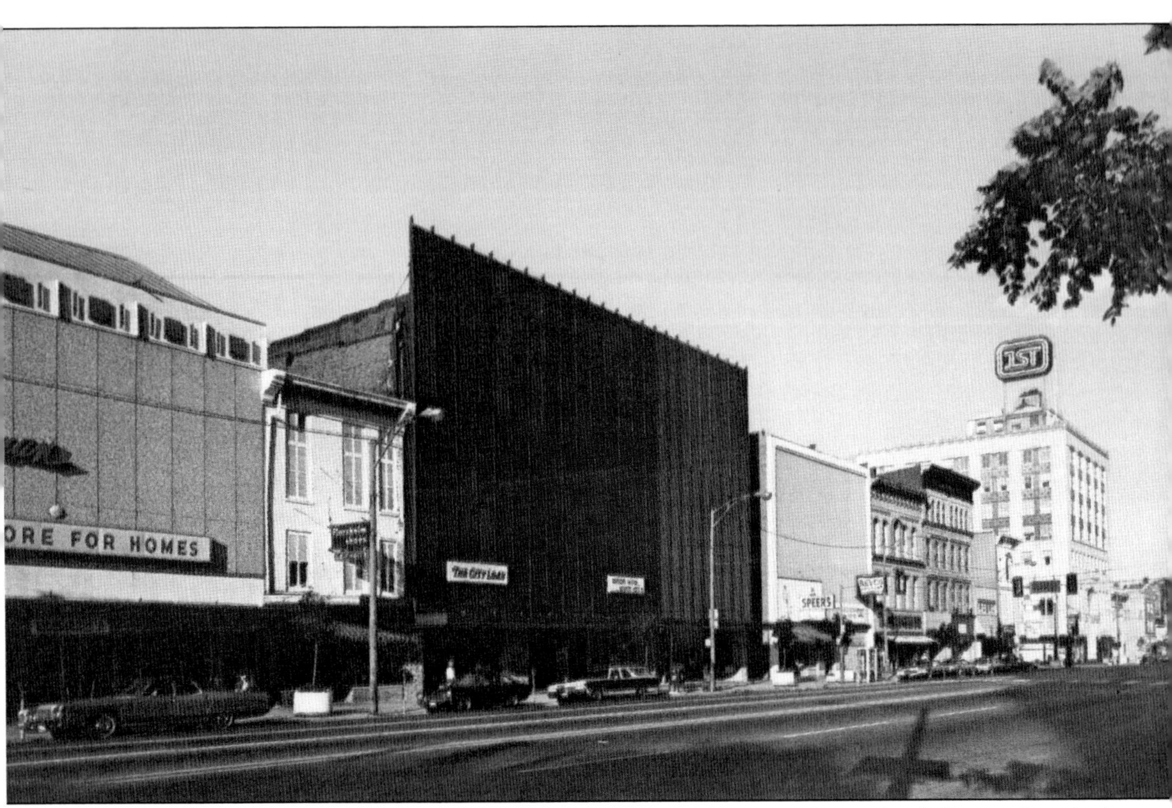

Today's view of the north side of High Street looking east looks vastly different than it does in this view from the 1970s. The Elder Beerman Furniture Store (left) is now an urban green space, the oppressive metal grating that covered the facade of the Mehrum Building (center) has been removed, and the face of the old Second National Bank Building, which housed Revco Pharmacy and Speer's Shoe Store at the time, is also now visible once more.

Two

The Monument and the Courthouse

As early as 1897, talks were underway to construct a monument commemorating Butler County soldiers and sailors. After two years of planning, a ballot petition was submitted for the November 1899 election to place six-fifths of a mil on all taxable property in Butler County to aid in construction. The measure passed within the city and failed in the rest of the county, but passed overall by over 1,200 votes. Designed by Hamilton architect Frederick Noonan, the structure is 50 feet square with 10-by-16-foot wings on the north and south. It is three stories in height, including a basement, and faced with cut stone. The interior marble walls bear the names of 4,500 pioneers and veterans, all hand-chiseled. Over 100 feet in the air stands a bronze statue of a cheering soldier titled *Victory*, but affectionately called "Billy Yank." Designed by Rudolph Thiem in his South A Street workshop, the statue is 17 feet tall and weighs in at 3,500 pounds. The cornerstone was laid on Thanksgiving 1902, and the monument was officially dedicated on July 4, 1906.

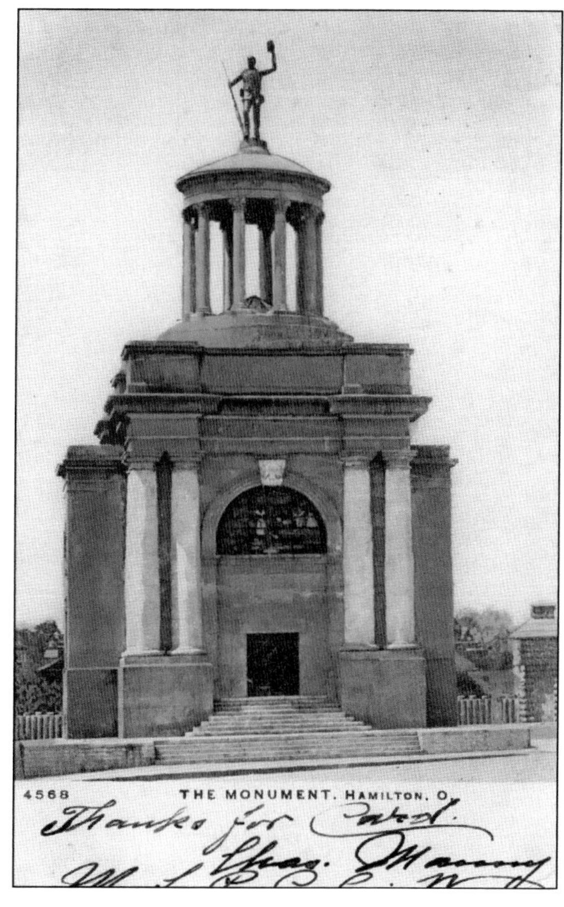

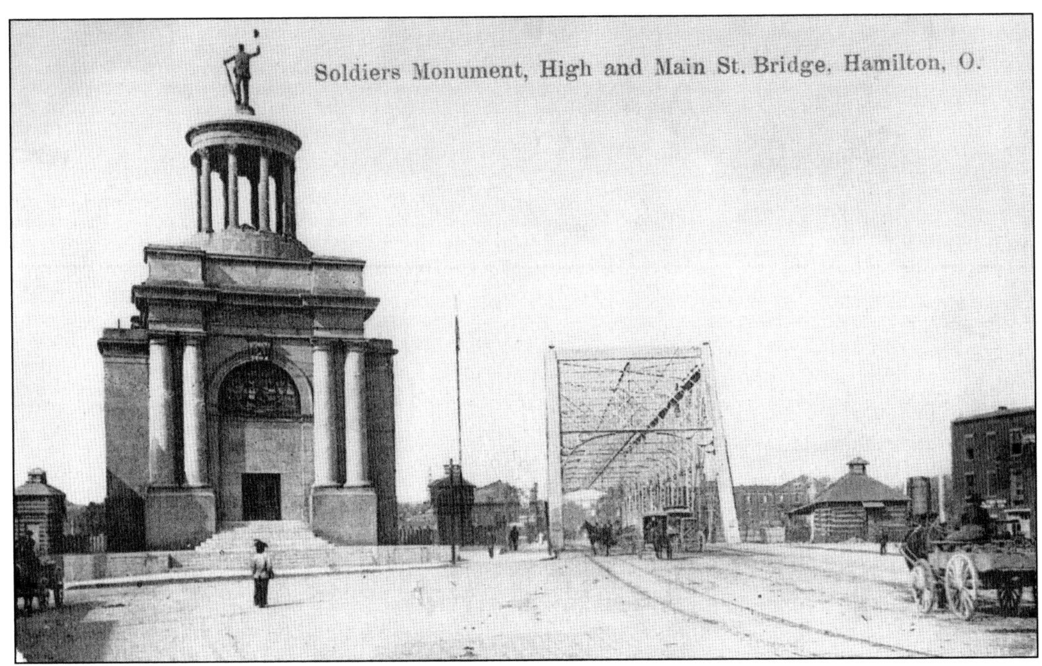

Offered here are similar vantages on High Street looking west. The view above is from 1908, two years after the monument was opened. The metal span bridge over the Great Miami River is intact and would remain until March 1913. The second view is from about 1918. The wagon traffic has diminished, the new concrete bridge arches over the river, and electric poles have proliferated. Note also that the original Fort Hamilton Blockhouse in the above view (right of bridge) is now missing, as are the buildings to the right. Both were swept away by the floodwaters of 1913, never to be replaced.

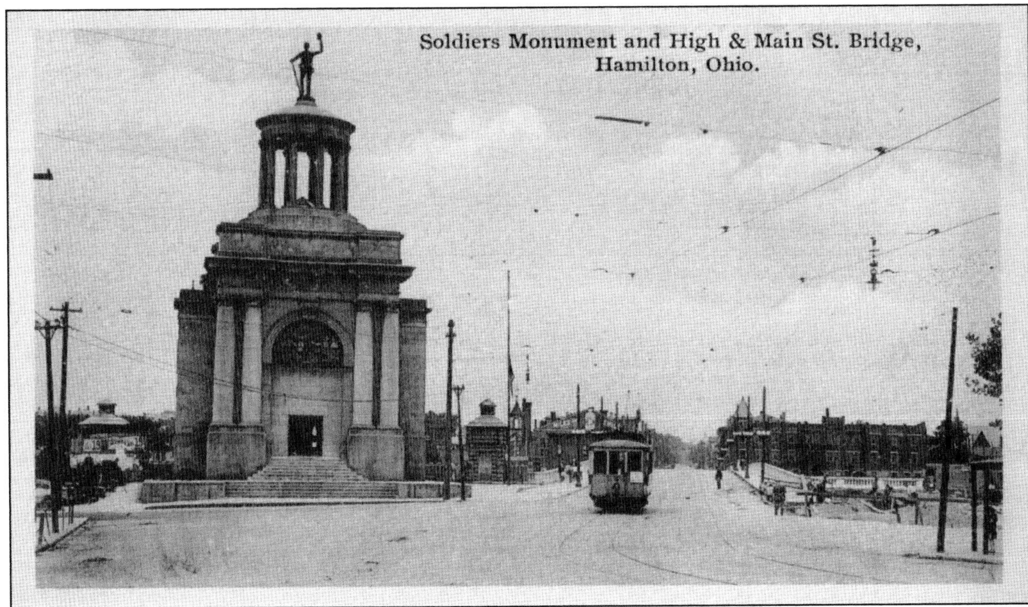

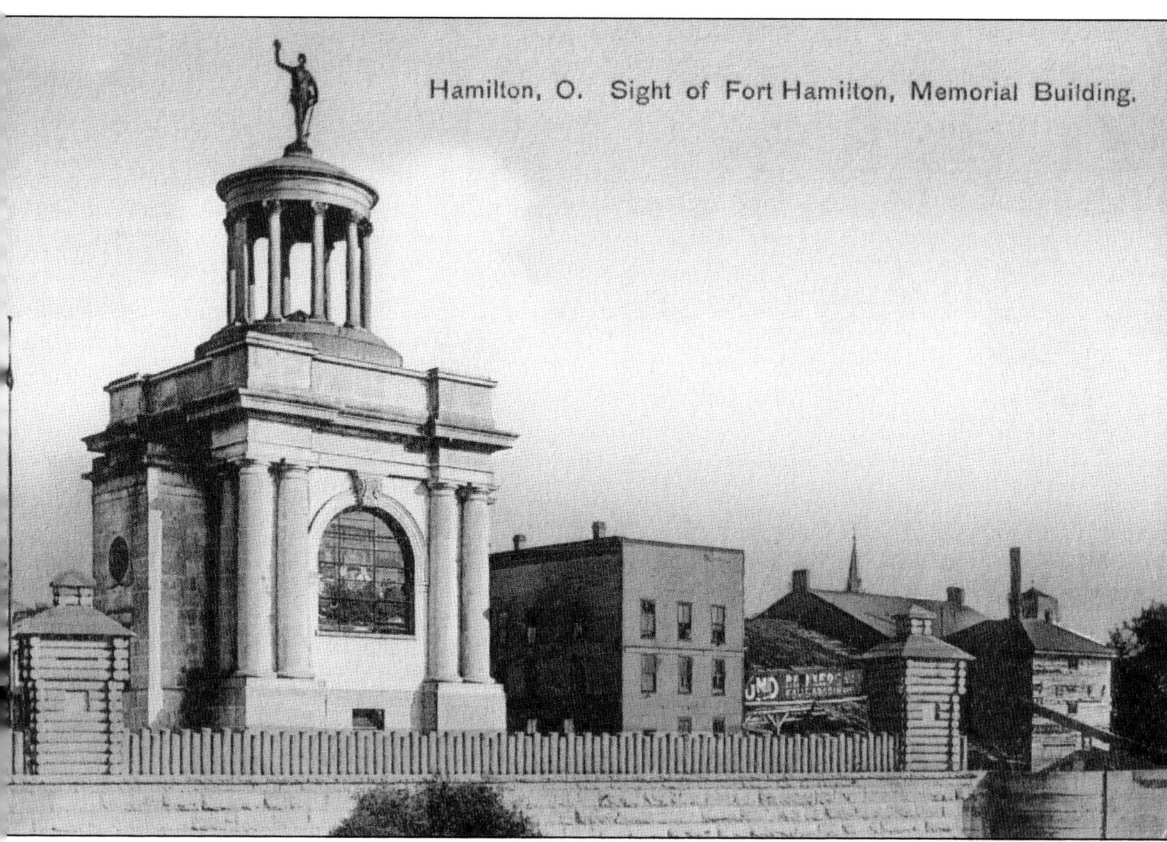

This view shows the back side of the monument as seen from the High and Main Street Bridge. A large art glass window titled *The Woman's Relief Corps* adorns the west face of the monument and depicts Civil War–era women and children performing services, such as packaging bandages, for soldiers. There are four such windows on the building. The east window depicts women tending to wounded soldiers, while the north and south windows feature the Grand Army of the Republic Seal and the Great Seal of the State of Ohio, respectively. Today, the area to the south of the monument has been transformed into a park-like setting, as all of the buildings shown here (left) are long since gone. (Courtesy of BCHS.)

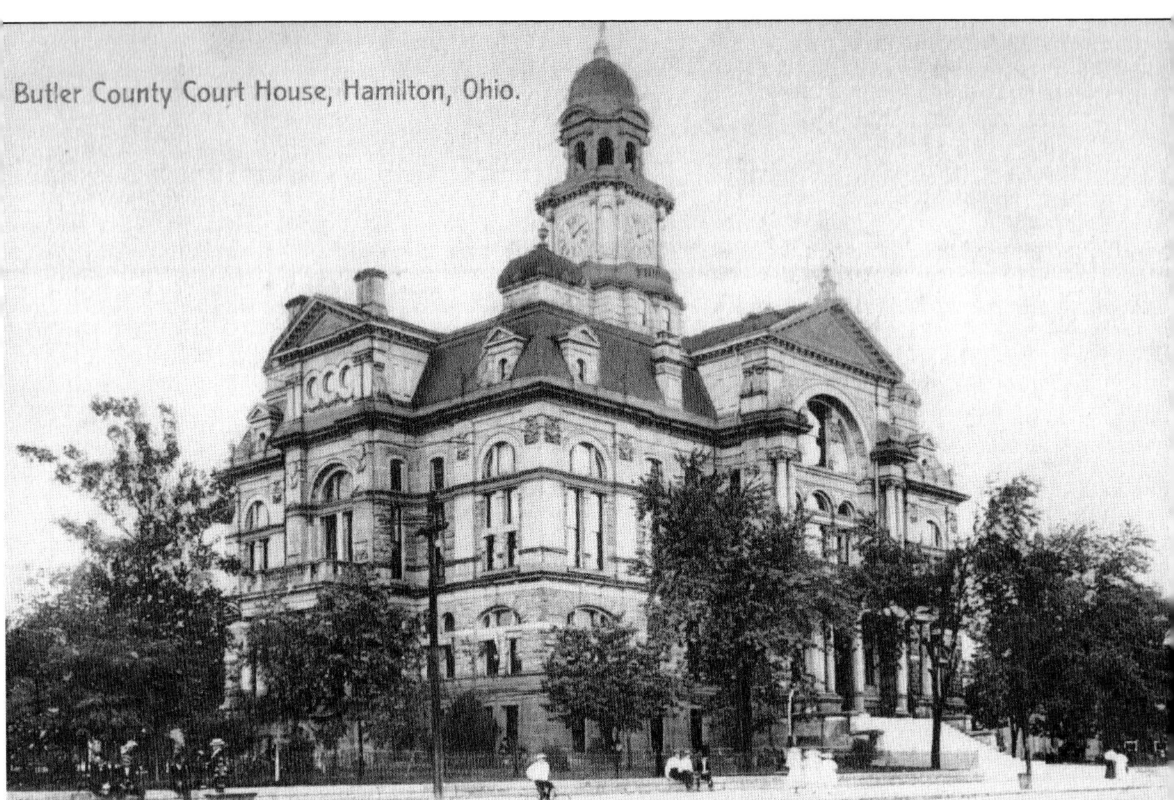

The current Butler County Courthouse, the focal point of Hamilton's downtown, was completed in 1889. This view from 1909 shows the building's first and original clock tower structure. The tower would be destroyed by fire in March 1912. Today, the building houses only a few local government offices and courts, but the sidewalks and grounds surrounding the sandstone landmark are still a gathering spot for community events.

Taken from the roof of the Rentschler Building and dated October 1906, this image looks down upon the finely manicured lawn of the county courthouse (left). The Soldiers, Sailors and Pioneers Monument (center) had been dedicated three months earlier on July 4, commemorating county veterans and settlers. The fine homes of Rossville can be seen across the river in the distance.

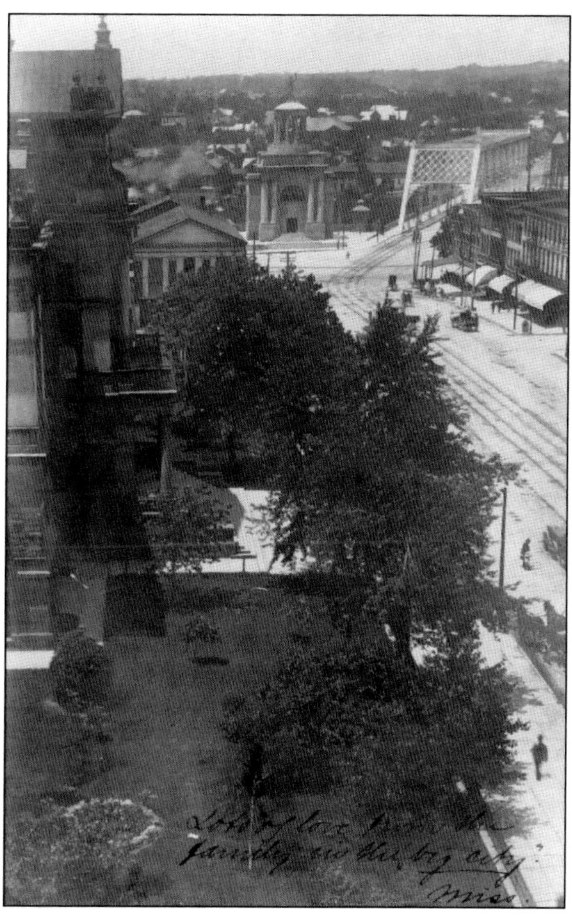

This is another view taken from the Rentschler Building looking southwest with Court Street below. The First Baptist Church (left) is in the foreground with the steeple of Zion Lutheran rising behind it. Directly across the street from the courthouse is the county jail. St. Mary Catholic Church (center) sits on Front Street, while the CH&D railroad bridge and arched viaduct stretch to the hills of Rossville to the west. (Courtesy of BCHS.)

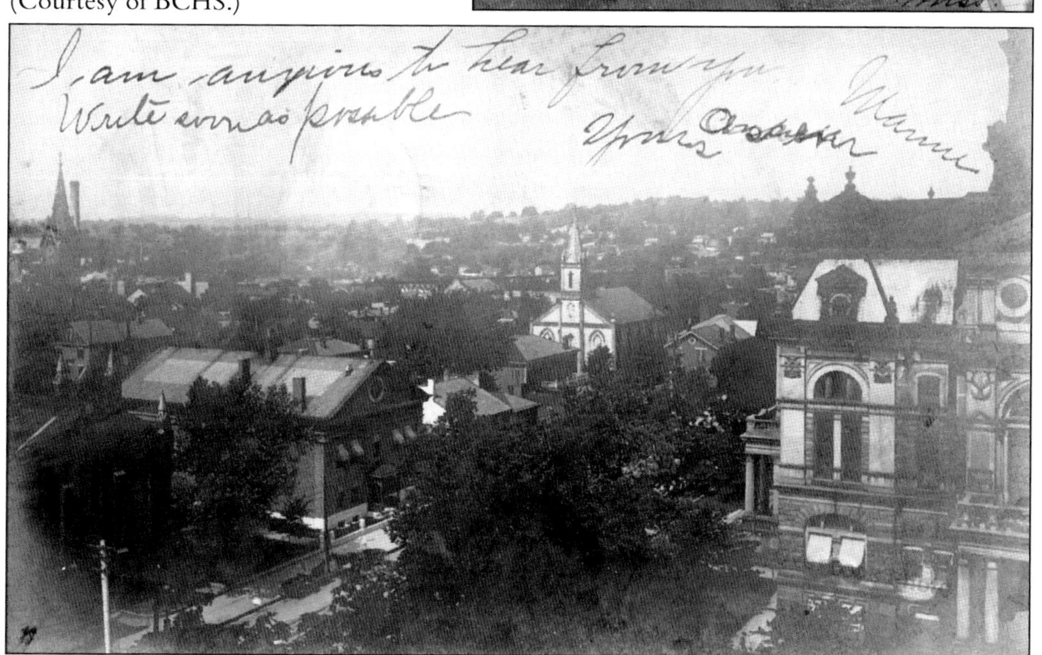

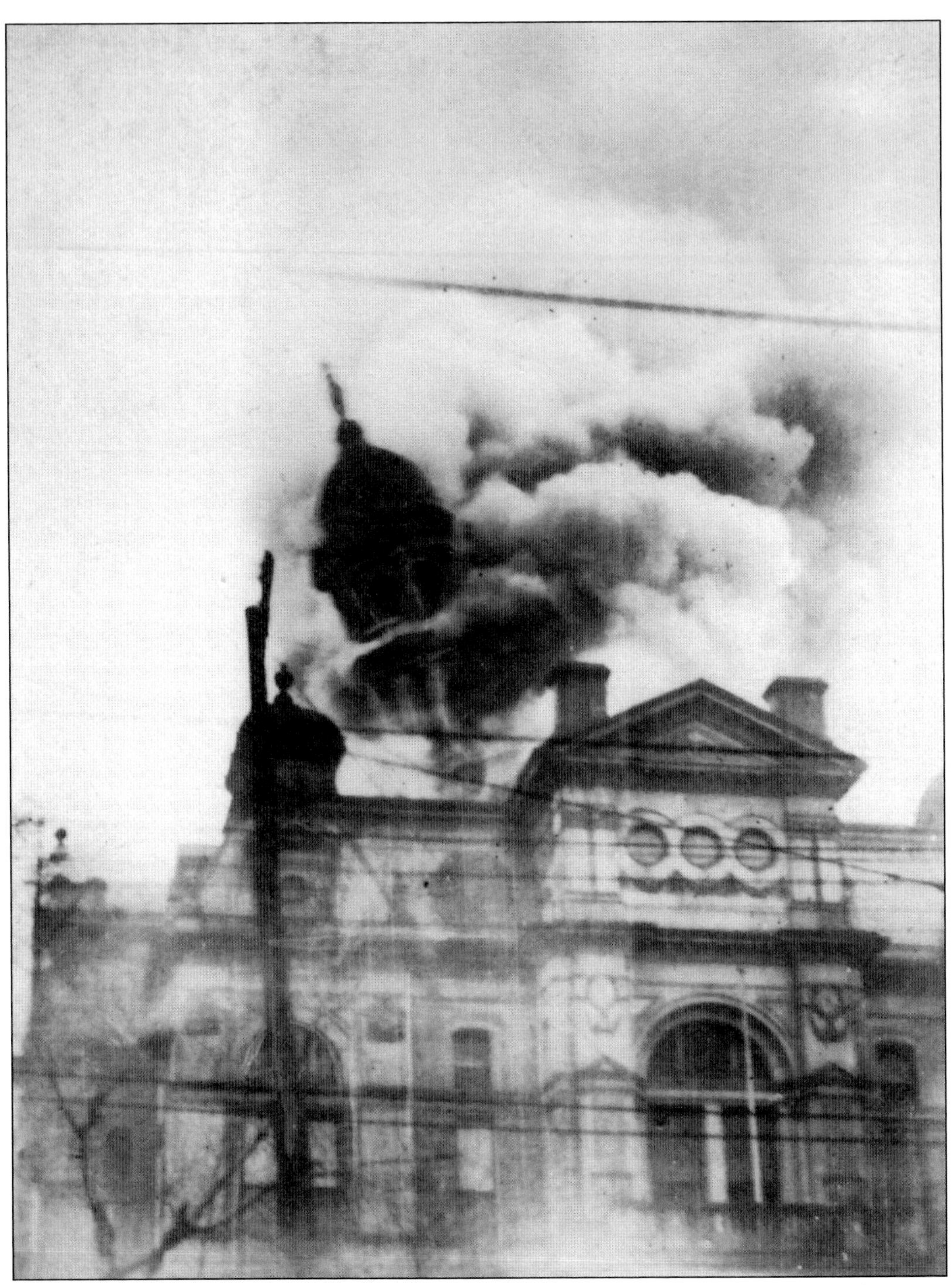

On March 14, 1912, fire roared through the upper floors of the Butler County Courthouse. It is believed the fire may have been smoldering for some time, as occupants reported smelling smoke for several days before the actual event. This dramatic view shows the clock tower and cupola just beginning to collapse. As this occurred, the tower bell sliced through the floors below and landed in the basement.

This view of the courthouse faces Second Street and was taken from the roof of the Rentschler Building. The bodies of the injured and dead firefighters are being removed from the still-burning building. Note that damage to this side of the building is almost nonexistent.

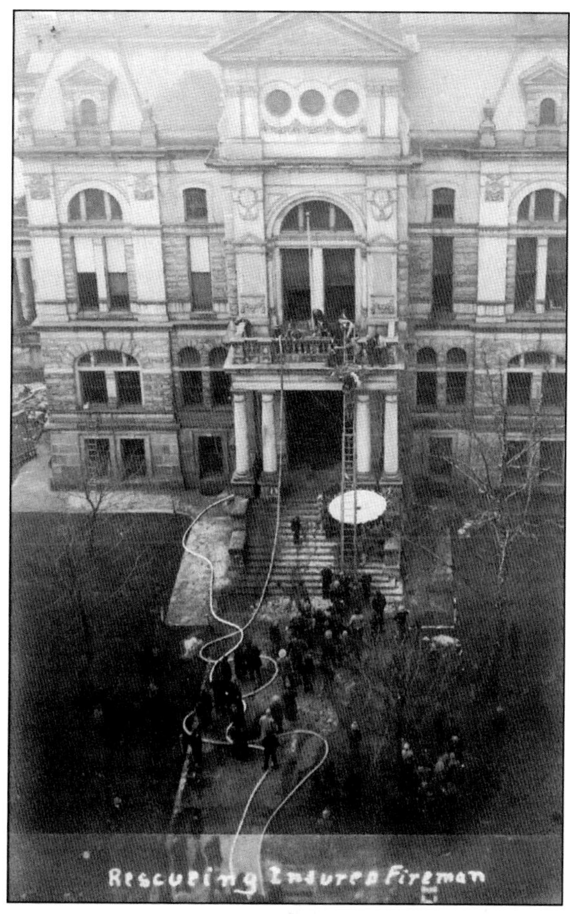

Three members of Hamilton Fire Department's Hose Company No.1 lost their lives fighting the 1912 courthouse fire. John Hunker died at the scene, while William Love and George Fritz succumbed to their injuries at Mercy Hospital. In this photograph, one of the men is being removed by fellow firefighters as dozens of onlookers watch with curiosity. A year later, another disaster, in the form of a flood, would test the building again.

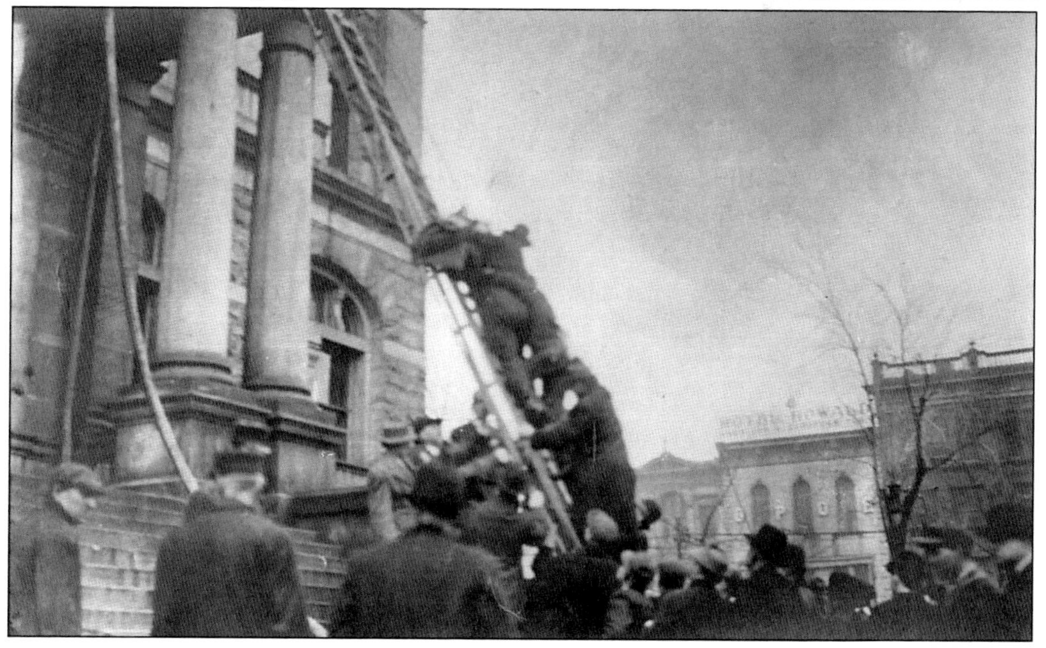

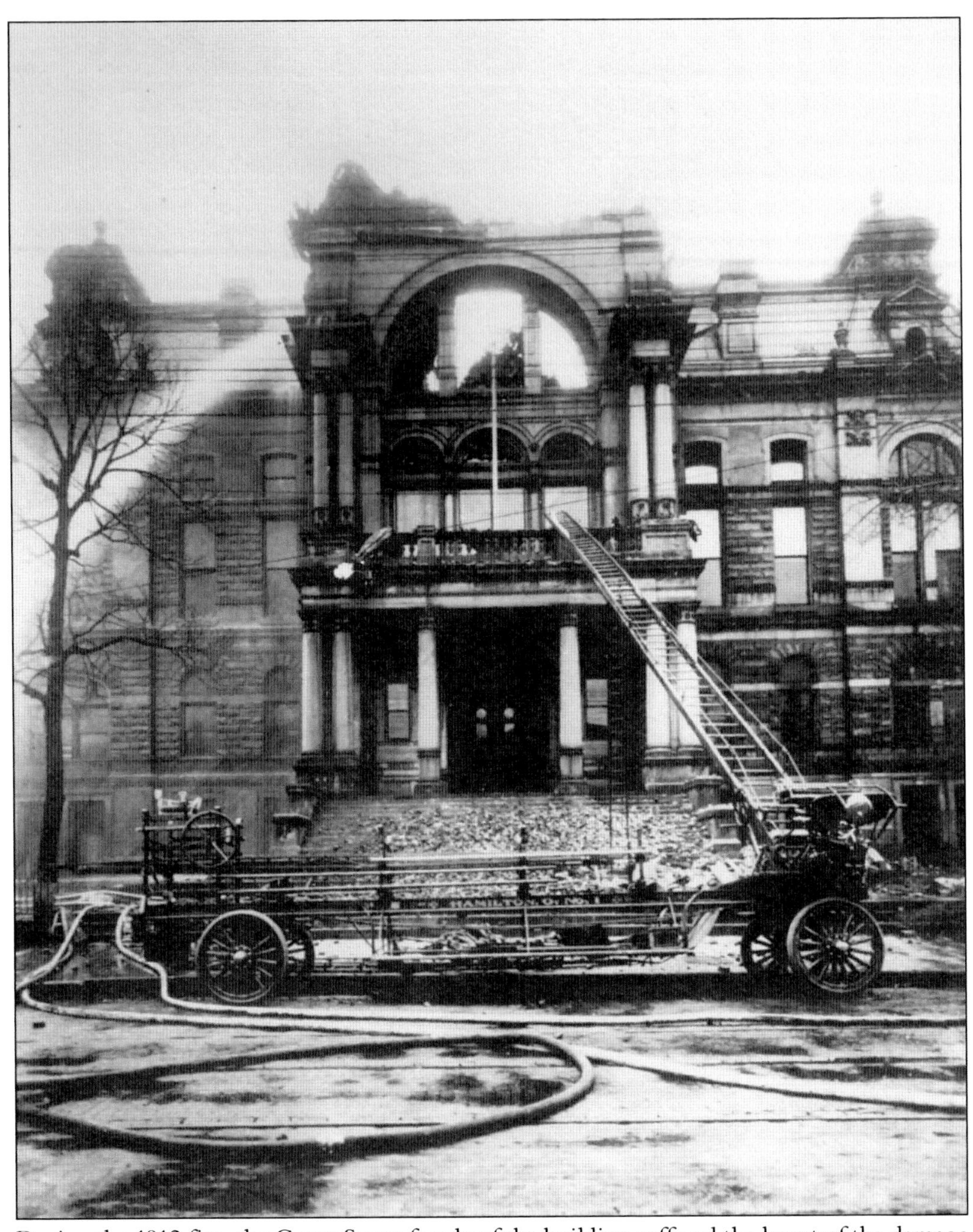

During the 1912 fire, the Court Street facade of the building suffered the brunt of the damage when the tower and cupola fell. Seen here sometime in the aftermath, the hoses and ladder truck from Hose Company No. 1 sit unattended. As the caption on the card reads, "the bronze statue of the Goddess of Justice that once sat atop the building is now shattered into pieces on the steps."

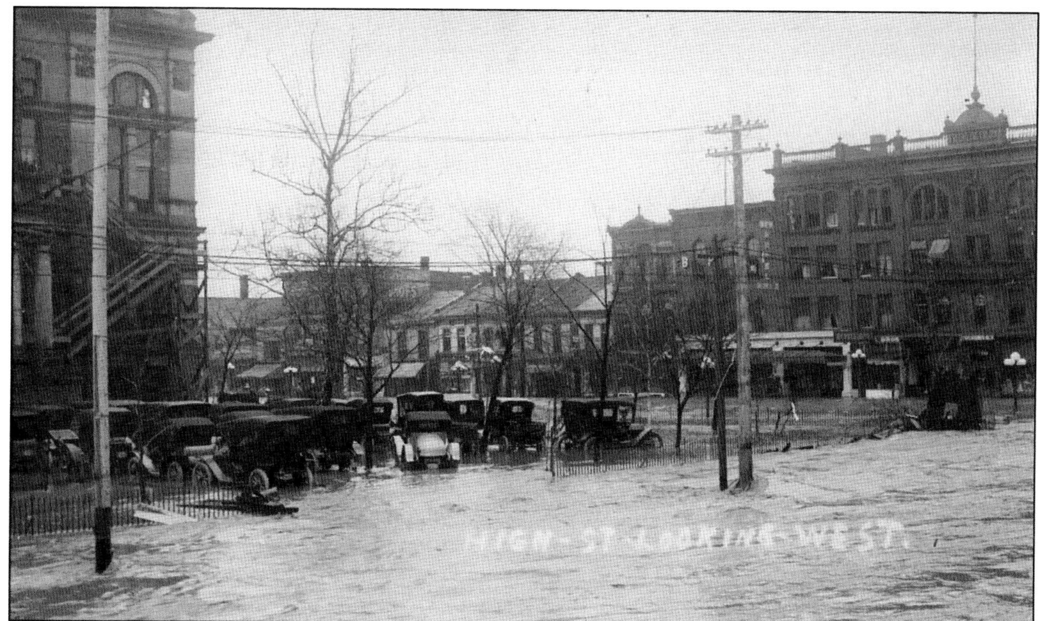

In March 1913, Hamilton endured the greatest flood it would ever know. This view shows a collection of automobiles parked inside the fencing on the courthouse lawn. Products still neatly stacked in the store windows across High Street indicate that the water is rising. Several people and a horse were trapped inside the building as the waters rose. The building served as the temporary morgue for flood victims.

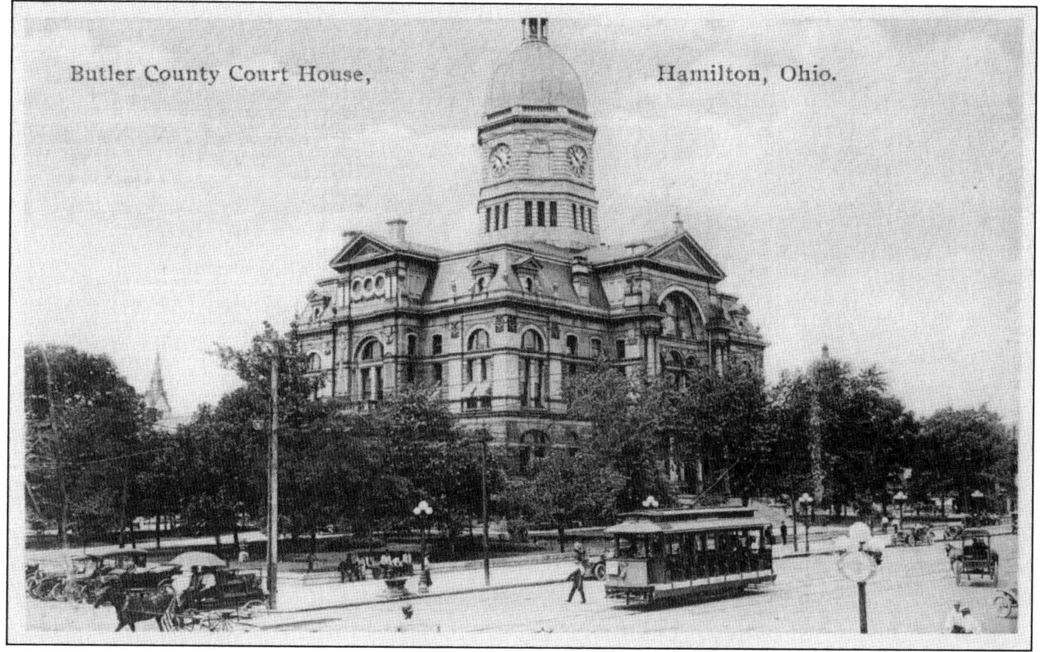

After the 1912 fire, the courthouse received a new clock tower and dome, completed in October 1913; however, the new look was short-lived. Water leakage began as early as 1920, and by 1925 the steel elements were so rusted that their integrity was questioned. A lightning strike in May 1926 was the proverbial straw. A month later, commissioners ordered the removal of the dome.

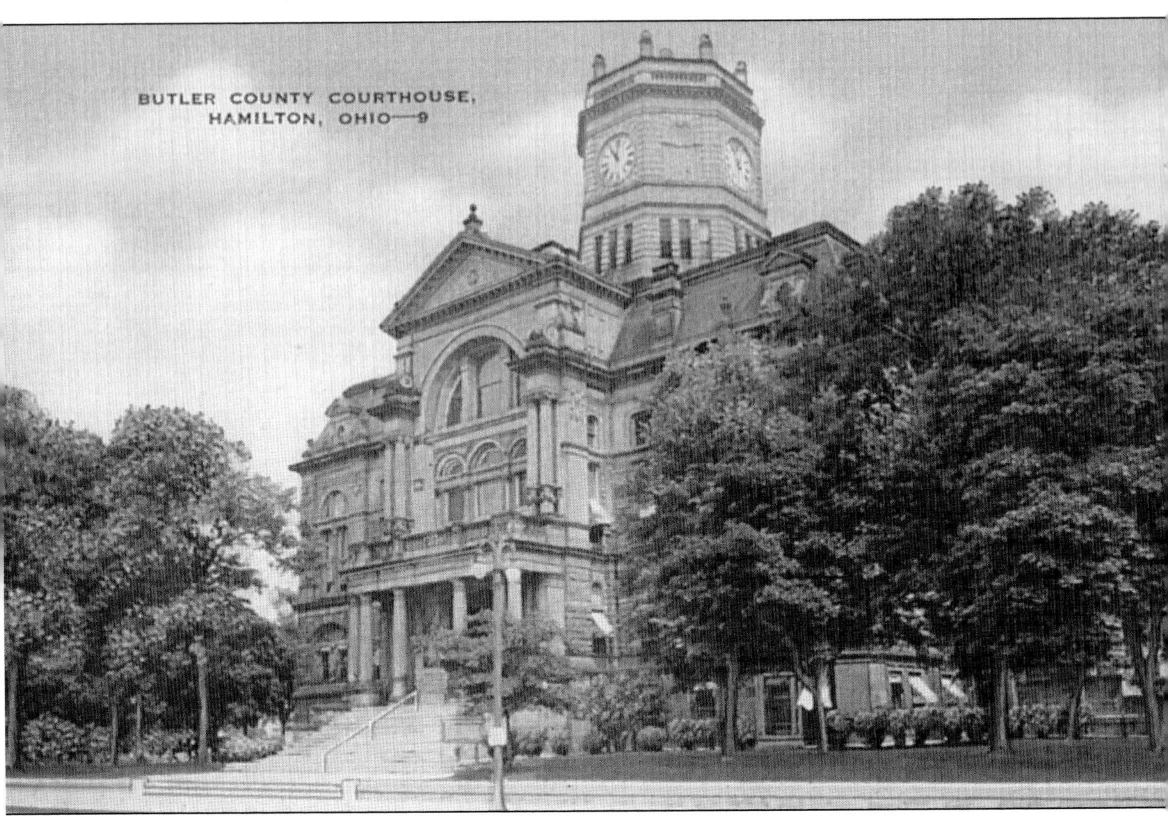

In March 1927, the last remnants of the failing upper dome portion of the clock tower were removed. A new flat copper roof took its place, and this is the look that the courthouse boasts yet today. A $1 million renovation to the building was completed in 1980, and the building was listed in the National Register of Historic Places. This card dates from the 1930s.

Three

Bridges

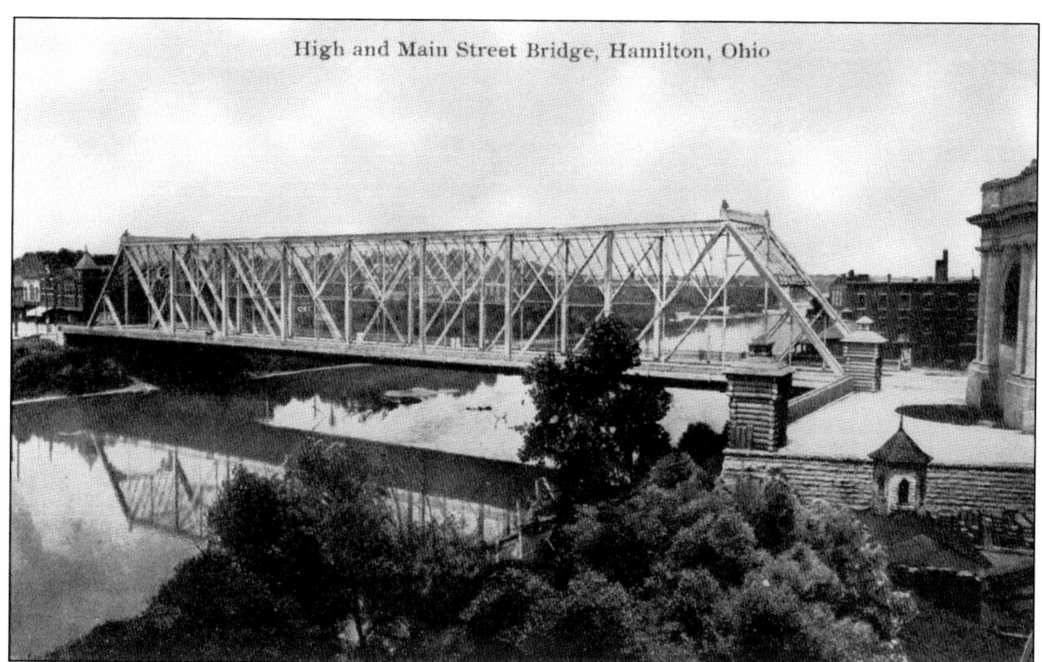

Built in 1895 with a 440-foot span, the Main and High Street Bridge was billed as the longest single-span bridge in the United States at the time of its construction. Designed by local engineer John C. Weaver and built at a cost of $109,000 by the Toledo Bridge Company, the structure sustained moderate damage during the 1898 flood, but remained standing. In March 1913, the placid waters shown here turned violent and brought this structure down with a vengeance.

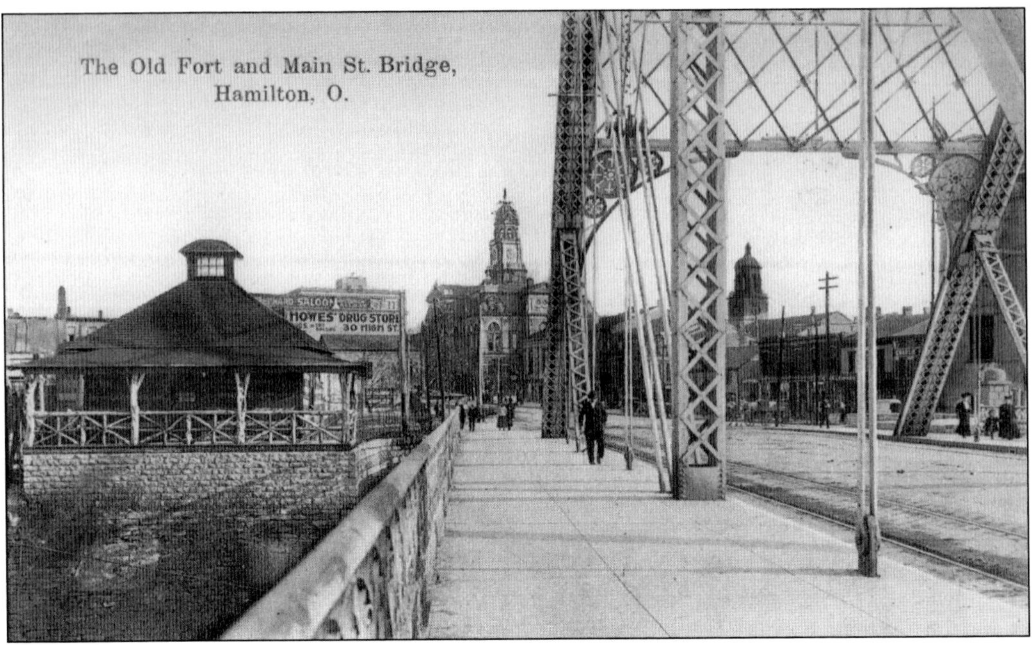

This view from about 1910 shows the intricate ironwork and detail that went into the design and construction of the Main and High Street Bridge. This bridge was the third to span the Great Miami at this location. Its predecessor was a suspension-style bridge built in 1866; before that, a covered wooden toll bridge built in 1819 provided passage between Hamilton and Rossville.

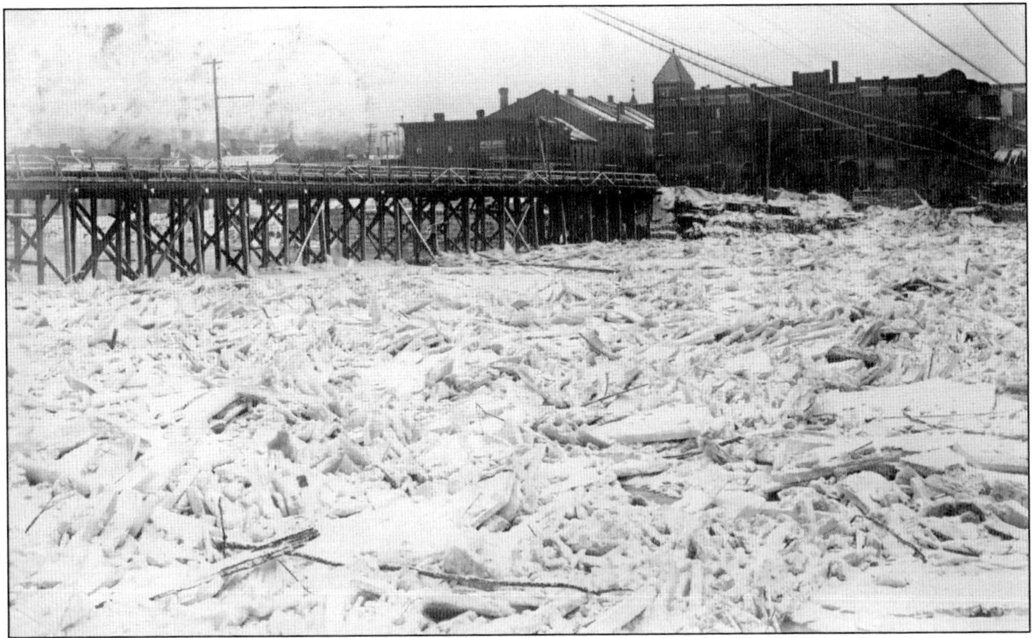

This card, postmarked February 24, 1914, shows the temporary High and Main Street Bridge and the Great Miami inundated with ice. On February 15, the bridge was closed when pilings and cross-braces began to snap under the pressure of the ice. The day this card was posted, an additional 13 inches of snow fell on the city. Four days later, with the help of dynamite and warmer temperatures, the ice began to dissipate.

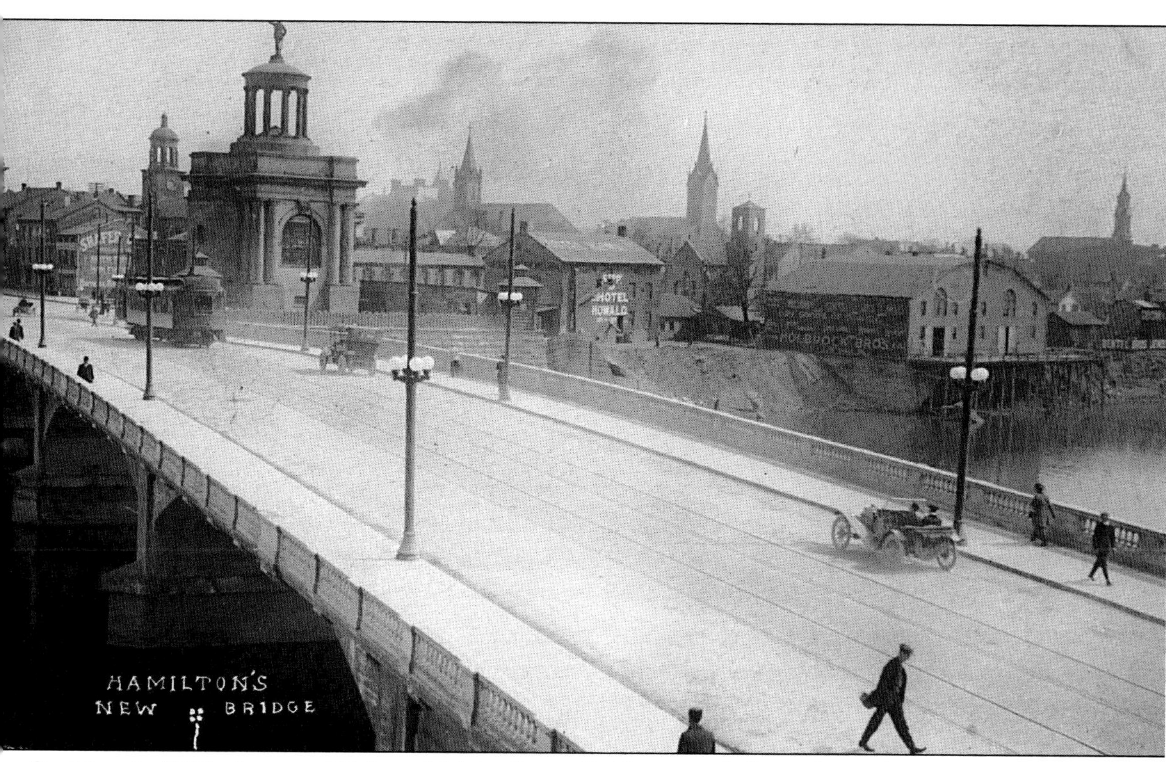

On May 6, 1915, the new High and Main Street Bridge was dedicated. By then, the horse-drawn carriage was slowly fading away, and more modern forms of travel such as streetcars and automobiles began to populate local streets. As this card demonstrates, however, nothing can replace the simplicity of just relying on one's own two feet. Even after the flood, businesses still hugged the banks of the Great Miami. (Courtesy of BCHS.)

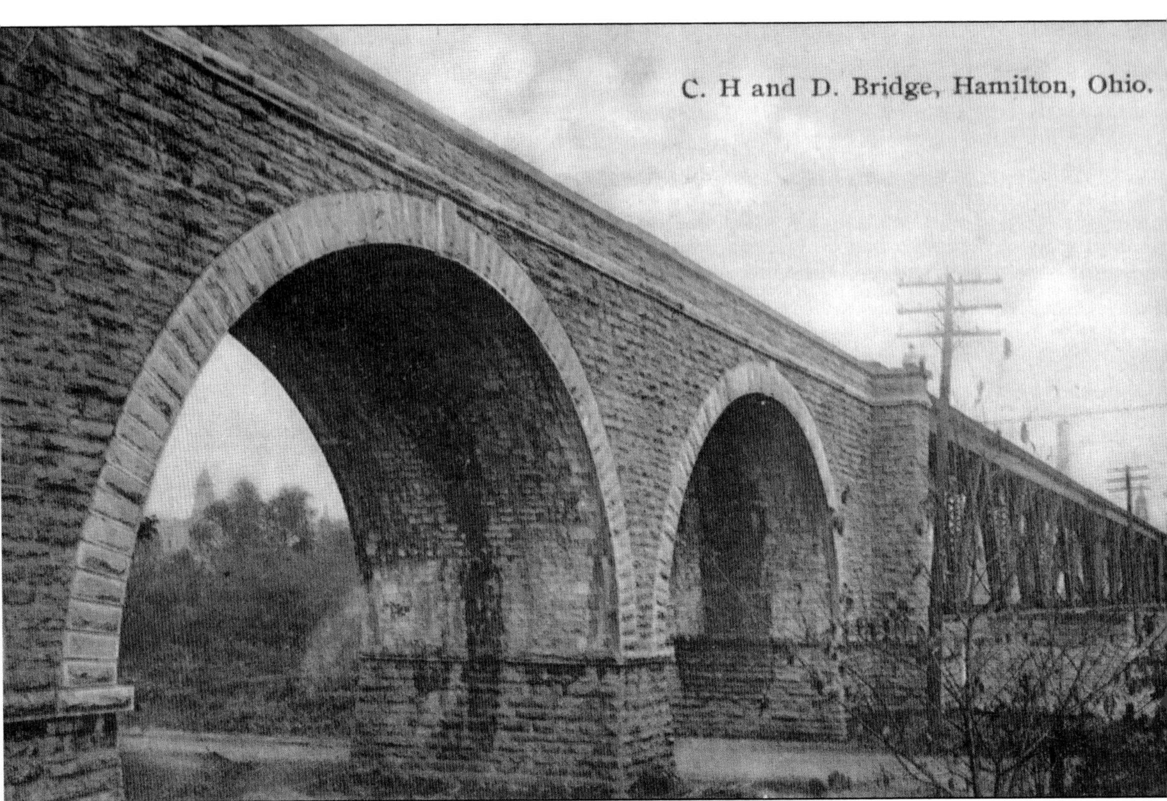

Designed by local engineer John Earhart, the original Cincinnati, Hamilton and Dayton Railroad Bridge is a design marvel. The 665-foot, 17-arch viaduct was constructed to connect Hamilton with Oxford, College Corner, and eventually Indianapolis. Completed in 1859, the original arches still form the basis of the railroad access across the Great Miami in Hamilton today.

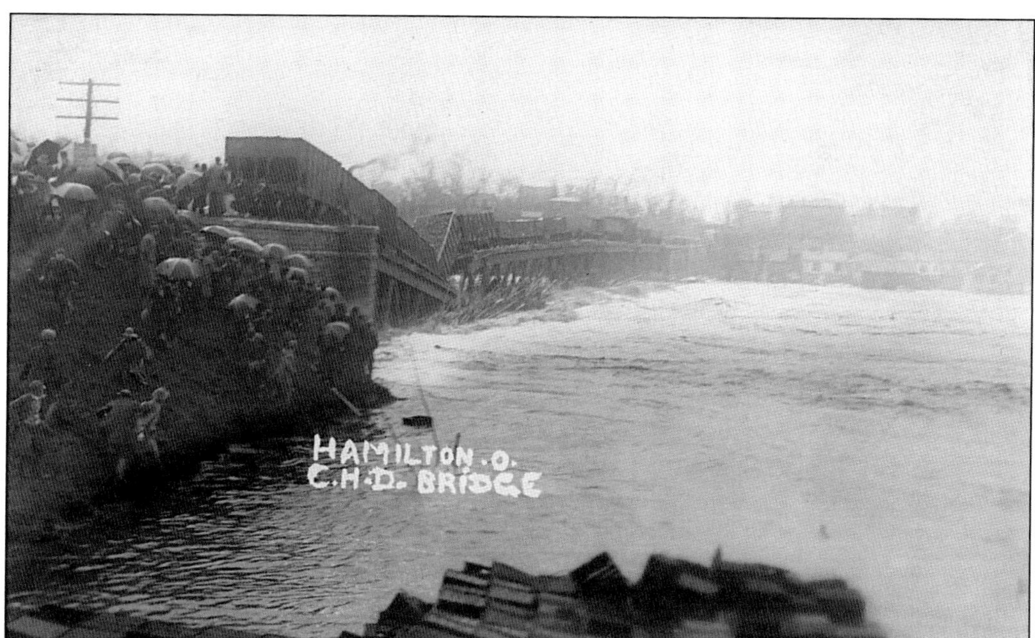

A huge crowd has gathered to witness the collapse of the Cincinnati, Hamilton and Dayton Railroad Bridge during the 1913 flood. This image captures the moment the bridge gave way, sending railcars full of coal into the torrential waters.

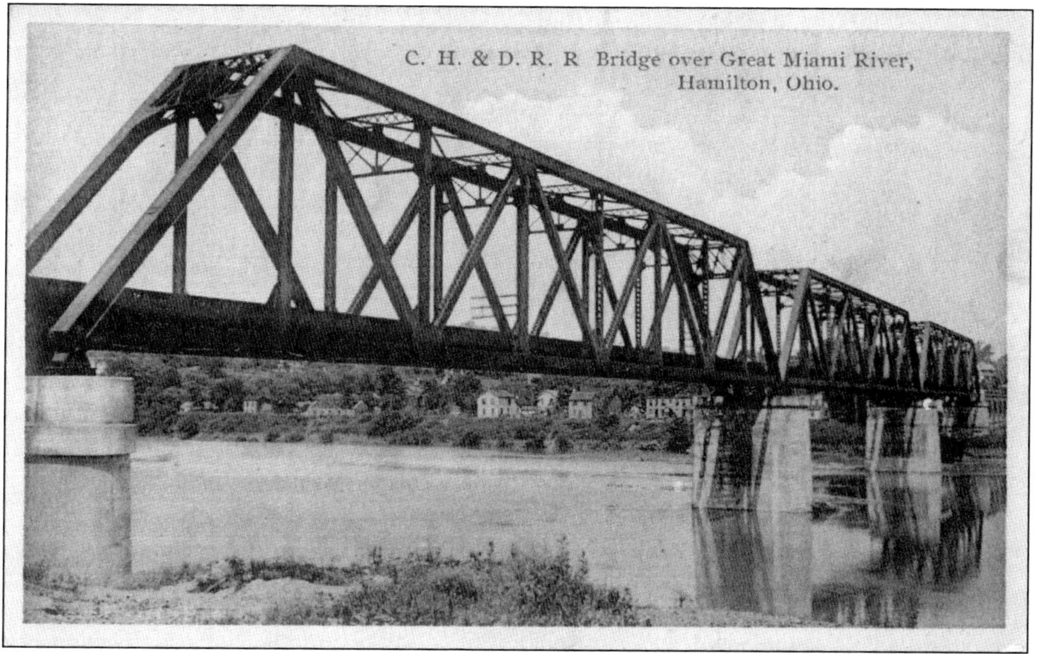

When the original ironwork of the Cincinnati, Hamilton and Dayton Railroad Bridge was washed away by the 1913 flood, work soon began on a replacement. The length of the bridge was increased to 835 feet, yet it still used the arch viaduct system from the previous bridge. This bridge was the first to be rebuilt after the flood, opening on January 18, 1914.

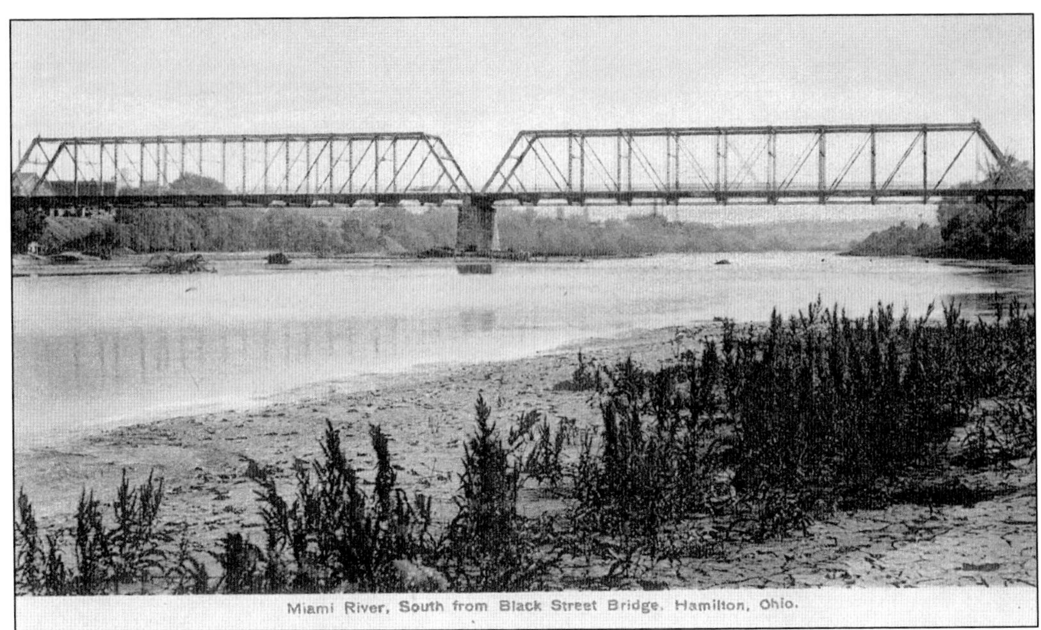
Miami River, South from Black Street Bridge, Hamilton, Ohio.

Another of Hamilton's bridges to not survive the floodwaters in 1913 was the Black Street Bridge. In fact, it was the first to collapse. Connecting east and west sides at the Champion Paper Mill and the Niles Tool Works near North Second Street, the iron-truss bridge was replaced with a more modern concrete arch design.

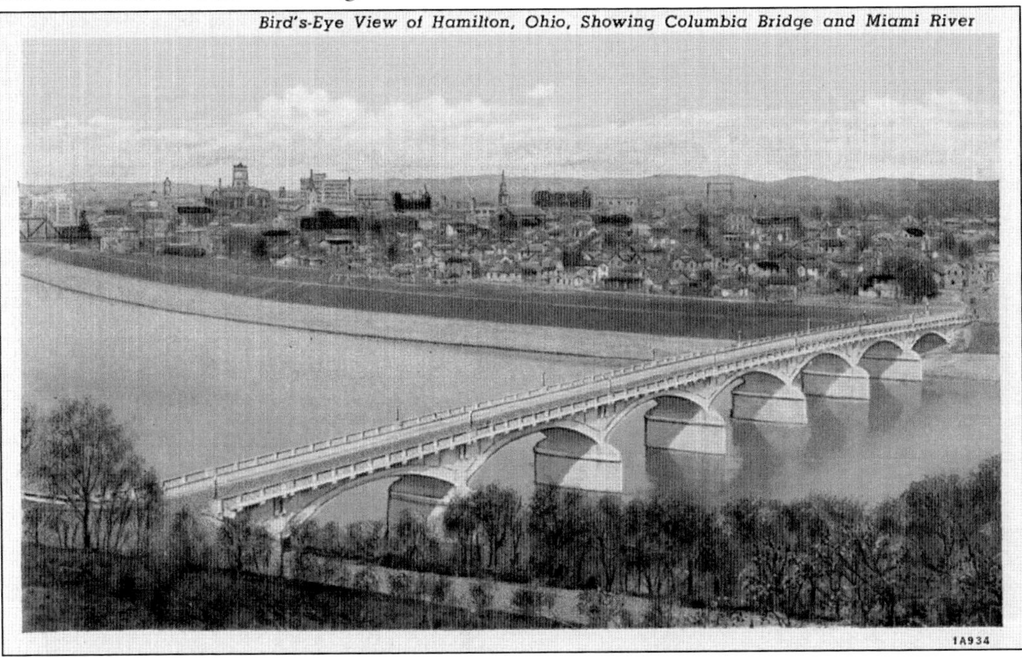
Bird's-Eye View of Hamilton, Ohio, Showing Columbia Bridge and Miami River

1A934

The Columbia Bridge was destroyed when large portions of the Coliseum, a local sports and entertainment venue located at Park Avenue and North A Street, was lifted off its foundation during the flood and swept downstream into the bridge. This view from the 1940s shows the new bridge along with a widened river channel and concrete walls built by the Miami Conservancy to help prevent another flood disaster.

Four

INDUSTRY

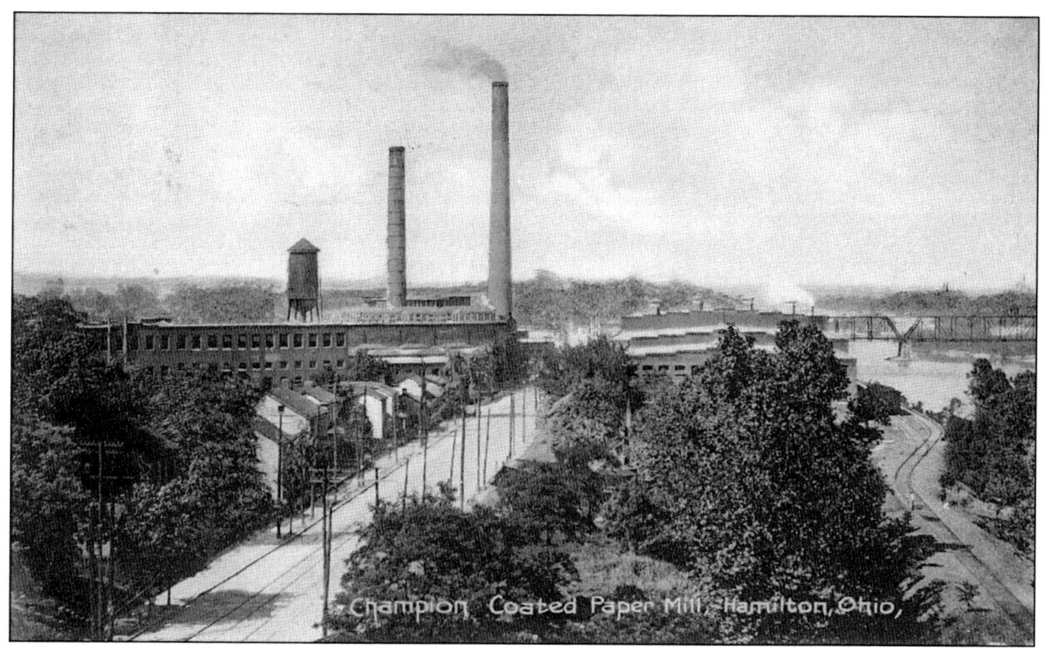

In 1900, Champion Paper Coating Mill was named by the publication *American Printer* as "The youngest and also the largest" of the 21 paper coating mills operating in the United States. This view from about 1908 looks north up Seven Mile Pike (North B Street). Railroad spars laid by the Belt Line Railroad in 1898 can be seen, and the original Black Street Bridge is in the distance (right). The plant had seen significant damage due to flooding in 1898 and was destroyed by fire in December 1901. More flooding visited the facility in 1907, and another fire razed large portions of the mill in March 1913 as a result of floodwaters entering the facilities yet again. In June 2000, economic and corporate forces accomplished what fires, floods, wars, and depressions could not. The Champion name ceased to exist, as International Paper purchased the plant. Less than six months later, the mill was sold and operated as Smart Paper LLC. In March 2012, the Hamilton industrial legend locked its doors forever. Selected demolition began in 2014.

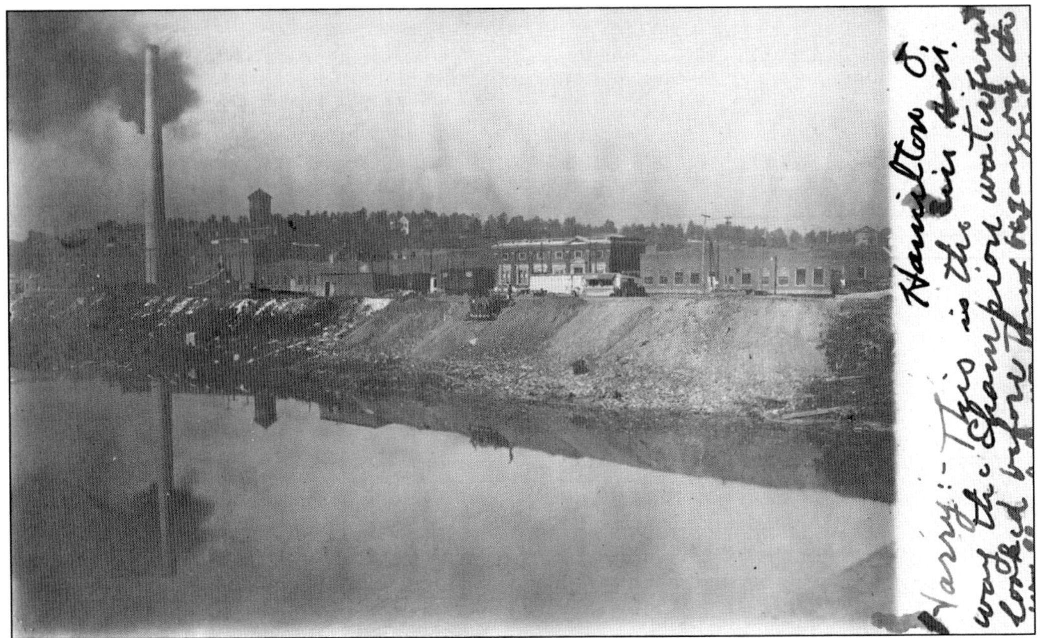

Postmarked in 1905, this card shows the Champion riverfront prior to the construction of the concrete river wall, which would run the length of the new mill expansion completed around 1907. The office building (center) was completed in 1899 and was replaced in 1924 by the office building that currently stands on the abandoned site.

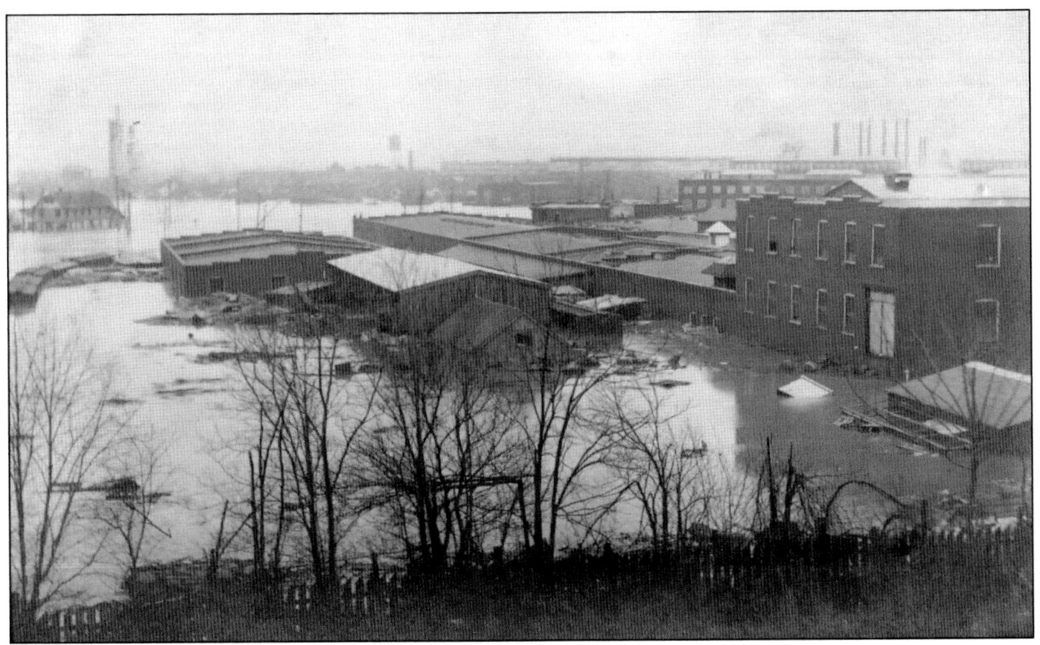

This real-photo postcard, taken from the hill to the west above the mill, shows the 1913 floodwaters engulfing the site. The railroad boxcars (left) are nearly completely submerged, indicating that the water depth is somewhere between 8 and 10 feet and still rising. This photograph was most likely taken during the early afternoon of Tuesday, March 25.

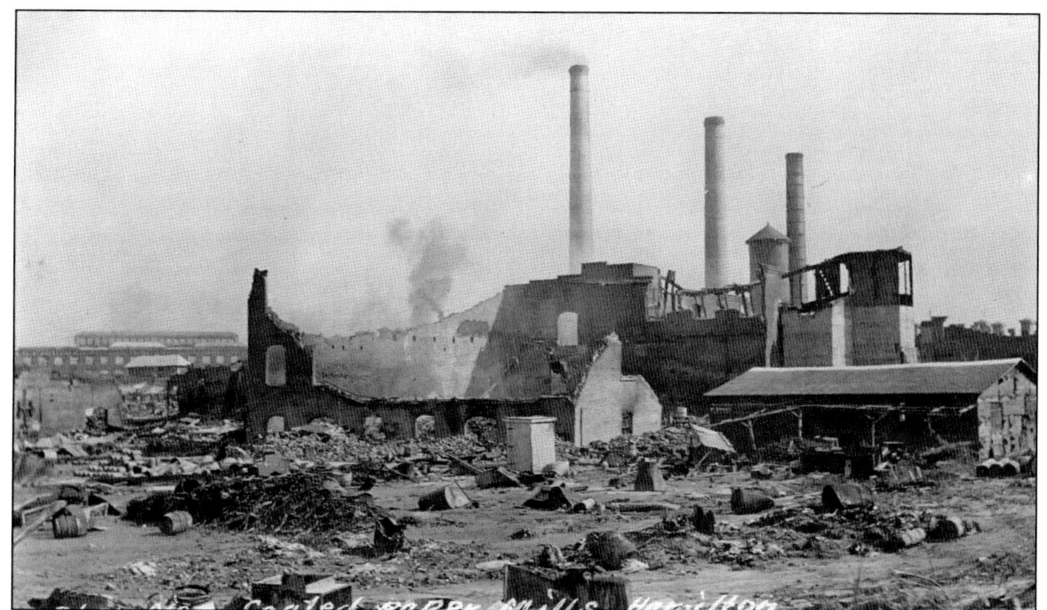

At approximately 1:00 a.m. on Wednesday, March 26, 1913, fire broke out at the Champion mill. Efforts to combat the blaze were difficult. The flood had isolated the Hamilton Fire Department. Eventually, equipment from Oxford arrived, and a valiant effort was put forth to douse the flames. Reported estimates of the fire damage were approximately $1.7 million.

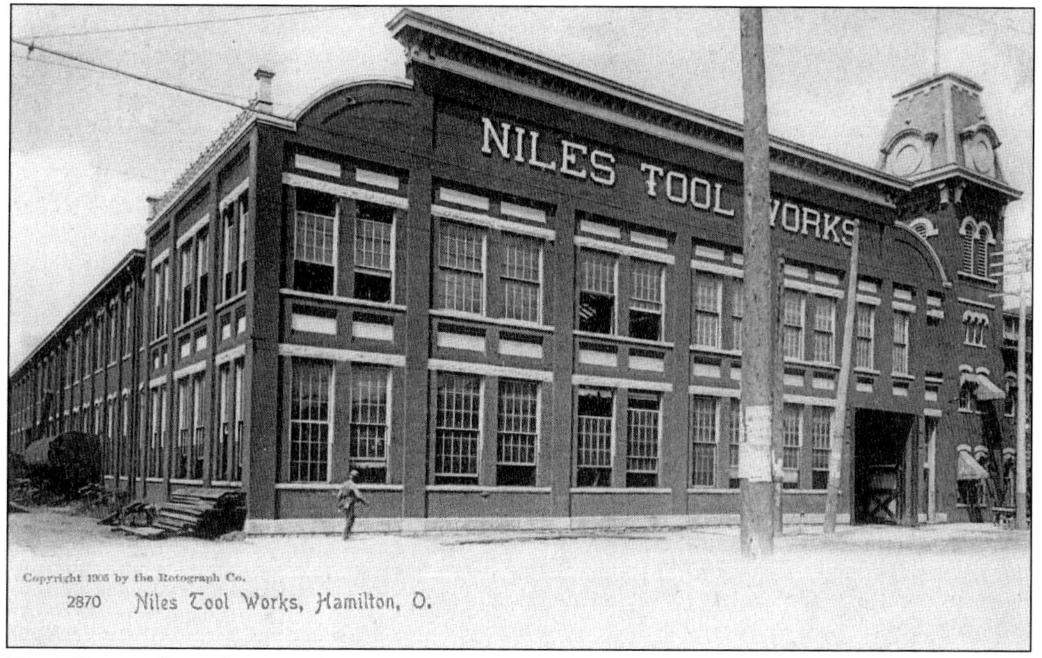

The Niles Tool Works moved to Hamilton in 1872. Land at the corner of Third and Mill Streets was donated by the city, as were the bricks and stone required to construct the tool manufacturing plant. In 1928, Niles merged with the Hooven, Owens, Rentschler Company to become the General Machine Company. Portions of the facility still stand today and are currently occupied by the Cohen Hamilton Recycling Center.

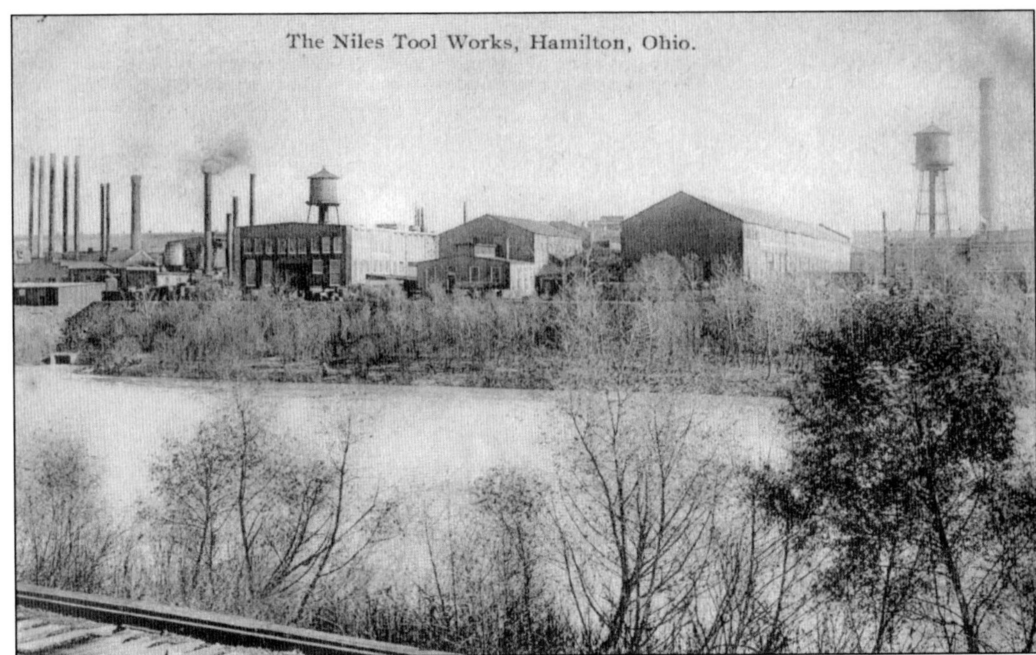

Here is a view of the Niles Tool Works looking east from across the Great Miami around 1908. The Beltline Railway spur heading into Champion Paper can be seen at the bottom of the card. Kraemer Art Company of Cincinnati, the premier card publisher in the region, captured this view and many others around the city.

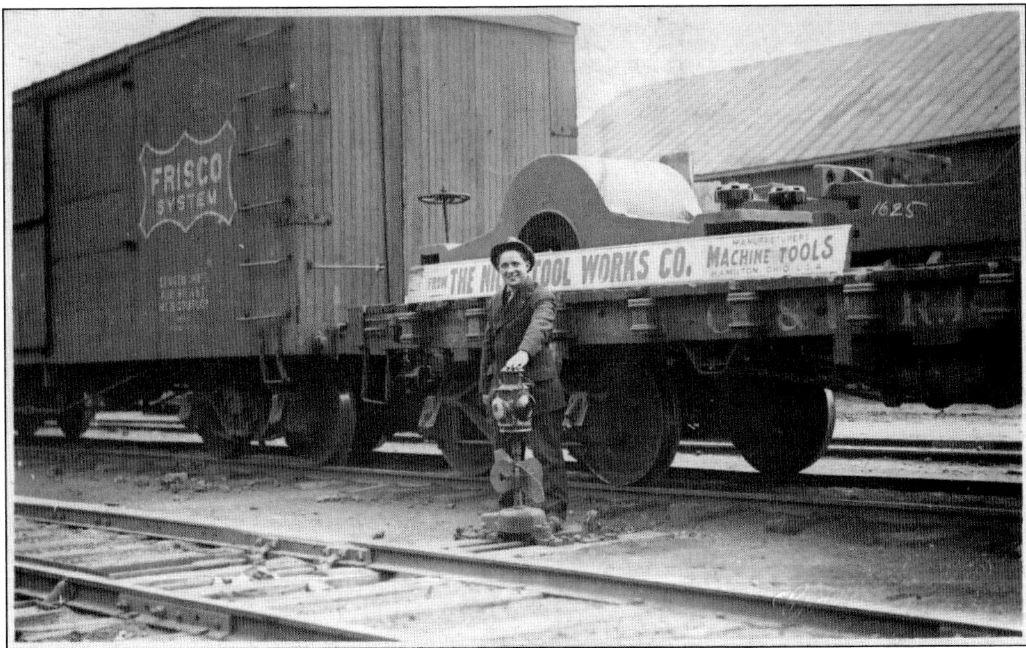

Although the location of this pre-1918 postcard is unknown, what is known is that a Niles Tool Works product was there. Shipments such as this left Hamilton for all points across the nation. In fact, US government contracts for machines for its arsenals, Navy yards, and machine shops required the "Niles Standard," meaning the best possible quality in manufacturing.

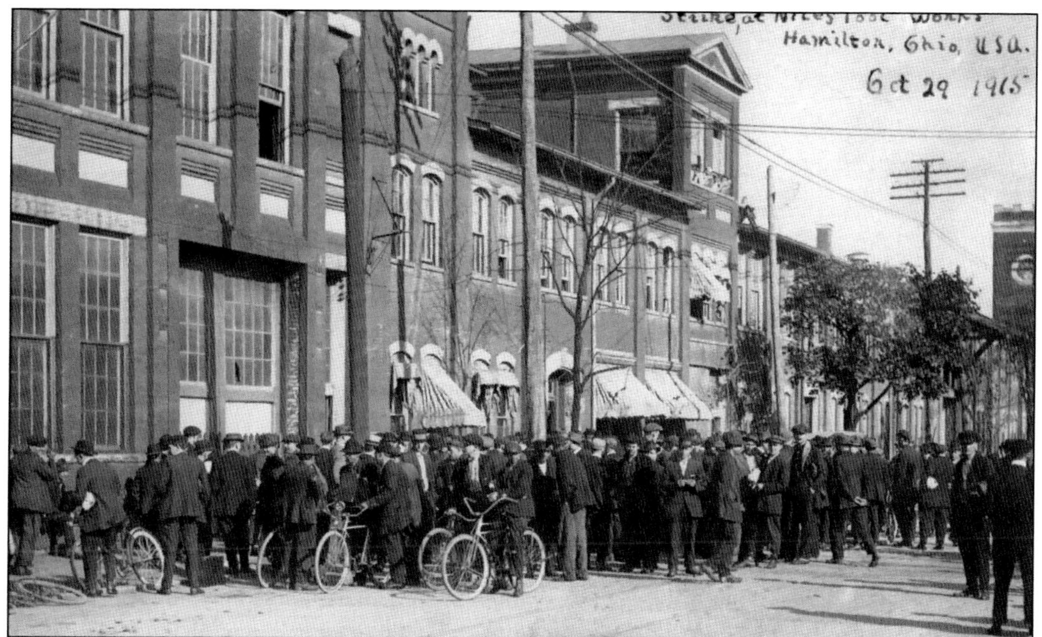

Just before 9:00 a.m. on October 29, 1915, machinists at the Niles Tool Works, totaling 360 men, walked off the job, as their overtime wage demands had not been met by management. The strike soon spread, and approximately 1,500 machinists from eight shops stopped work, causing a total loss in wages of over $40,000 per week. The strike lasted until January 13, 1916. (Courtesy of BCHS.)

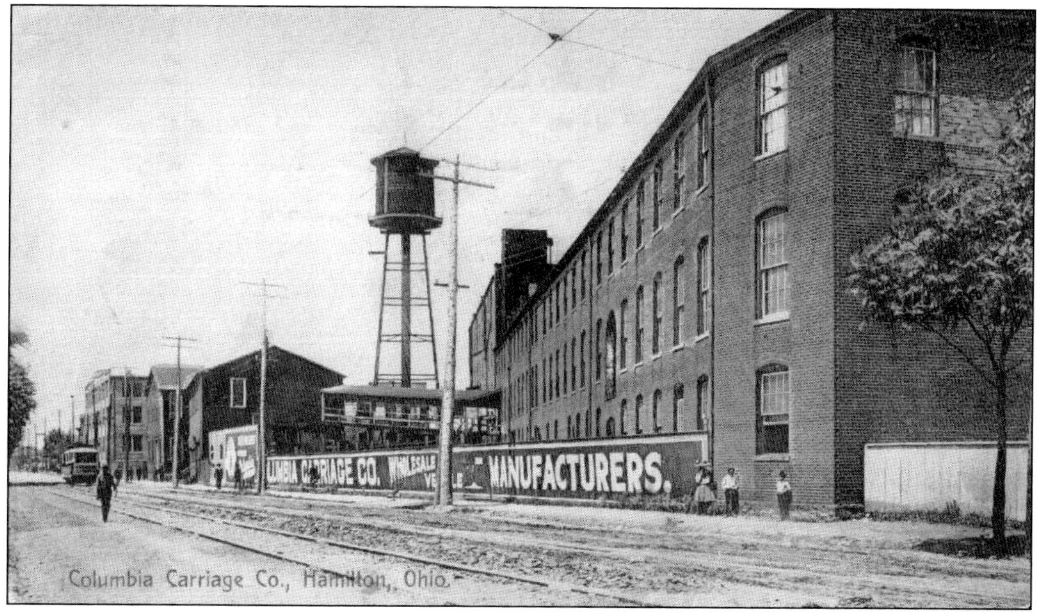

The life of the Columbia Carriage Company was a relatively short one. In 1891, the old Hamilton Distilling Company, located on Central Avenue near the South Hamilton Railroad Crossing, was leased and remodeled to manufacture medium- and high-grade carriages and buggies. In 1906, the company unveiled the "Hamilton." Essentially a buggy with a gasoline engine under the seat, the machine had a top speed of 15 miles per hour.

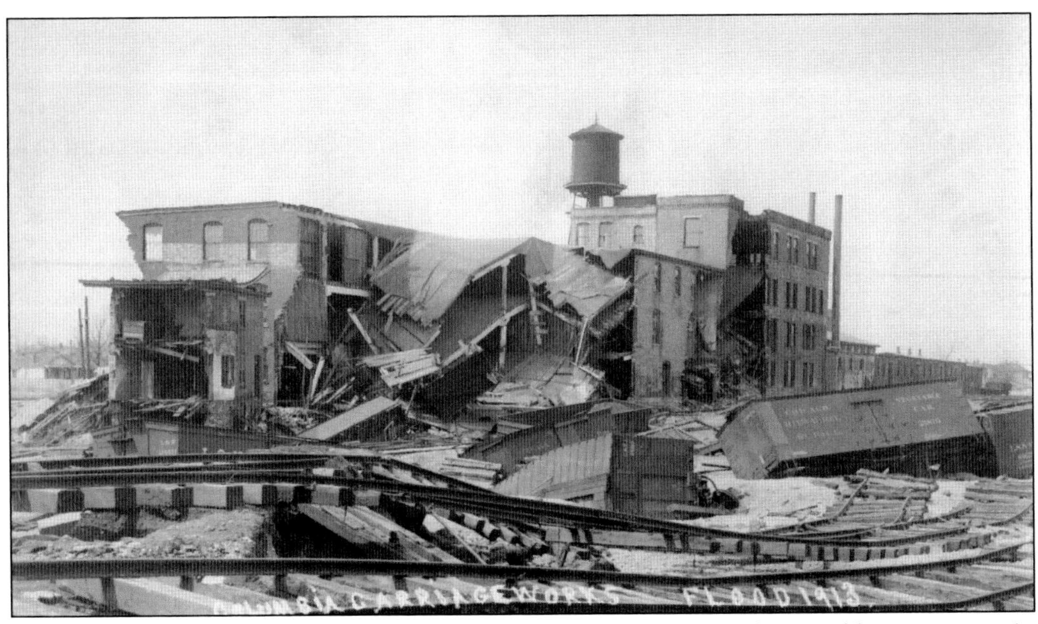

By 1911, the Columbia Carriage Company had closed its doors, no longer able to compete in the growing automobile market. In 1912, the Fostoria Company, a rival carriage manufacturer, purchased the facility and gutted it of equipment and machinery. By the time the 1913 floodwaters ripped through the facility, it was nothing but an empty shell.

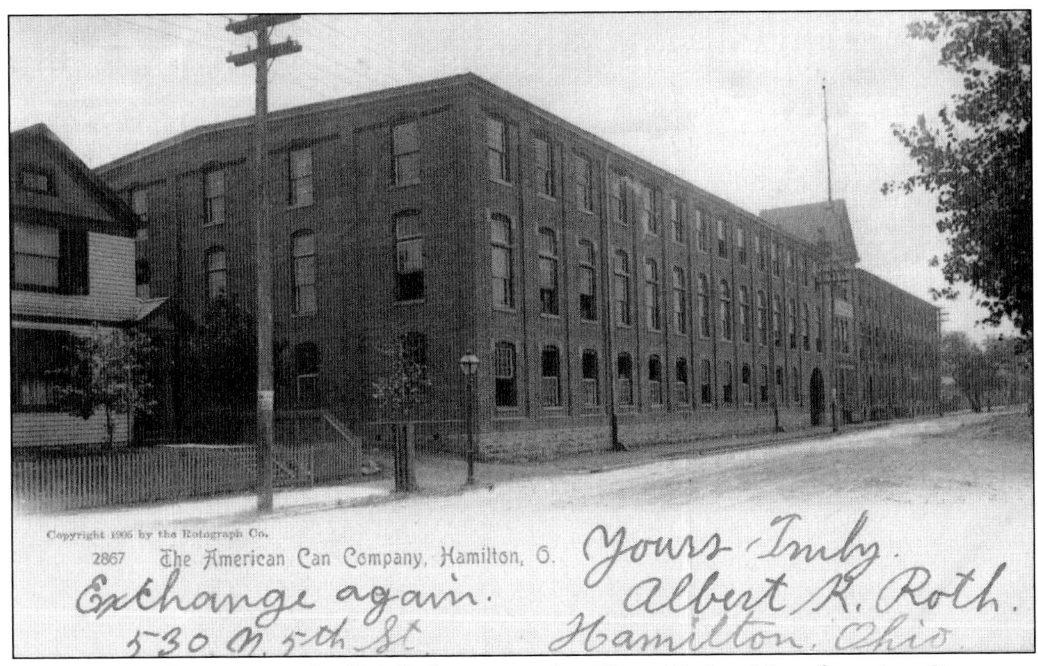

Originally built in 1889 and officially known as the Albert Fischer Manufacturing Company, the plant, located at 821 North Third Street, was referred to by locals as simply "the can works." Absorbed in 1901 by the American Can Company of New York, the facility manufactured numerous styles and sizes of cans for all types of uses, specializing in those for lard. The plant ceased operations in 1931.

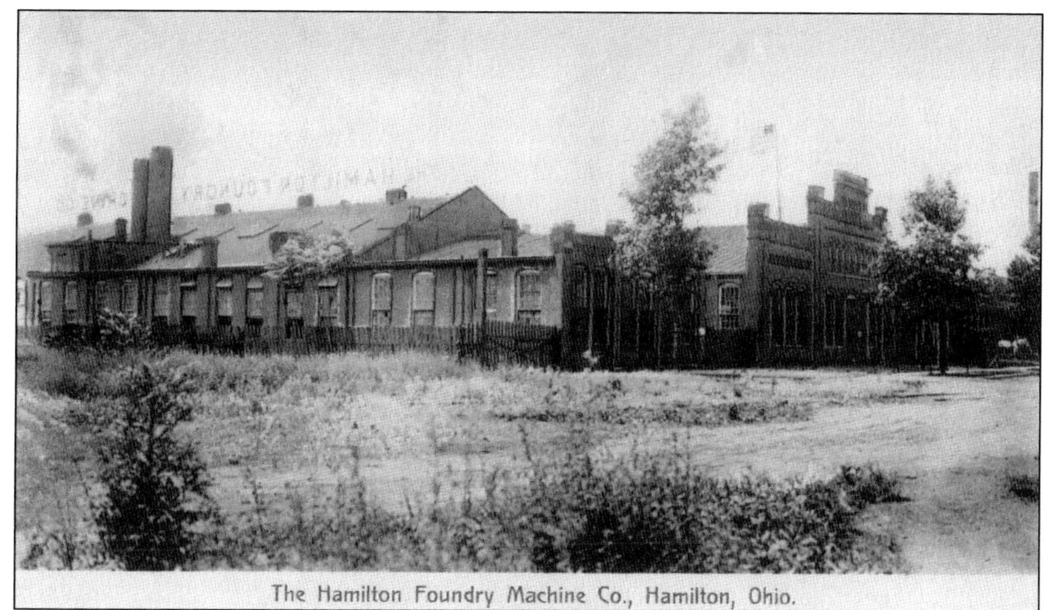

This view of Hamilton Foundry and Machine Company shows the plant before its expansion and rebuild in 1913. Specializing in light-iron castings, the plant melted 50 tons of metal per day in 1914 but never accepted an order for a casting weighing over 100 pounds. Founded in 1891 by George A. Rentschler and located on Lincoln Avenue in east Hamilton, the company closed its doors in 1984.

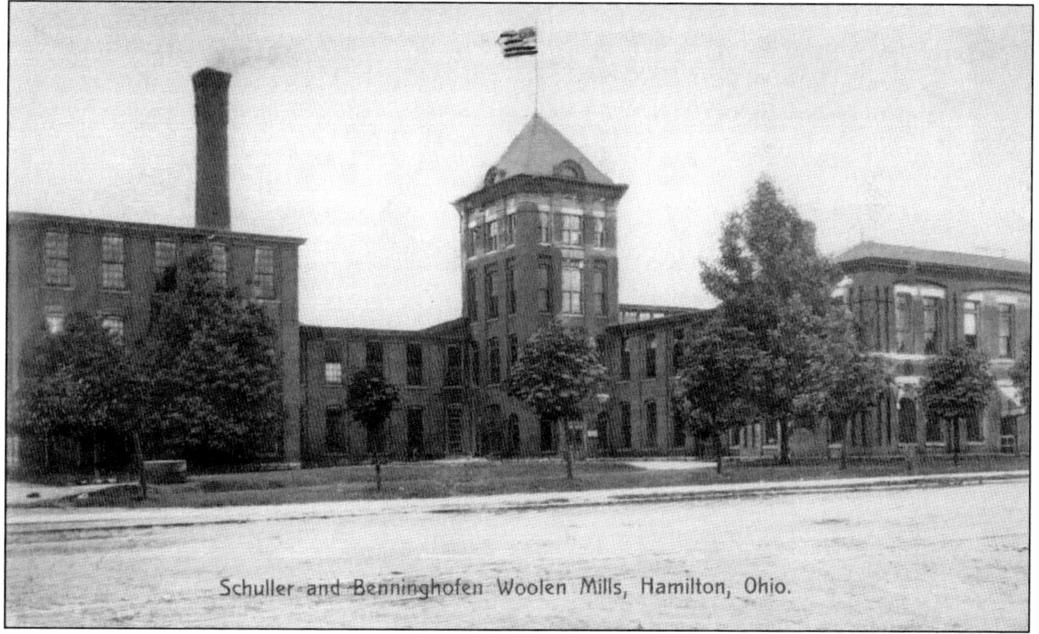

Originally started in 1858 by John W. Benninghofen and Asa Shuler, the Shuler and Benninghofen Woolen Mills Company built this plant in 1894 at Williams and Pleasant Avenues in Lindenwald due to increased product demand. Specializing in felt for the paper industry and the production of woolen blankets and shawls, the business was one of the longest family-held operations in the area. The facility closed in 1967, but the building still stands today.

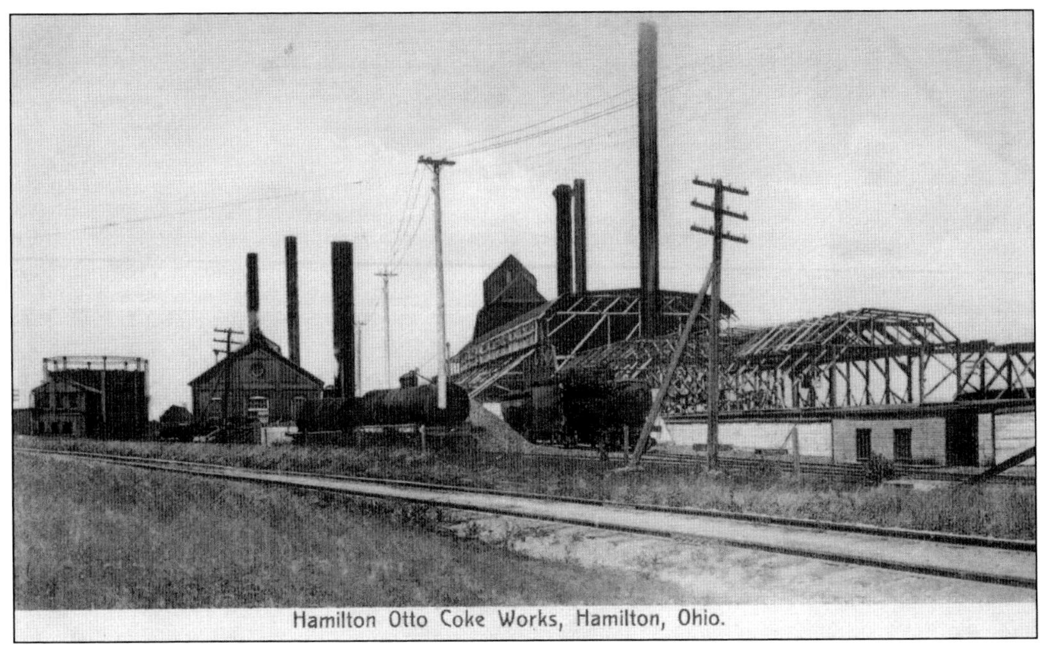

The Hamilton Otto Coke Company was constructed in 1900 in the small village of Coke Otto, named after the plant, now known as New Miami. The facility supplied a by-product gas, separated during the coal conversion process, which was piped to Hamilton to be used for heating and lighting. Electricity was also generated on-site and sold to the Hamilton Utilities Company.

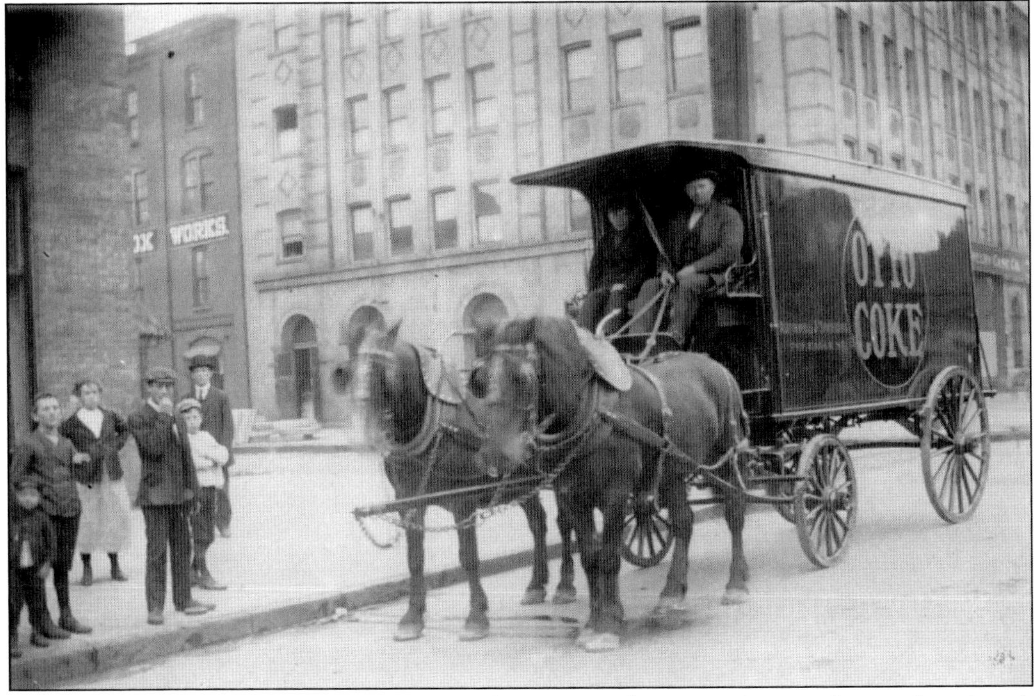

Here is an early 1900s real-photo postcard of an Otto Coke wagon in an unknown location; it appears to be carrying a father and his young son. By this time, coke was beginning to close the gap on hard or anthracite coal for household use.

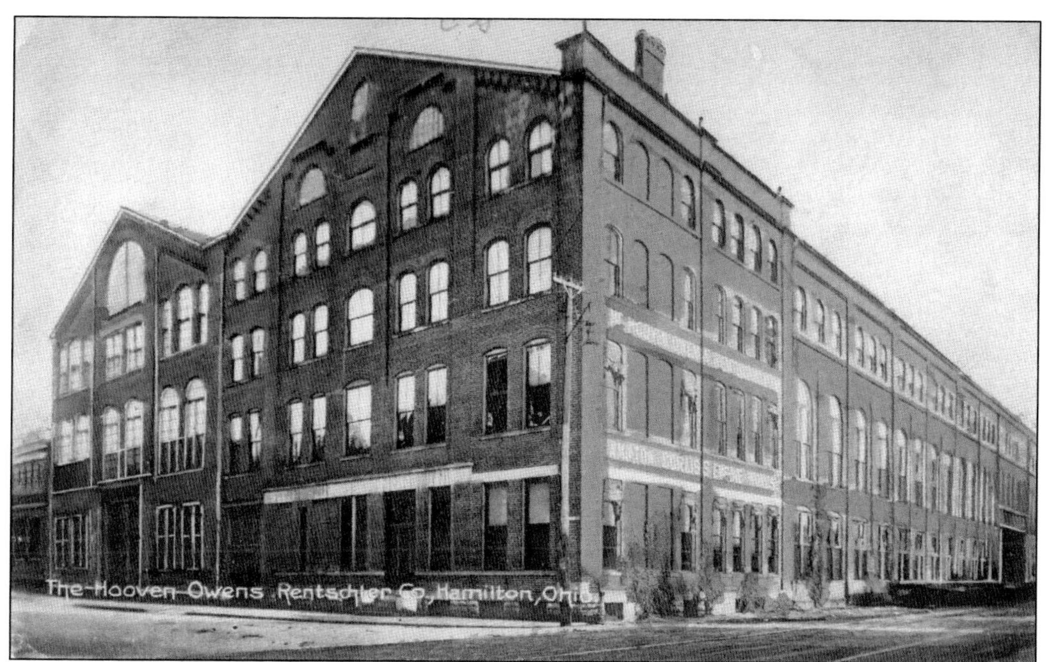

Incorporated in 1882, the Hooven, Owens, Rentschler Company gained fame in manufacturing the Hamilton Corliss Steam Engine as well as other gas, pumping, and blowing engines. The foundry also created heavy semi-steel and gray iron machine castings with the ability to melt over 250 tons of metal a day in 1914. The facility, located on over two full blocks at Heaton and Fourth Streets and bounded by Buckeye and Vine Streets, enjoyed many decades of prosperity and innovation. George A. Rentschler merged the company with Niles Tool Works in 1928 and formed the General Machinery Corporation. After additional mergers in the 1940s and 1950s, the facility ceased engine manufacturing operations in 1959. When Henry Ford expanded his Model-T assembly facilities, he selected Hooven, Owens, Rentschler Company's Hamilton-Gray gas engines to power his plant. The 6,000-horsepower engines were the largest internal-combustion engines built to date. Ford eventually ordered 12 such engines, and one is on display at the Henry Ford Museum.

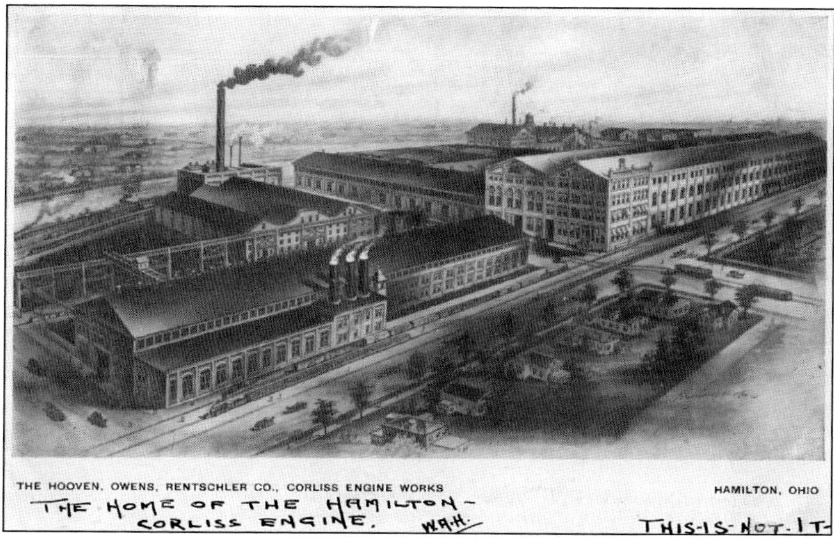

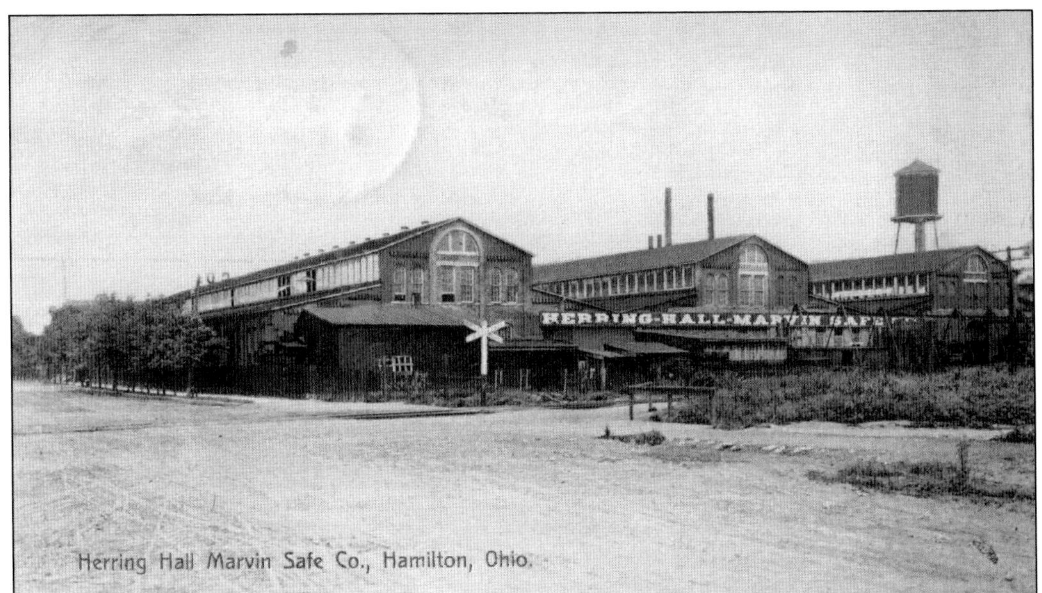

Located on Grand Boulevard, directly across from the Mosler Safe Company, the Herring Hall Marvin Safe Company was established in Hamilton in 1896. The merger of three existing companies created the entity that was the first to use electric protection of bank vaults and was involved in uranium machining for the Manhattan Project. The facility was purchased by Diebold Corporation in 1959, and the facility closed in 1991.

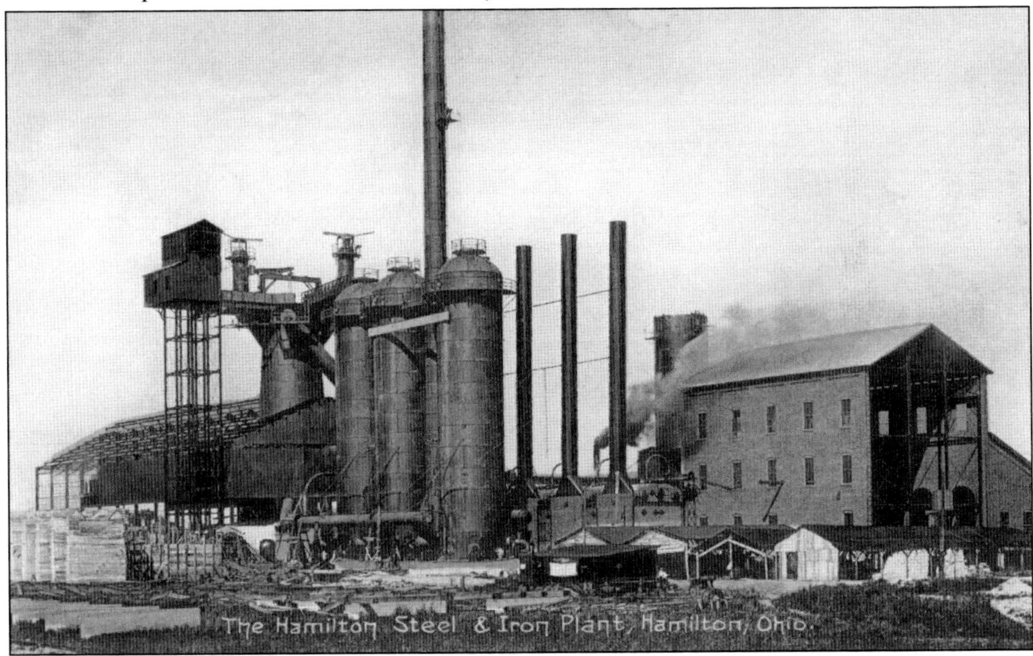

Constructed in 1908, the Hamilton Steel and Iron Company was located in the small village of Coke Otto (present-day New Miami), to the north. Employing over 1,000 men when it opened, the facility consisted of blast furnaces, a rolling mill, and a cement plant. The American Rolling Mill Company purchased the site in 1937 for the manufacture of coke and iron. The plant completely ceased operations in 1994.

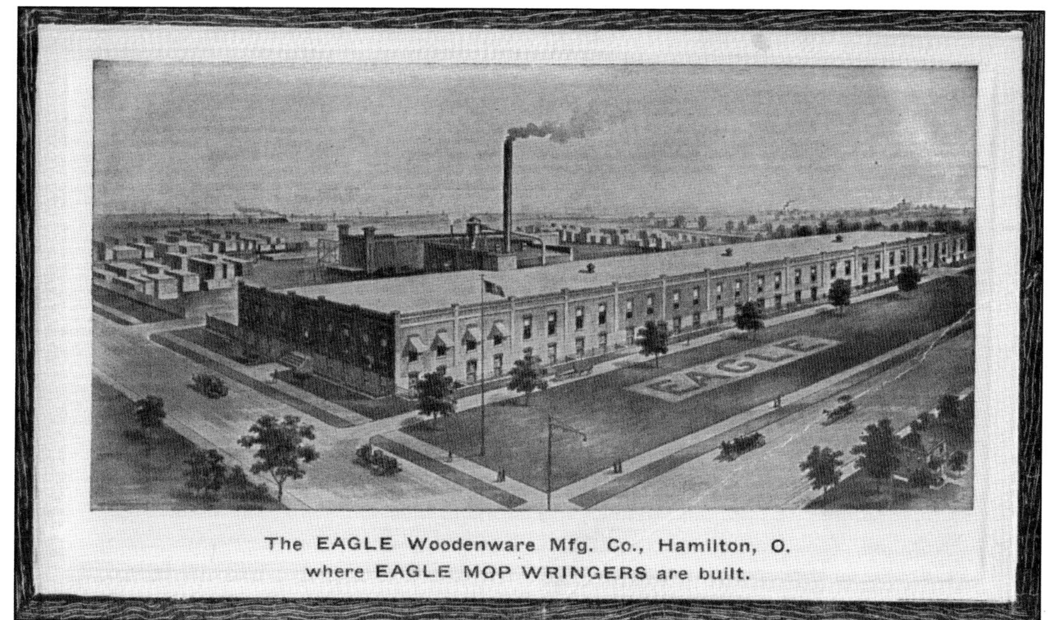

Originally based in Circleville, Ohio, the Eagle Wooden Ware Manufacturing Company moved to Hamilton in 1911 and built the plant pictured here, located on Dayton Street near the canal, for better distribution purposes. Even though Eagle manufactured a variety of products, including washing machines, ice-cream makers, and a general line of wooden wares, the company was best known for its combination mop wringer and bucket.

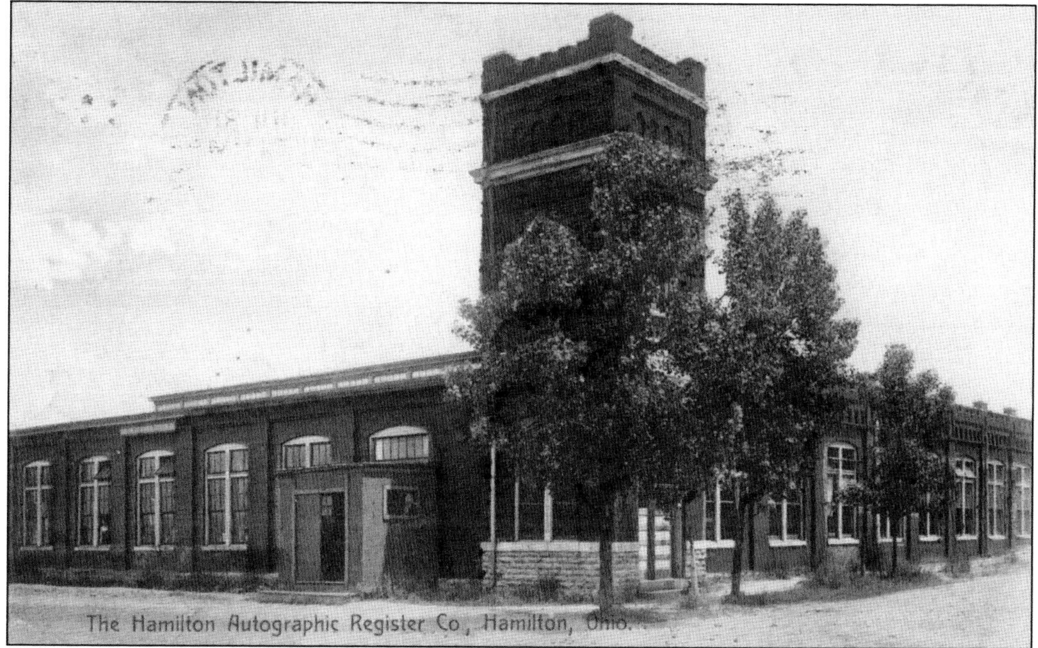

Situated on the northeast corner of Symmes and Millikin Avenues in Lindenwald, the Hamilton Autographic Register Company was owned and operated by Christian and Peter Benninghofen. Beginning in 1887, the company manufactured carbon-rolled devices for duplicating bills and receipts for businesses. The facility still stands, though the company is now defunct.

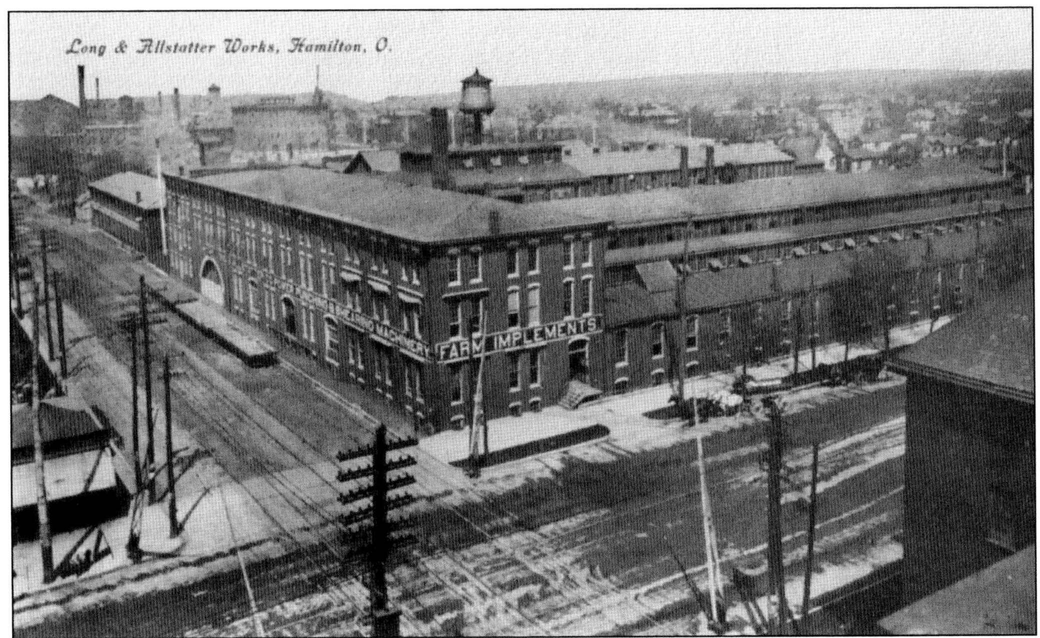

In 1858, the Long, Black & Allstatter Company sold 65 of its patented "iron harvesters." In 1873, the company moved its operations to the corner of Fourth and High Streets, Peter Black retired, and the company name became Long & Allstatter. The facility would become a leader in the manufacture of shearing and punching machines as well as farm implements. The plant closed in the 1930s.

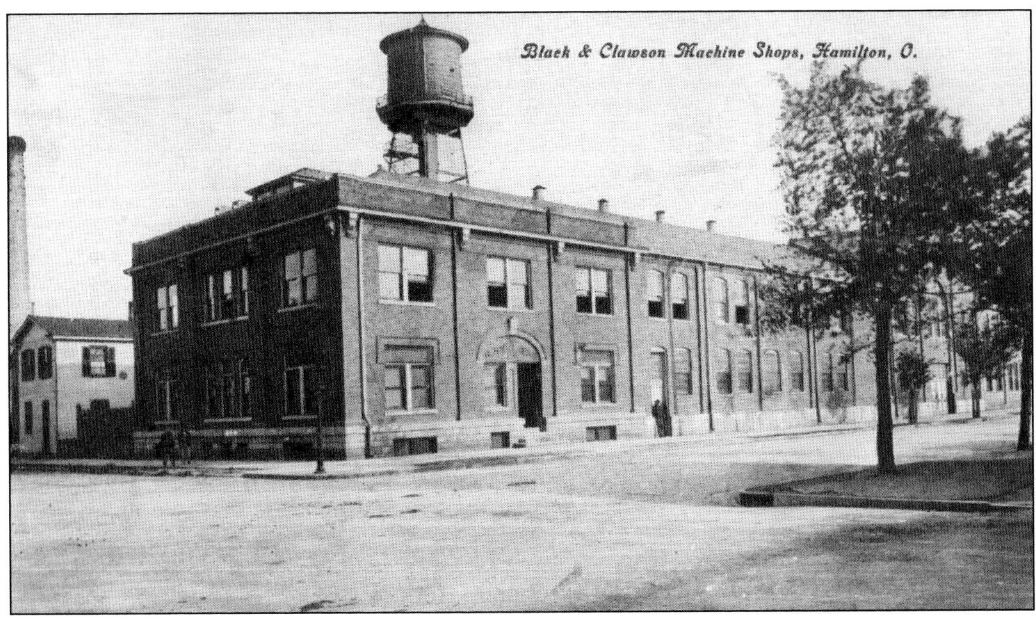

The enormity of the manufacturing processes for the Black-Clawson Company filled two city blocks at Second and Vine Streets. Makers of a variety of paper-mill machinery, the company was begun in 1875 and reached peak performance and reputation by 1904. Machines weighing as much as one million pounds were constructed in the works and hauled across the county in as many as 30 rail cars per machine.

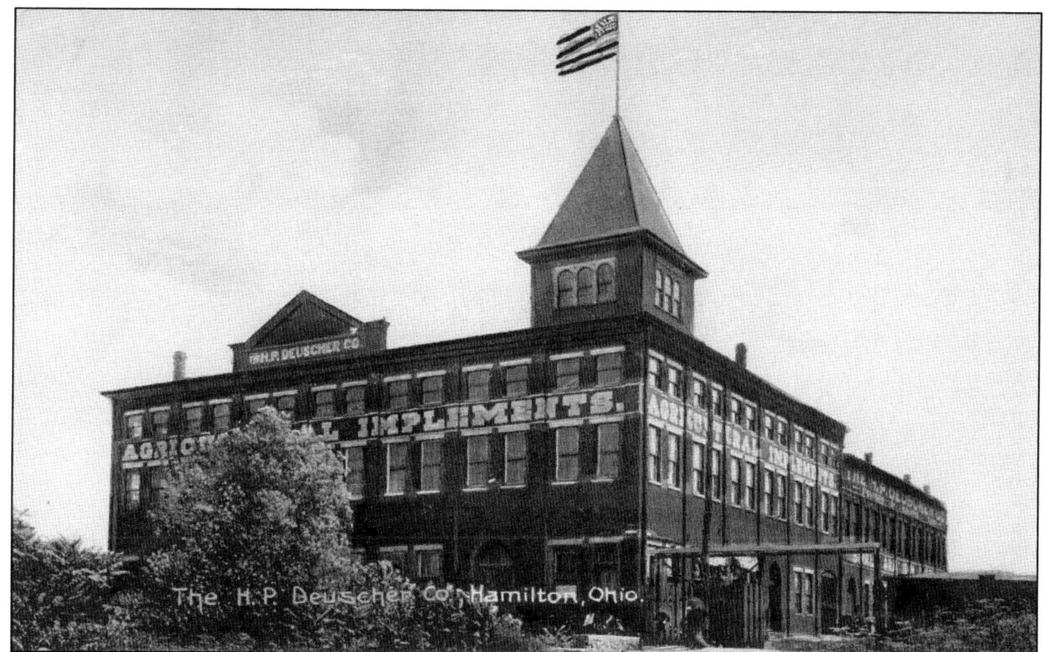

Incorporated in 1888, the H.P. Deuscher Company can trace its roots back to 1879 with the Variety Iron Works, a venture begun by Civil War veteran Henry P. Deuscher. By 1891, the company was bringing in upwards of $1,000 per day in orders and contracts. The factory, located on the southeast corner of Seventh and Hanover Streets, closed its doors in 1990.

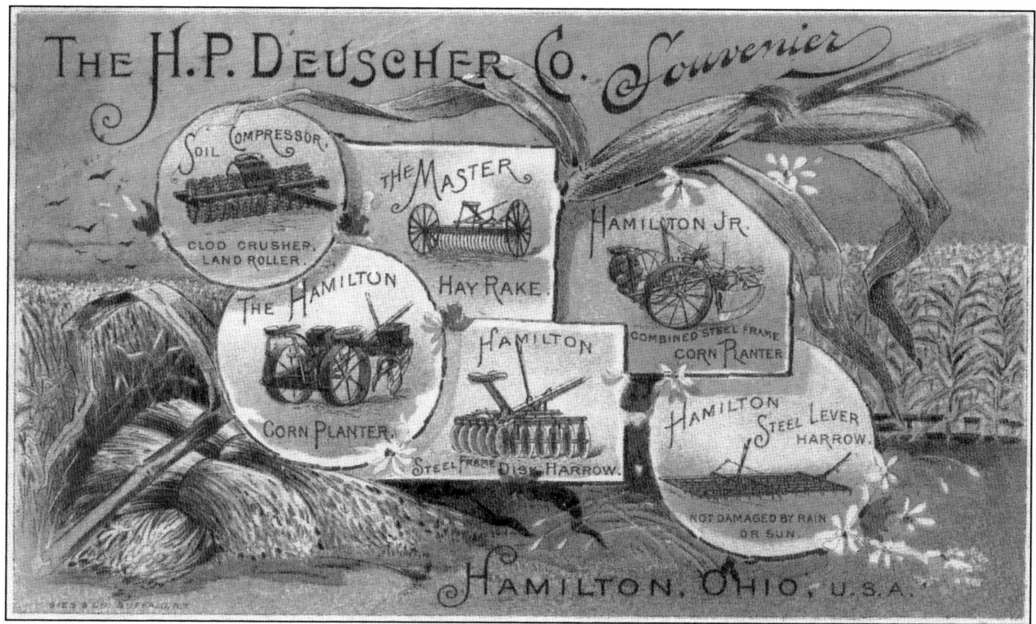

This advertising card shows a few of the agricultural implements being manufactured by the H.P. Deuscher Company. Though farming equipment made up the bulk of the company's business early on, it also manufactured school desks, heating and ventilating appliances, and eventually gray iron castings.

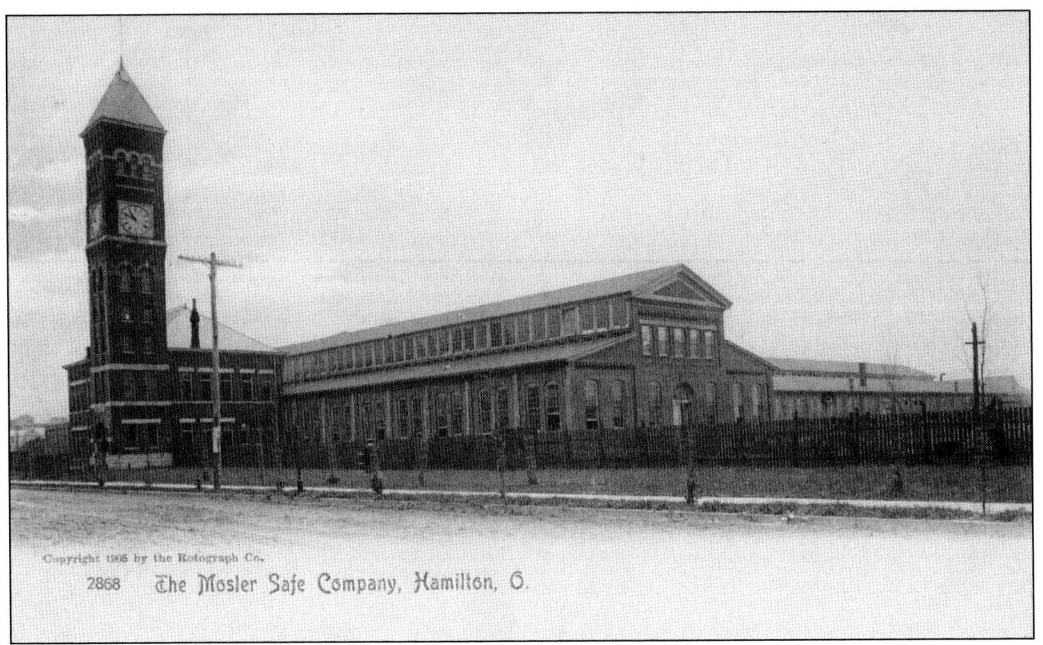

Brothers Moses, Julius, and William Mosler opened their new Hamilton operations is 1891 after outgrowing their facilities in Cincinnati. The Mosler Safe and Lock Company soon became the largest and most respected safe and vault manufacturer in the world. The large complex faced Grand Avenue in east Hamilton. The company ceased operations in 2002 after 134 years.

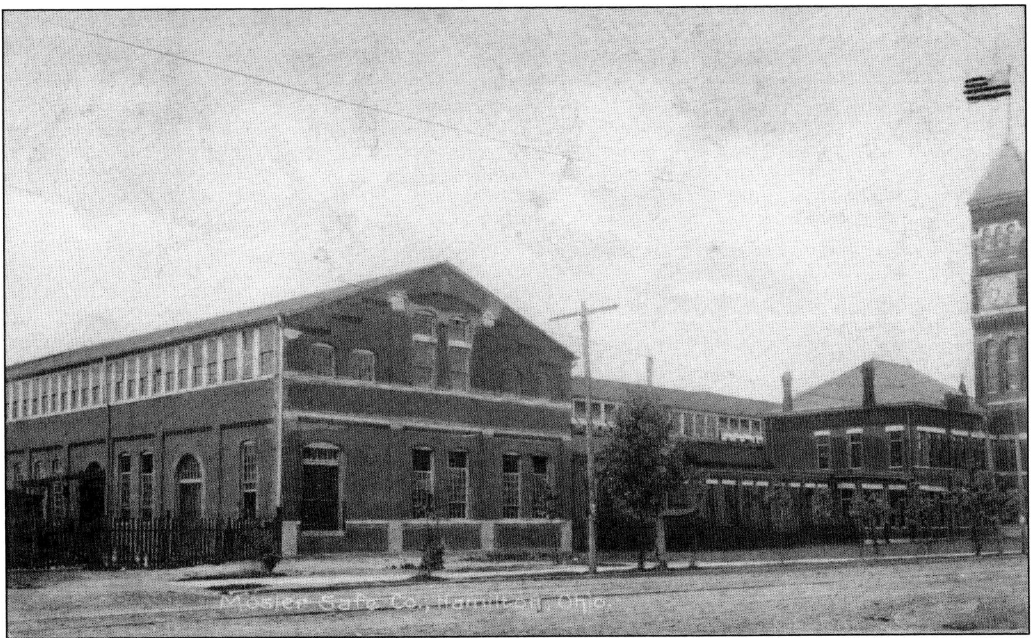

In 1915, some 50 percent of the banks in the United States were using, or had contracted to use, Mosler safes and vaults. The company provided security cases for the Bill of Rights, the Declaration of Independence, and the Constitution at the National Archives during the 1950s, manufactured the security vaults at Fort Knox for the gold supply, and built parts for Sherman tanks during World War II.

Though headquartered in Hamilton, Mosler Safe Company had global markets. This card advertises the company's New York City offices and showroom on Fifth Avenue as well as Mosler's exhibit at the 1939 New York World's Fair. The back of the card indicates additional offices in Chicago, Boston, Dallas, Kansas City, Los Angeles, Pittsburgh, Portland, Oregon "and other principal cities."

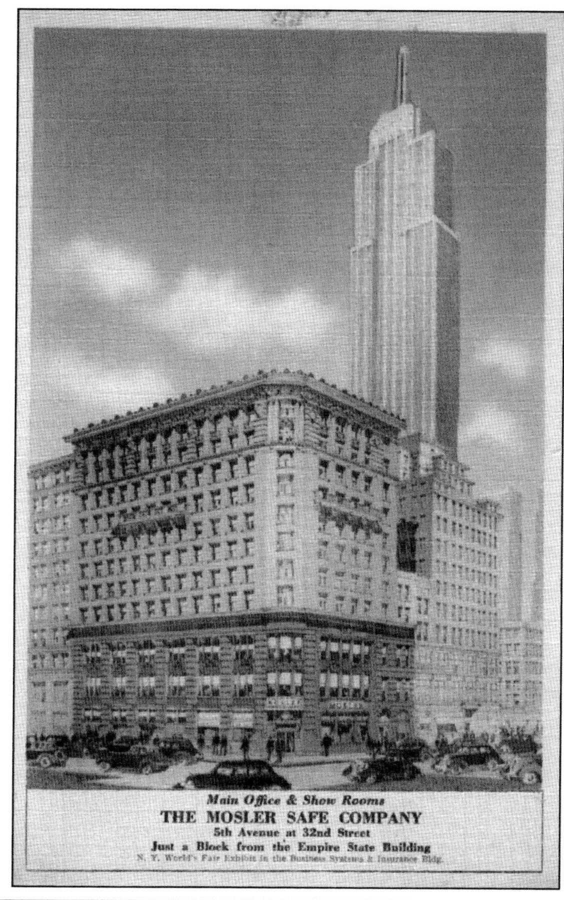

The Republican Publishing Company was incorporated in 1892 and originally headquartered in the St. Charles Hotel on High Street. In 1898, the company acquired the *Hamilton Daily News* and moved into this facility, located at the corner of North Third and Market Streets. Catalogs, newspapers, and books were published in the facility. The building was razed in the early 1970s to make way for the municipal parking garage.

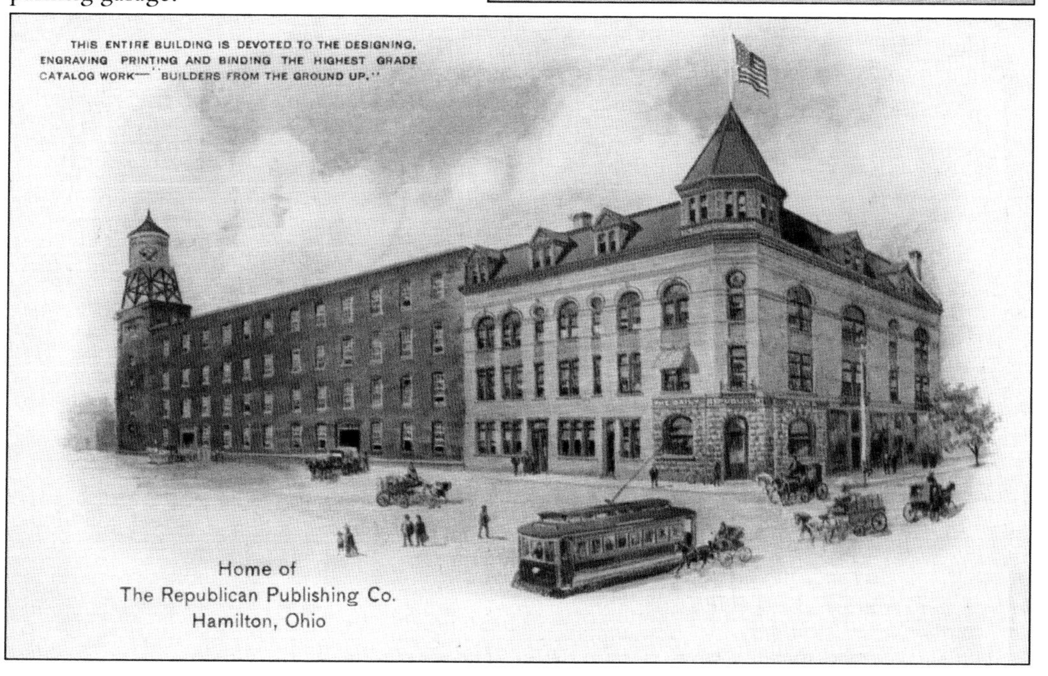

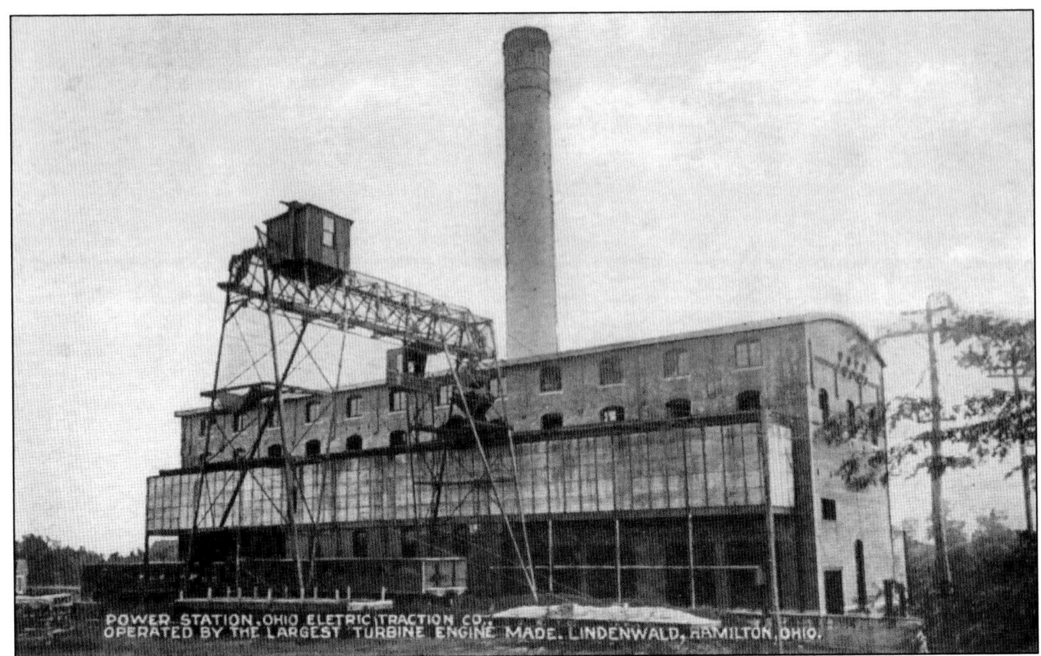

Between 1907 and 1910, the Ohio Electric Railway Company spent over $1 million on projects located on its line from Hamilton to Cincinnati. One such project was the construction of a new power station between Williams and Fairview Avenues in Lindenwald. Currently, the site is home to athletic fields and Safety Town. Only a concrete tower remains to indicate the presence of former industry.

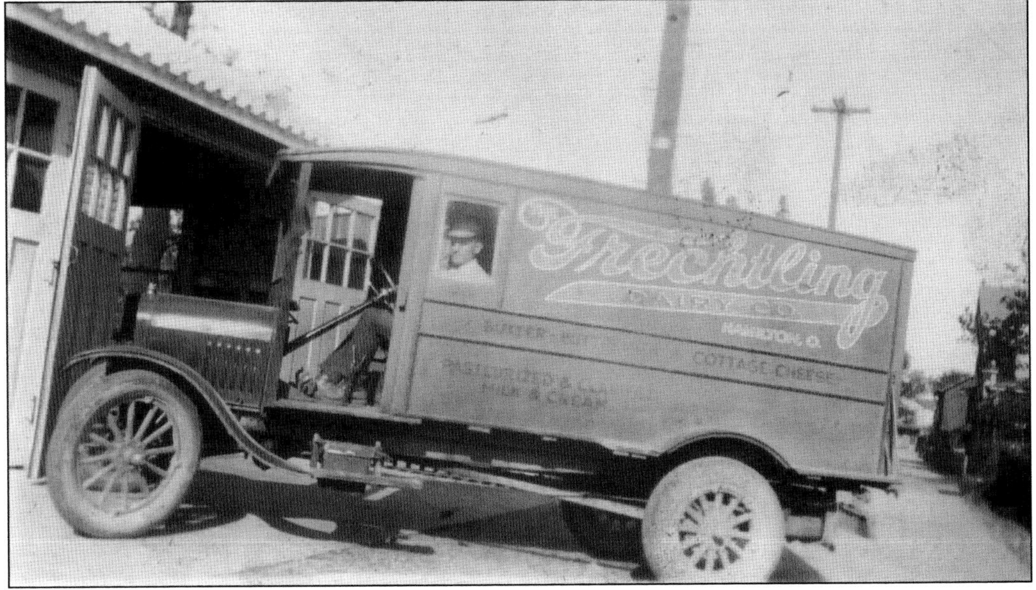

This view shows a 1926 Ford Panel Truck owned by the Frechtling Dairy Company. By the time this truck was moving raw milk from surrounding farms to the plant on South Front Street and then delivering finished product throughout the city, Frechtling Dairy had been in business for 18 years. In 1907, some 100 gallons of milk were processed per day. By 1925, capacity had increased to 10,000 gallons per day.

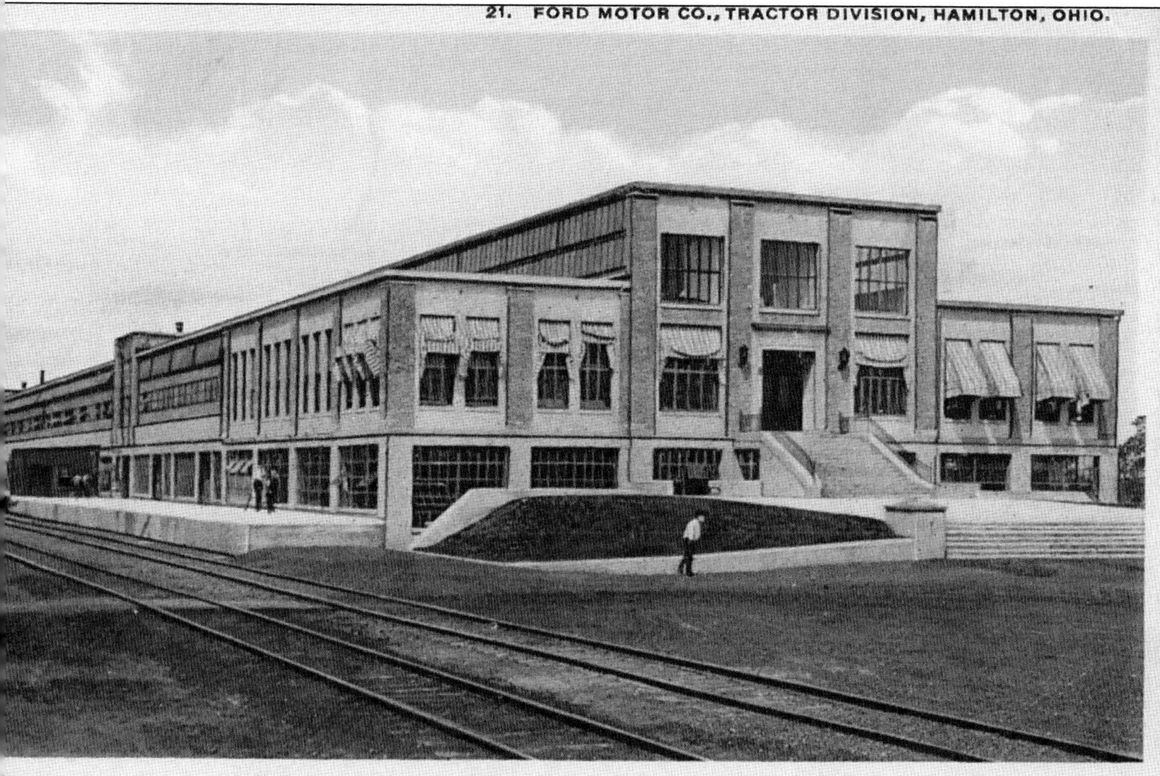

Henry Ford opened his tractor plant in 1920, and it remained in operation for 30 years, though tractor production lasted only the first six months. The plant was retooled and became a massive producer of Model-T and Model-A wheels. During World War II, aircraft parts were manufactured here. Ford closed the plant in 1950. In the 1970s, it became the site of the infamous Chem-Dyne toxic waste controversy.

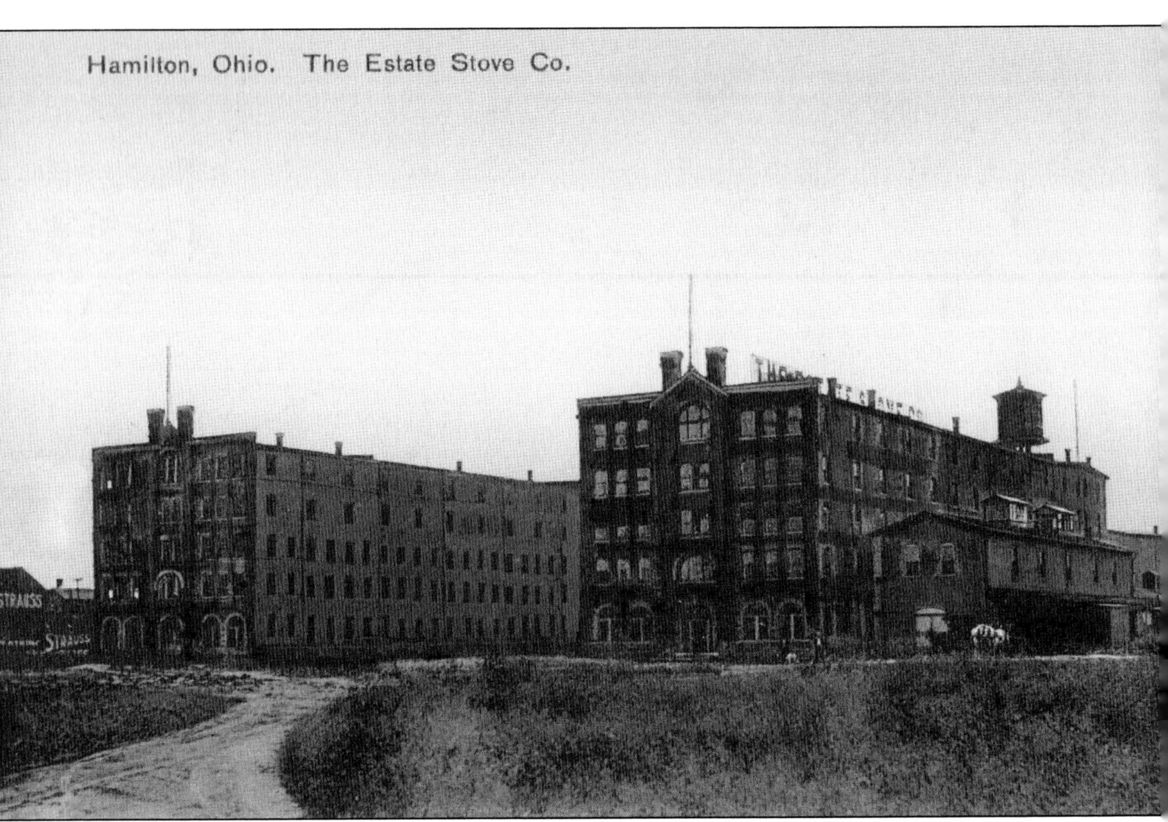

Founded in 1845, the Estate Stove Company had risen to the pinnacle of business success by 1915. Furniture stores, gas companies, and retailers in small towns to large cities across the country carried the Estate line of heating and cooking stoves. Some argued that Estate products were the most widely known of any Hamilton-made product. The factory was located on the west side of East Avenue near Grand Boulevard.

Five

ARCHITECTURE

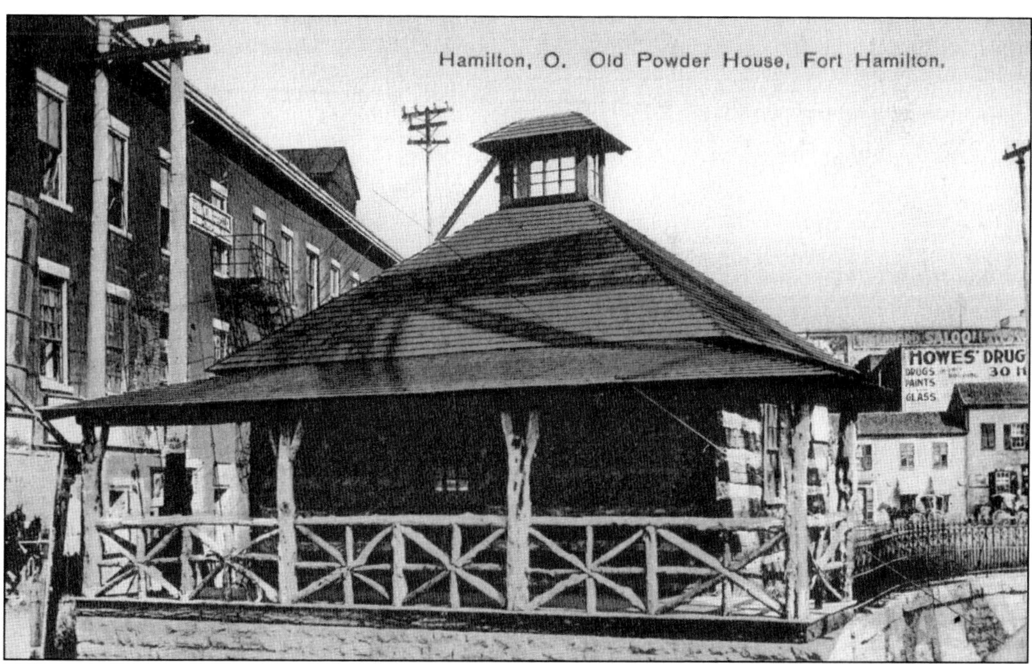

The John Reily Chapter of the Daughters of the American Revolution conducted a renovation project on the old Fort Hamilton Powder House in 1903. The organization had use and control of the structure by permission of Hamilton's Board of Control. Exterior wood weatherboarding was removed to expose the original rough-hewn logs, and a new porch was constructed facing the river. Interior renovations were also made, including a new stone fireplace and the addition of a second level. The organization held its chapter meetings and other small events in the building. Between 1903 and 1909, numerous lawsuits were filed by Mary A. Morey, an adjacent property owner, claiming that, according to the *Hamilton Telegraph*, the DAR's "ugly, dilapidated building of old, decaying second-hand logs" was wrongfully and unlawfully maintained and operated, and had changed the grade of her property as well as that of the street. The Circuit Court in Eaton, Ohio, found against Morey on all occasions. In 1909, the chapter turned the property over to the city, and Morey's troubles were solved in March 1913 when the flood washed the historic structure away.

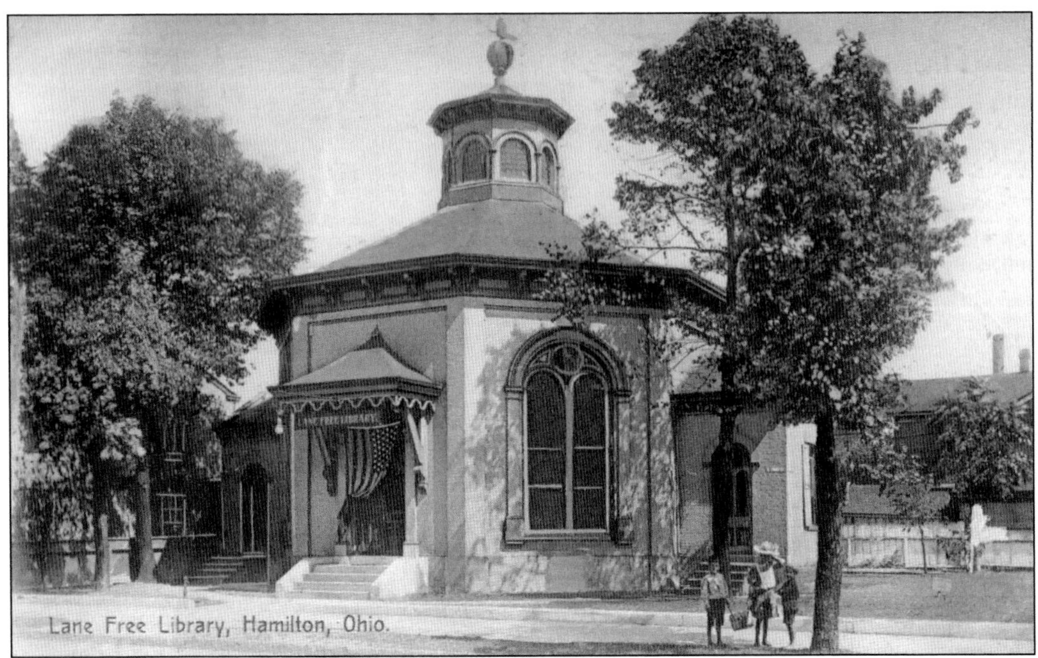

When constructed in 1866 by Hamilton industrialist, philanthropist, and abolitionist Clark Lane, the Lane Free Library was the first of its kind west of the Allegheny Mountains. The octagonal building, similar to his residence directly across North Third Street, was personally financed by Lane until he donated it to the city in 1868. The library was originally stocked with over 2,000 titles he personally selected.

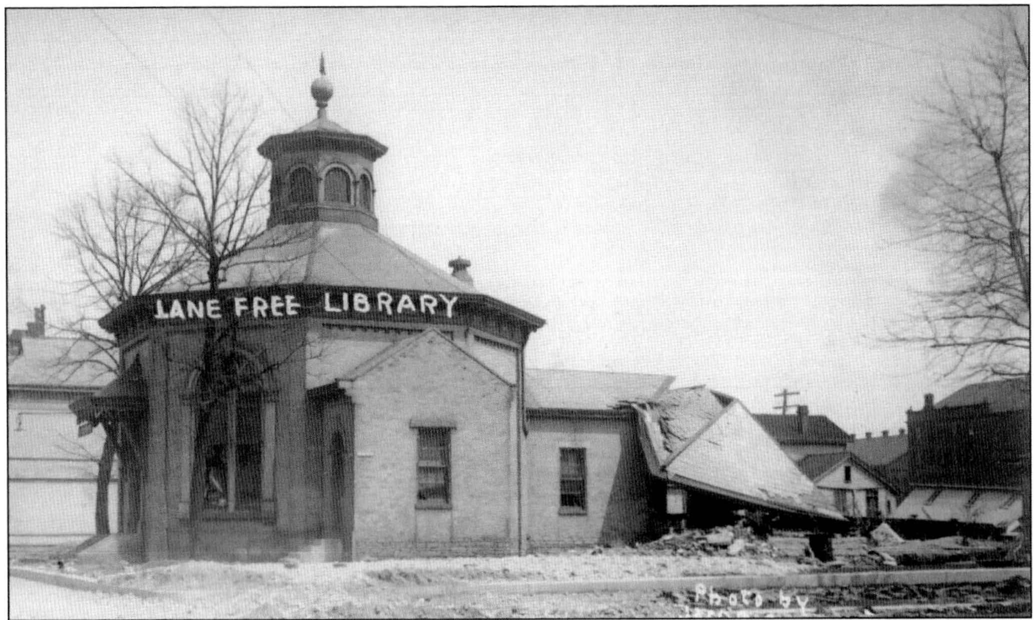

The damaged Lane Free Library is pictured here after the 1913 flood. Losses at the library were estimated at $30,000. The flood swell, which reached 12 feet in this neighborhood, and the strong current mercilessly damaged or destroyed the numerous volumes of books and reference materials. As shown here, the rear of the building also received considerable damage.

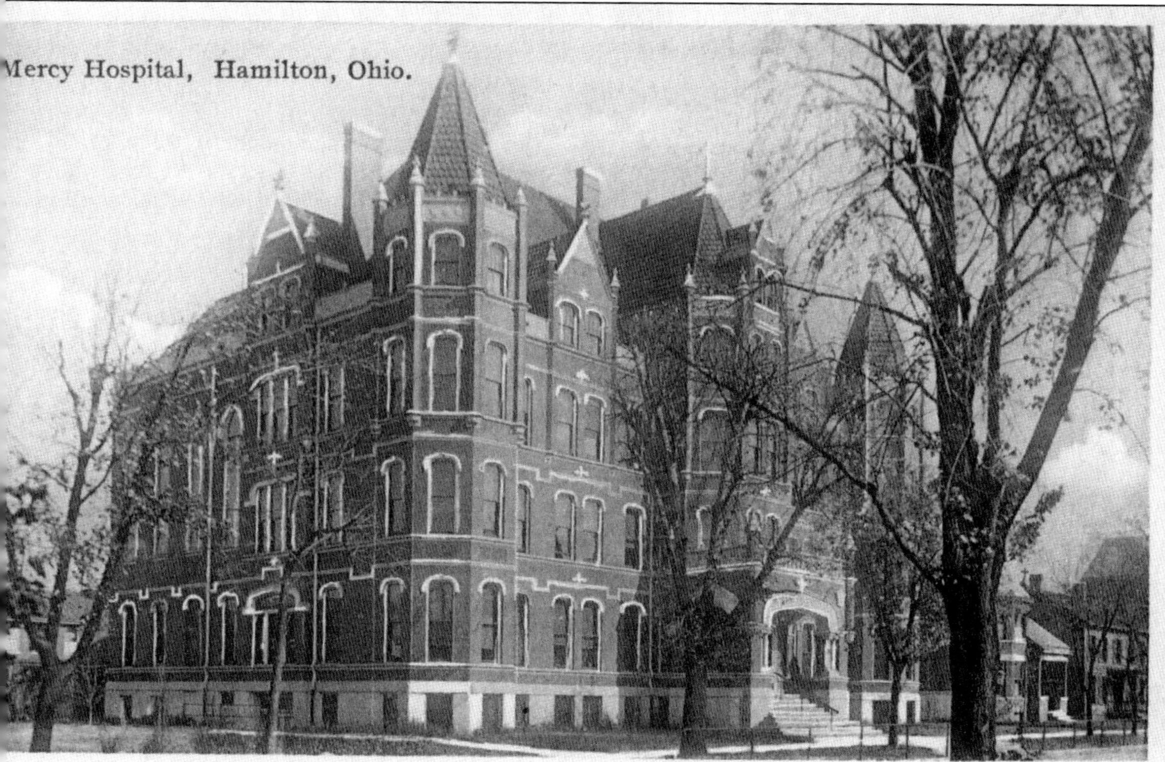

The original Mercy Hospital began service in 1892 in the former residence of William Hurm at 116 Dayton Street. It could house 15 patients and was staffed by six nuns of the Sisters of Mercy. By 1903, it was obvious to trustees that a new hospital was necessary. Opening in 1904 at a cost of $50,000, the new facility, shown here, had a maximum capacity of 100 beds. Experiencing numerous expansions throughout the decades, the hospital was closed in 2001, and demolition commenced in 2007. The site is now the home of RiversEdge Amphitheater and Marcum Park.

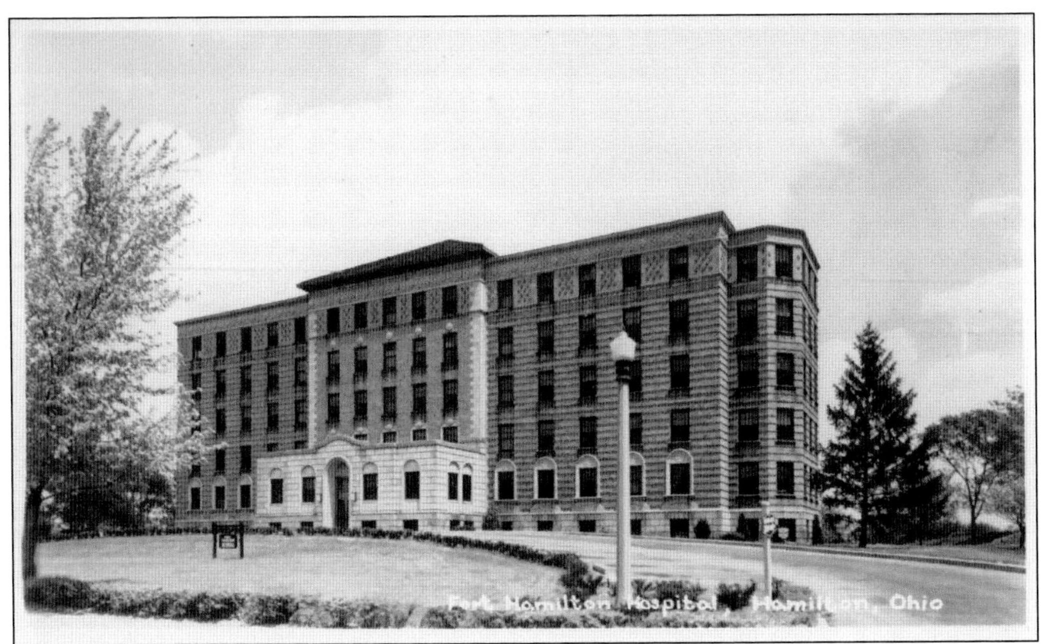

After over four years of planning and fundraising for a new medical facility, Marie Campbell was the first patient admitted to the new Fort Hamilton Hospital on May 1, 1929. She was also the hospital's first surgery. By the end of the day, five people had been admitted and treated in the new facility on the east side of Eaton Avenue. This view from the 1940s shows the expanded entry.

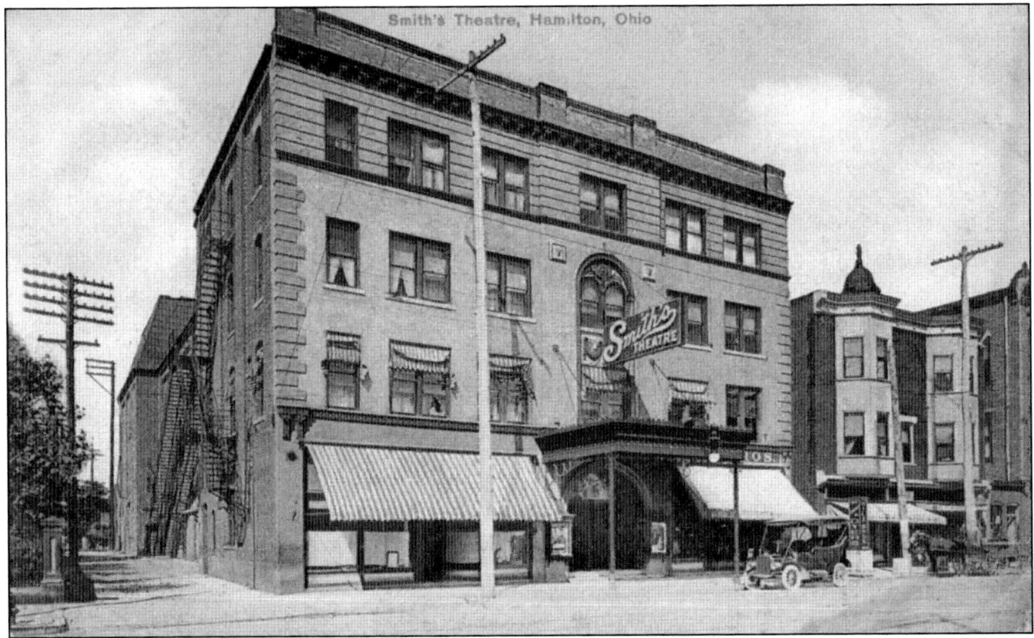

Opening in 1903 as the Jefferson Theatre, this entertainment hot spot on the west side of South Second Street between Ludlow and Court Streets became Smith's Theatre in 1908 and provided Hamilton with live vaudeville-style entertainment, lectures, concerts, plays, and more. By 1914, the name had reverted back to the Jefferson, until 1928, when fire erased the building from the city's landscape.

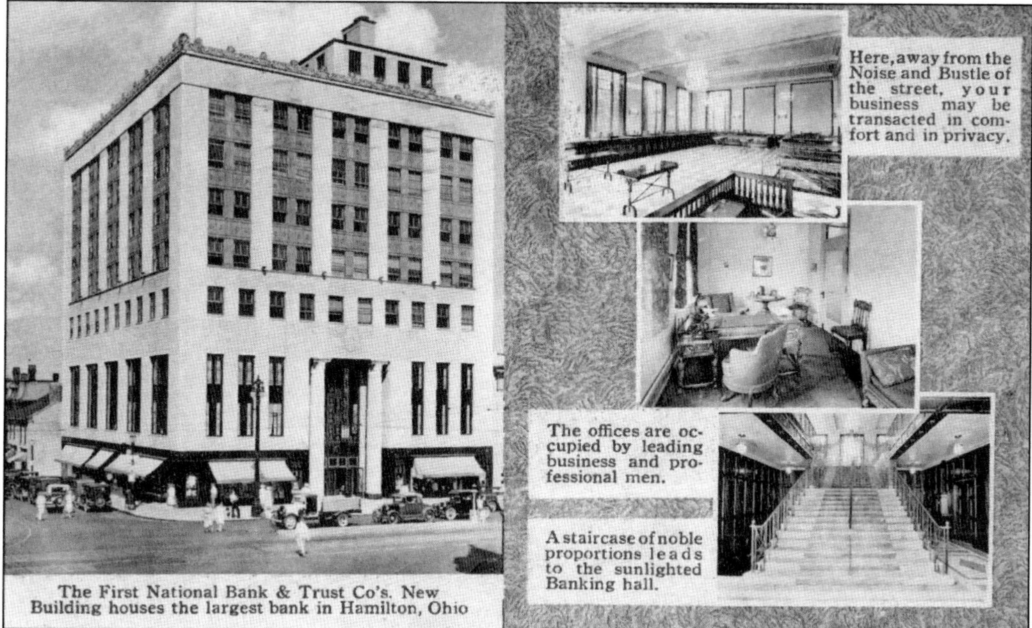

This card from 1930 celebrates the opening of the new First National Bank & Trust Company building. Situated on the corner of High and North Third Streets, the bank has roots back to 1863. Opening during the nation's worst economic crisis, the building was a symbol of the financial strength of Hamilton, as not a single bank or trust in the city went insolvent during the Depression.

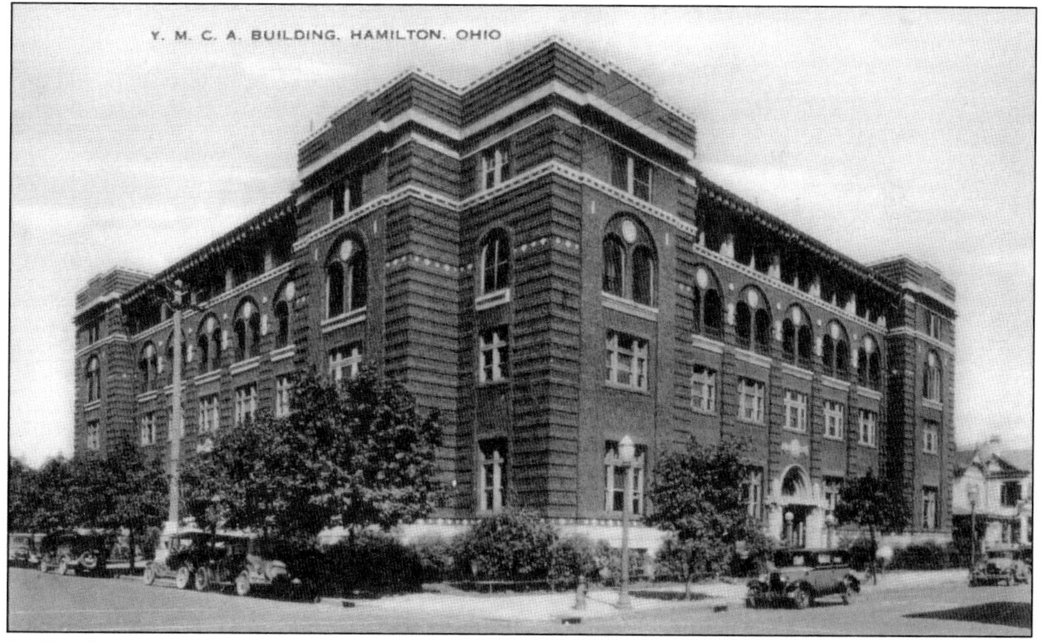

In October 1910, a committee of over 100 local businessmen organized a fundraising campaign to construct a new YMCA building. In eight days, $151,234.51 was raised. The new facility was constructed for $160,000 and dedicated on September 20, 1914. Facilities in the new building included a swimming pool, running track, cafeteria, gymnasium, auditorium, bowling alleys, an entire floor of dormitories, and numerous classrooms.

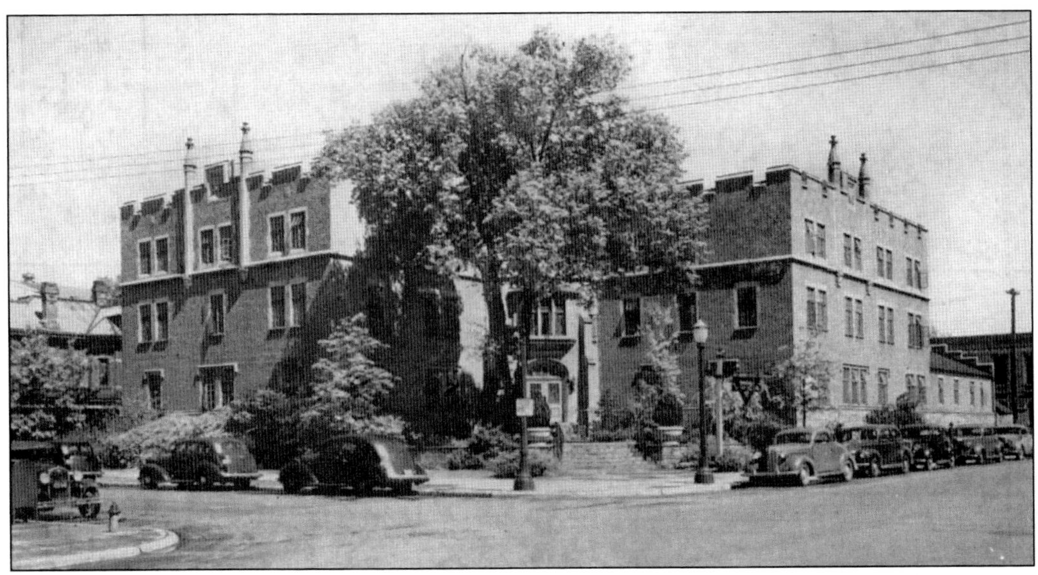

Sent in September 1941, this card served as a dinner invitation in celebration of the YWCA Building's 10th anniversary. The cost of the meal was 75¢. Looking like a Gothic castle situated on the northwest corner of Third and Dayton Streets, the facility was touted as an important instrument in developing "sound civic affairs" and "afforded Hamiltonians ample opportunities and facilities for meetings, banquets and other community gatherings."

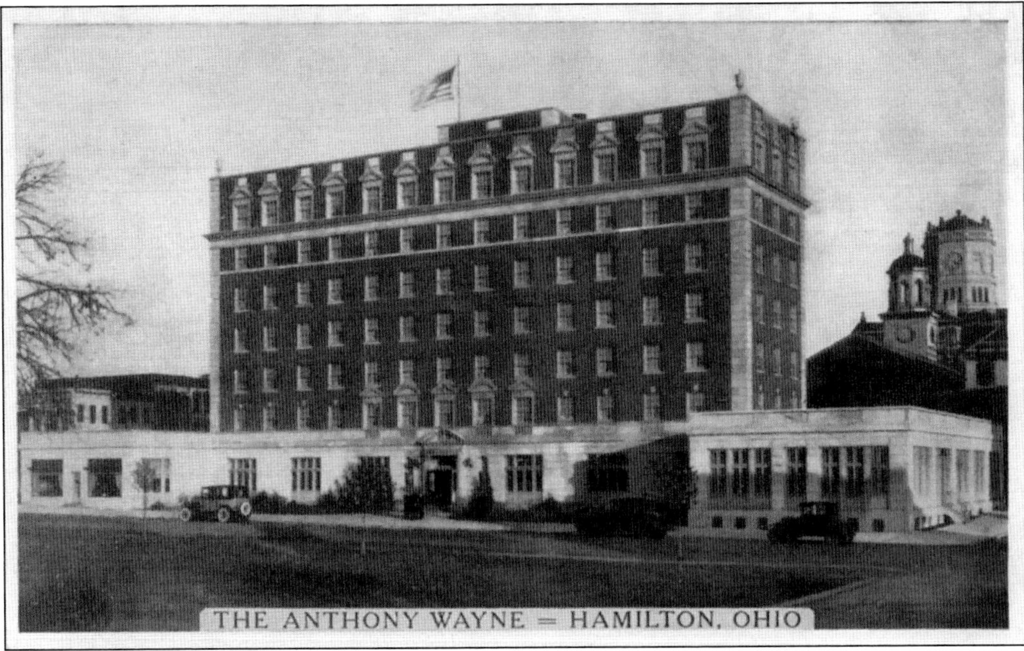

One of local architect Frederick G. Mueller's crown jewels was the Anthony Wayne Hotel, which opened in 1927. The 100-room hotel was praised for its combination of beauty and function. With offices located in the Rentschler Building, other notable local designs by Mueller include the municipal building, the Ford Tractor plant, the Champion Coated Paper office building, the First Methodist Episcopal Church, the Elks Club, and Fort Hamilton Hospital. He also had a hand in the drafting of the Masonic lodge.

This card served as an invitation to a "private inspection" of the new Bell Telephone office and exchange building on December 22, 1906. The new facility, located at the northeast corner of Second and Ludlow Streets, was advertised as the "most complete telephone exchange in the state." At the time, Bell was the only telephone company in town with direct lines to Middletown and to Cincinnati.

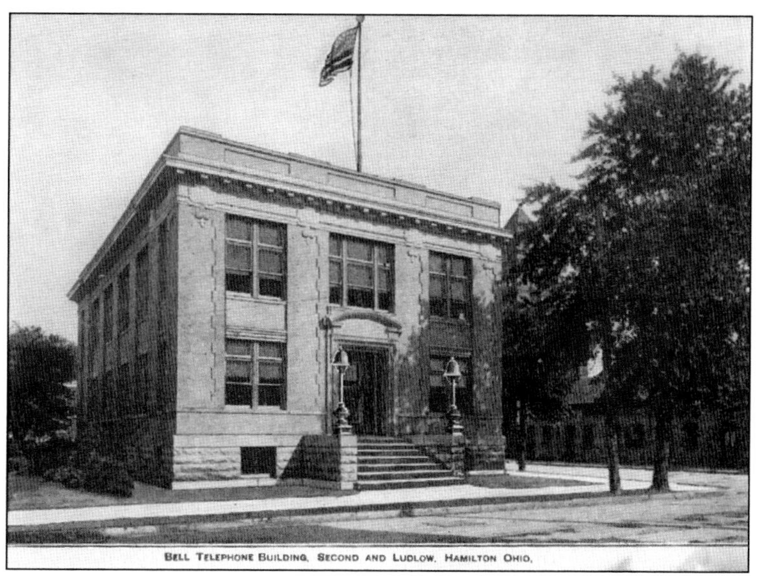
BELL TELEPHONE BUILDING, SECOND AND LUDLOW, HAMILTON OHIO.

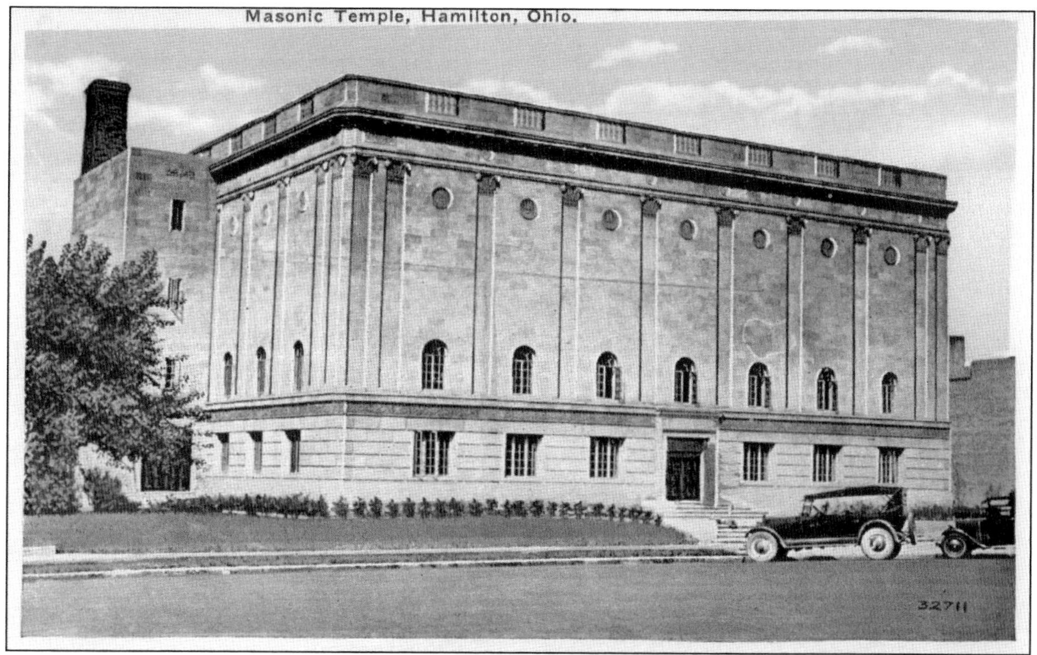
Masonic Temple, Hamilton, Ohio.

Freemasonry came to Hamilton in 1811, but a steady meeting place was not provided until 1887, when the Masons of Hamilton held their meetings for over 40 years on the third floor of the Reily Block on the southwest corner of High and Reily Streets. On November 24, 1928, a week-long dedication celebration began including a public open house for the new Masonic temple on the north side of High Street between Seventh and Eighth Streets. The facility is still used by the Masons today.

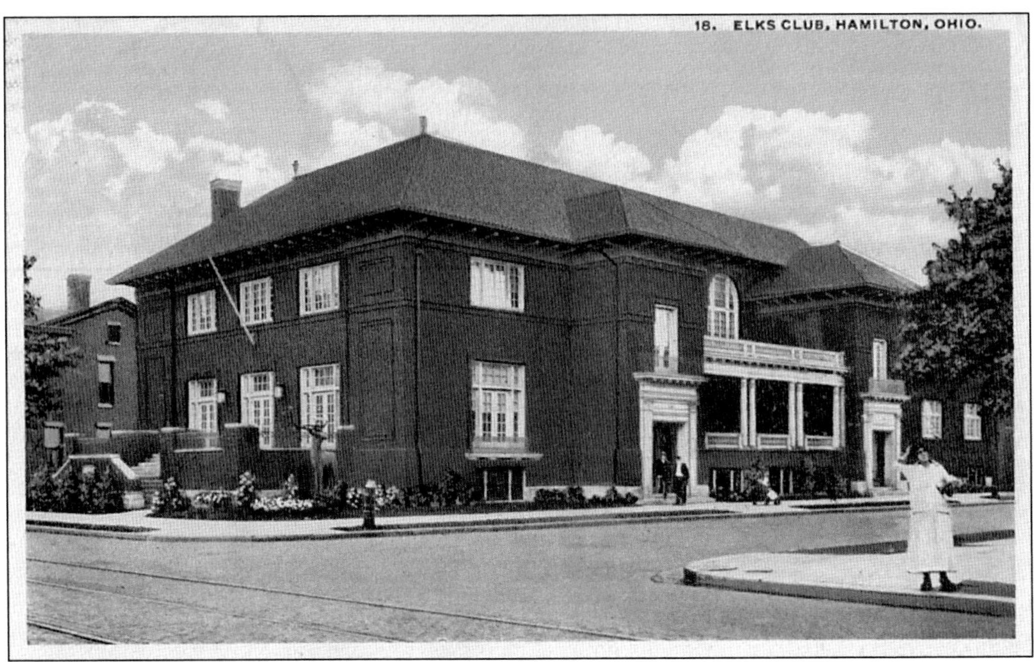

Completed in September 1915 on the southwest corner of South Second and Ludlow Streets, the new Hamilton Lodge 93 Benevolent and Protective Order of Elks Temple cost approximately $95,000. An interesting design feature of the building was that it was constructed with a concrete roof covered by red Spanish tile, to aid in fire protection. A two-day carnival dedicated the building in October with nearly 1,000 Elks in attendance from nearby cities.

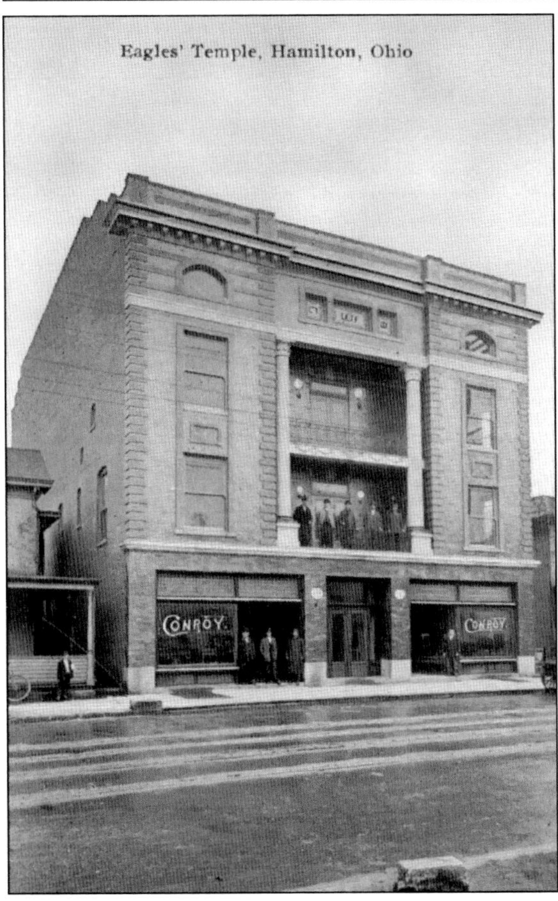

The Butler Aerie No. 407 of the Fraternal Order of Eagles was created in Hamilton in 1903. Located on the east side of South Second Street between Sycamore and Ludlow Streets, this three-story temple was completed in 1910. The first floor contained two storefronts, both occupied by the A.J. Conroy Company, dealers in furniture and household decor.

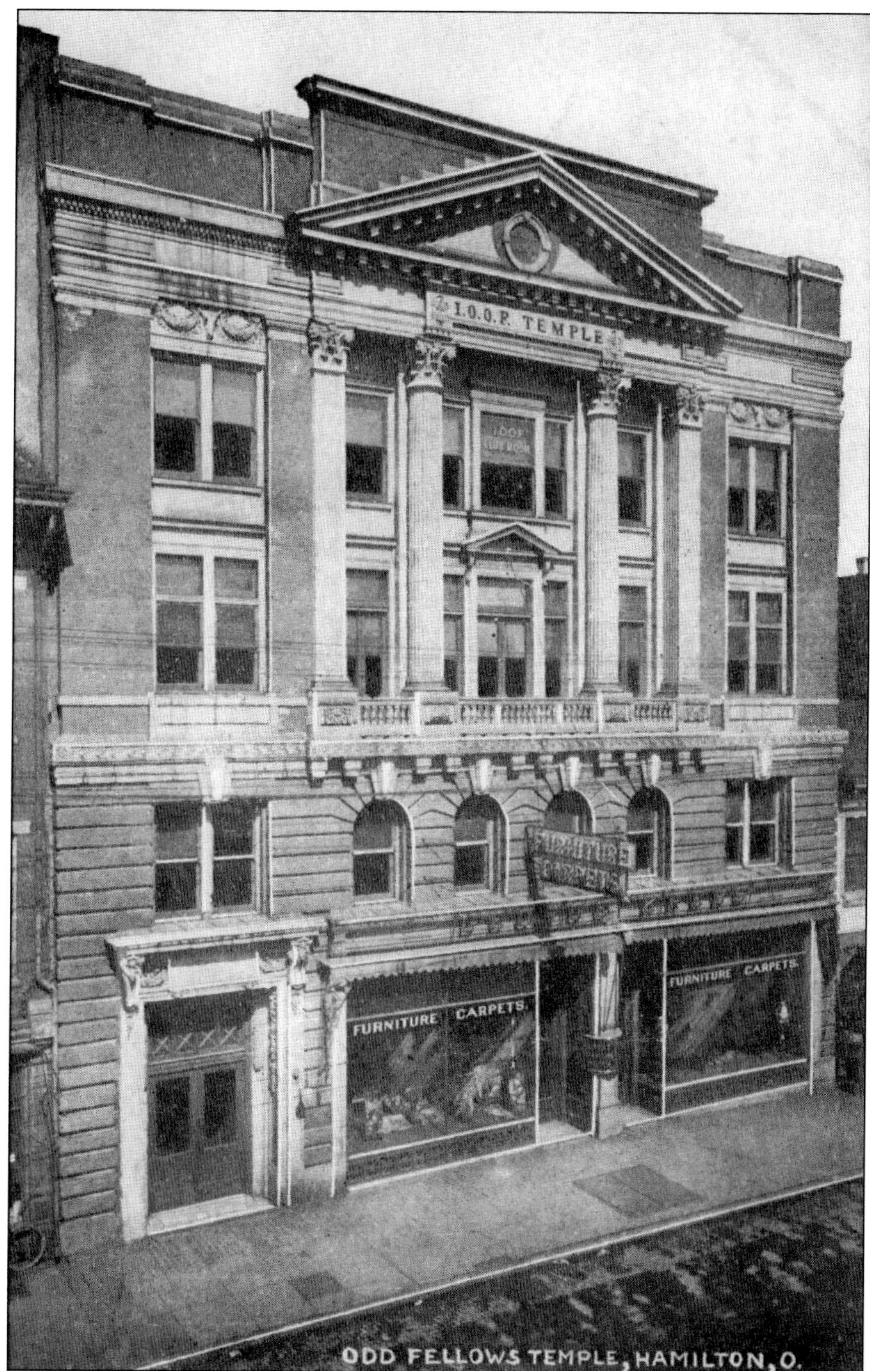

When former Hamilton mayor Brooks Sanders died in 1902, he willed his entire estate and property to Hamilton Lodge No. 17 of the Independent Order of Odd Fellows. This gift included land on the west side of South Third Street between High and Court Streets. In 1906, a new IOOF temple stood on the land. George Krebs ran his furniture and carpet business on the first two floors. In June 1912, the state delegation of the order held its 80th session of the Grand Lodge in Hamilton.

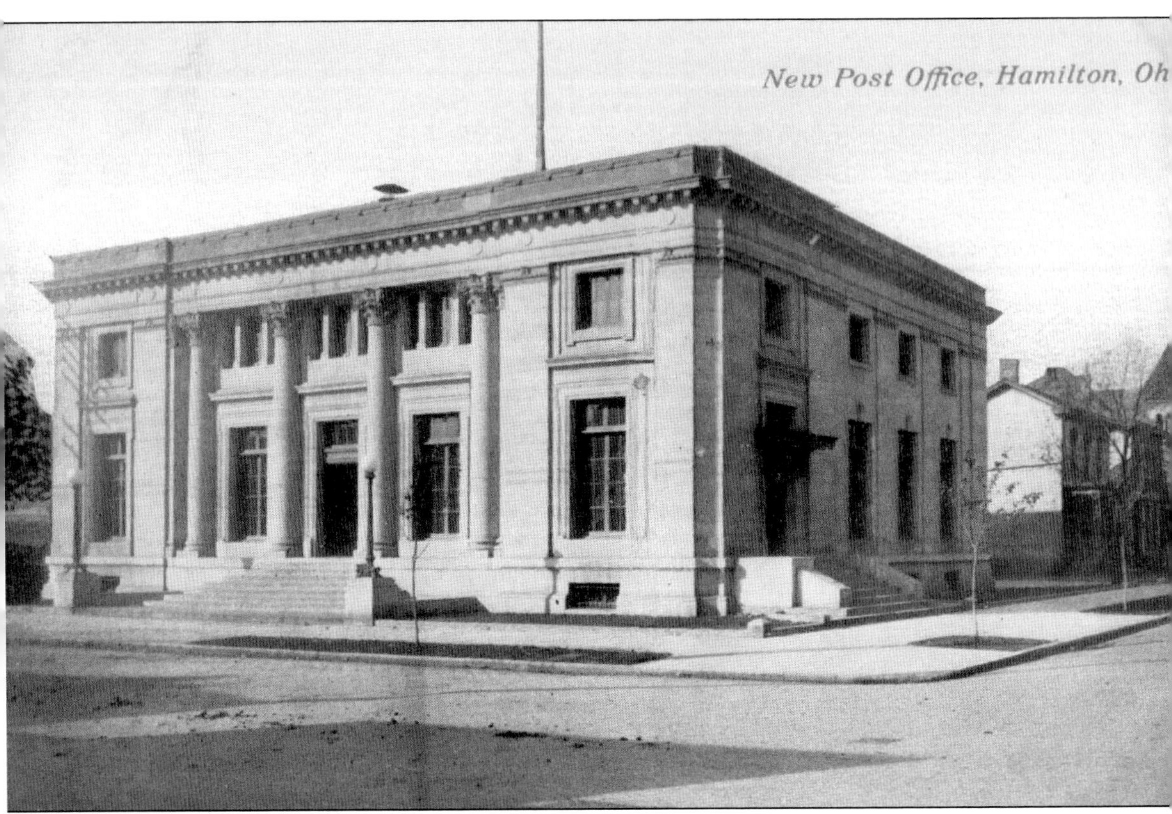

The Hamilton Federal Building, located on the southwest corner of South Third and Ludlow Streets, was opened for official business in 1909. Hamilton had petitioned the federal government for such a building since the 1880s. At one point, Congress approved the measure, but it was vetoed by President Cleveland. The post office was on the ground floor, while the second floor housed the deputy collector of the Internal Revenue Service. The facility is used for local government purposes today.

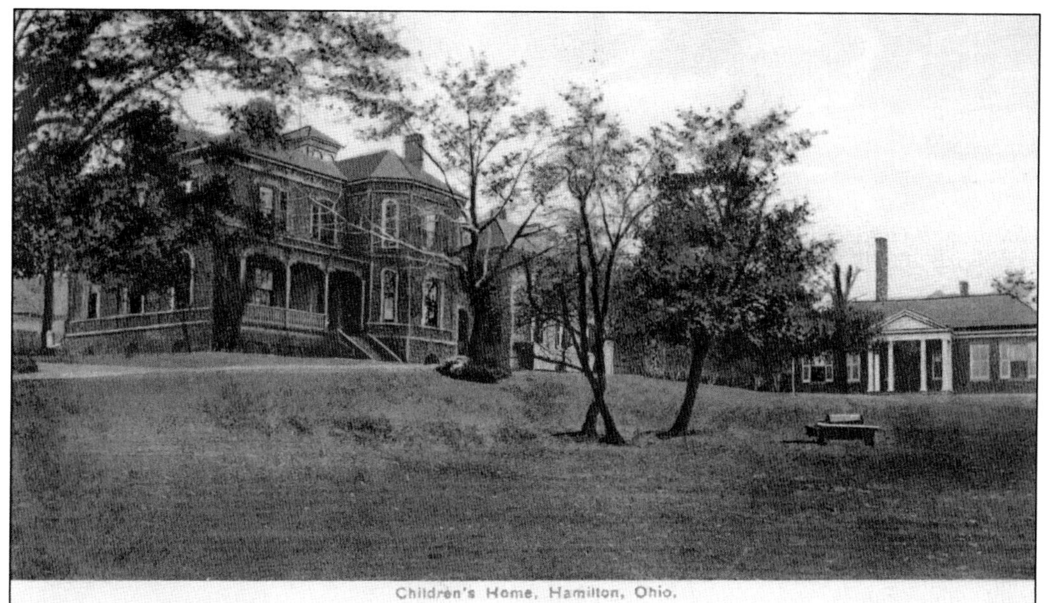

Children's Home, Hamilton, Ohio.

In 1875, Clark Lane and E.J. Dyer donated $10,000 for the purchase of Dyer's old family farm, located on South D Street, for the creation of a new home for the relief of poor and unfortunate children, many of whom had been left orphaned and homeless following the Civil War. Lane's son Harry, who was an invalid, lived there from age 18 until he died at the age of 29. The facility closed in 1985 but has since been recently reopened for charitable work.

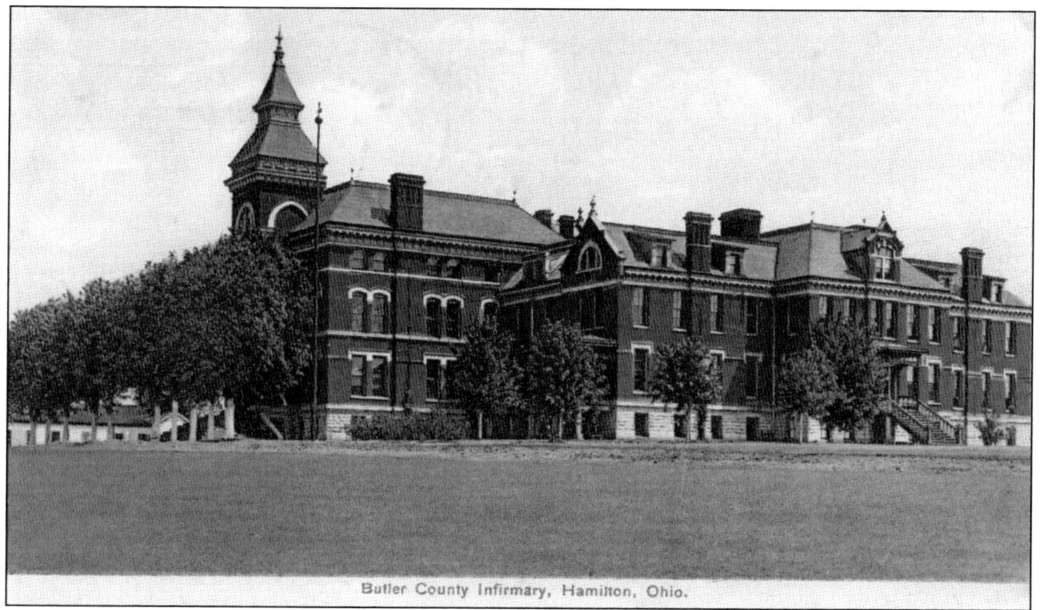

Butler County Infirmary, Hamilton, Ohio.

In 1875, the board of directors for the Butler County Infirmary pleaded with county commissioners for a new and expanded care facility for the poor, aged, orphaned, and diseased of the area. The current home was operating at over capacity. It would be nine years before they got their wish. The new facility was constructed atop a hill overlooking Hamilton from the east. It operated until 1976, when a new facility was constructed. Fire claimed the structure in 1983, and the remnants were demolished.

Originally organized and constructed in 1858, Fire Department No. 2 was located on the west side of South Third Street between Sycamore and Ludlow Streets. The station received the department's first sliding pole in 1893. In 1911, the department purchased its first motorized vehicles. Notice the ladder wagon is still using old-fashioned horse power. This station was in operation until 1936, when the company was moved to the new municipal building.

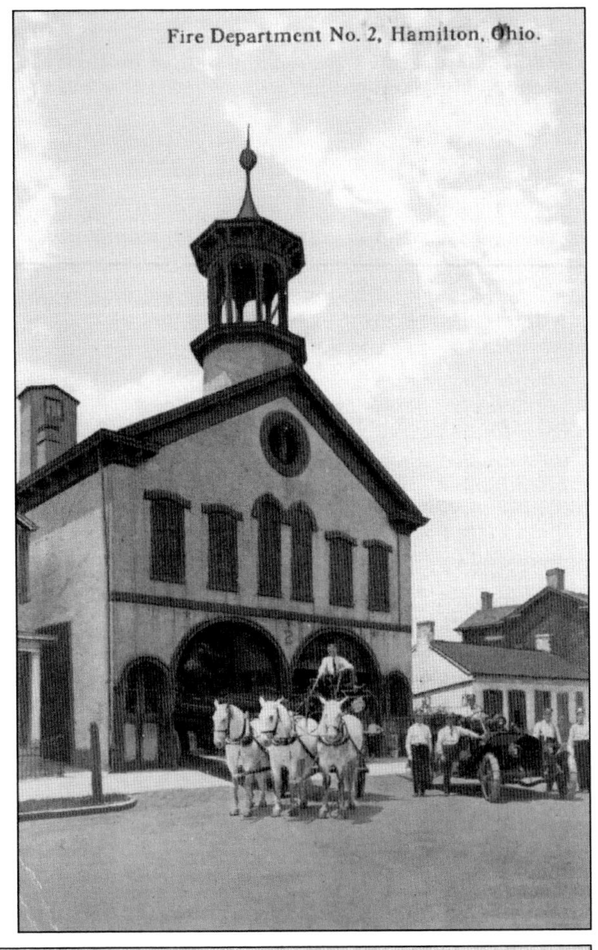
Fire Department No. 2, Hamilton, Ohio.

From its inception in 1851 until its disappearance in 1917, the Cincinnati, Hamilton and Dayton Railroad was the king of the rails in Hamilton. This depot, located at South Fifth and Henry Streets, began as a single-story brick structure built in the 1870s. In 1885, a two-story addition was added. The last B&O passenger train to leave this station was in 1971. Limited Amtrak service was available until 2005.

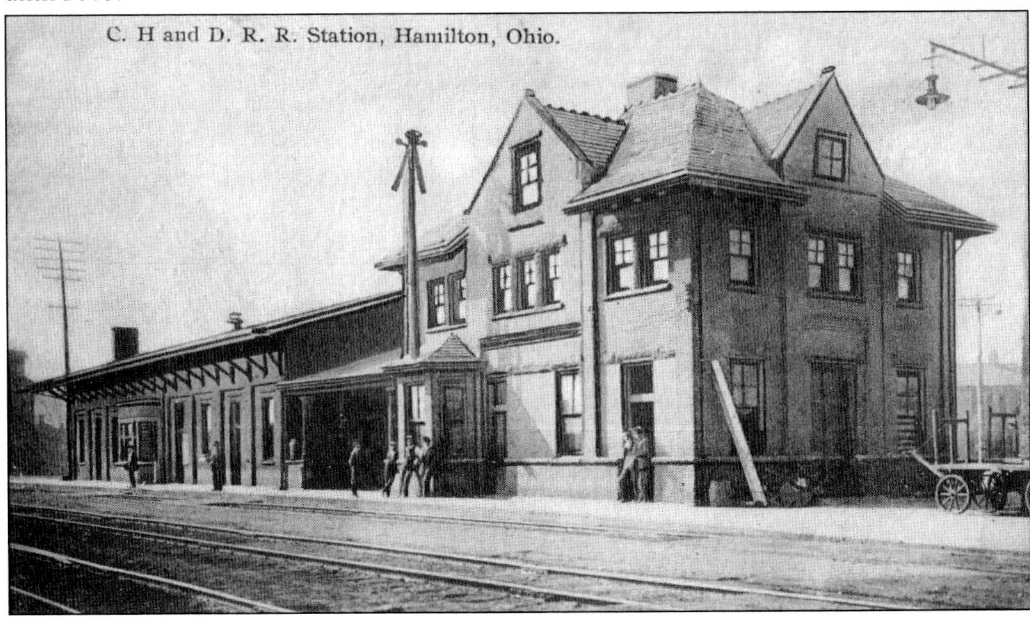
C. H and D. R. R. Station, Hamilton, Ohio.

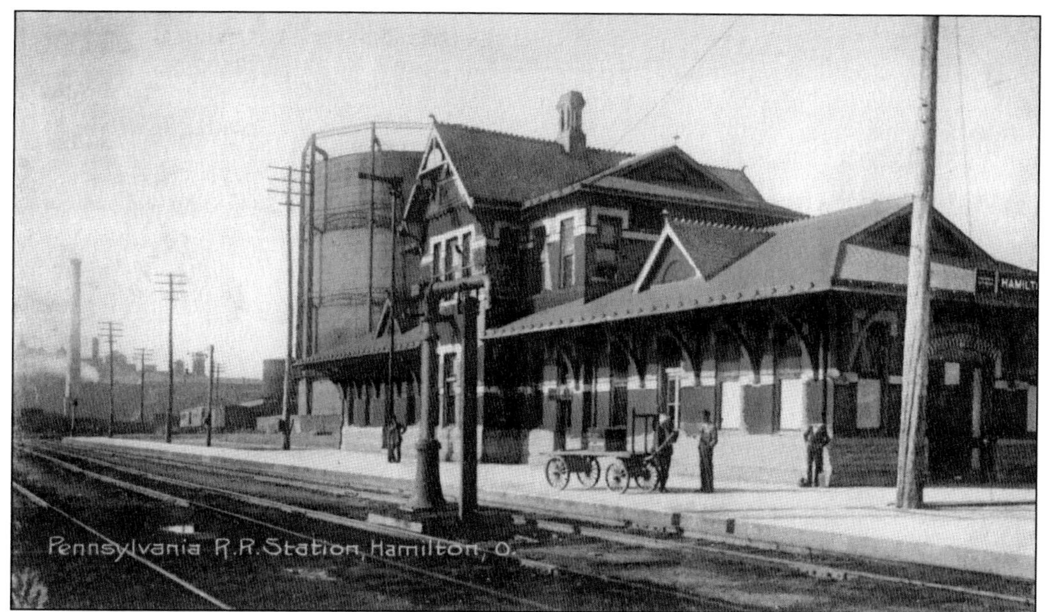

Originally constructed in 1888 for the Pittsburgh, Cincinnati, Chicago & St. Louis Railroad, this passenger depot later became part of the Pennsylvania Line. Located on South Seventh Street between High Street and Maple Avenue, the second story was removed during remodeling sometime after the 1920s. The last passenger train left the station in 1971, and in 1991 the building was torn down.

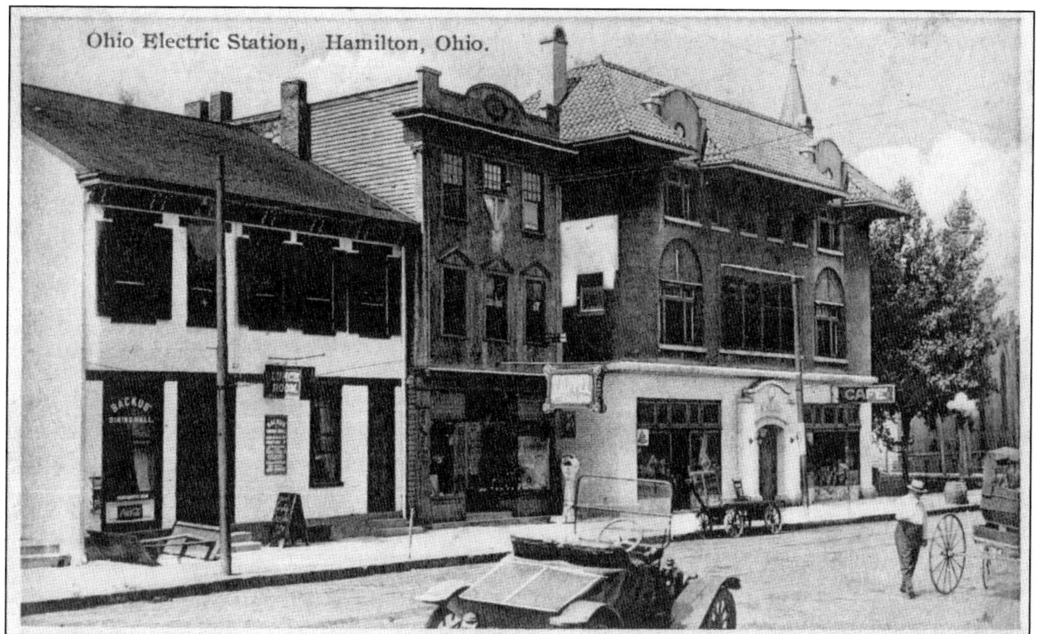

This view from 1916 shows the Ohio Electric Traction Station at 113 Court Street, which included a small café inside (right). Businessmen who needed repairs or alterations before or during their travels could see George Kappel, merchant tailor, next door (center). If the café at the station did not have a wide enough variety of food for one's liking, two doors west at 121 Court Street was Robert Backus's Dining Hall (left).

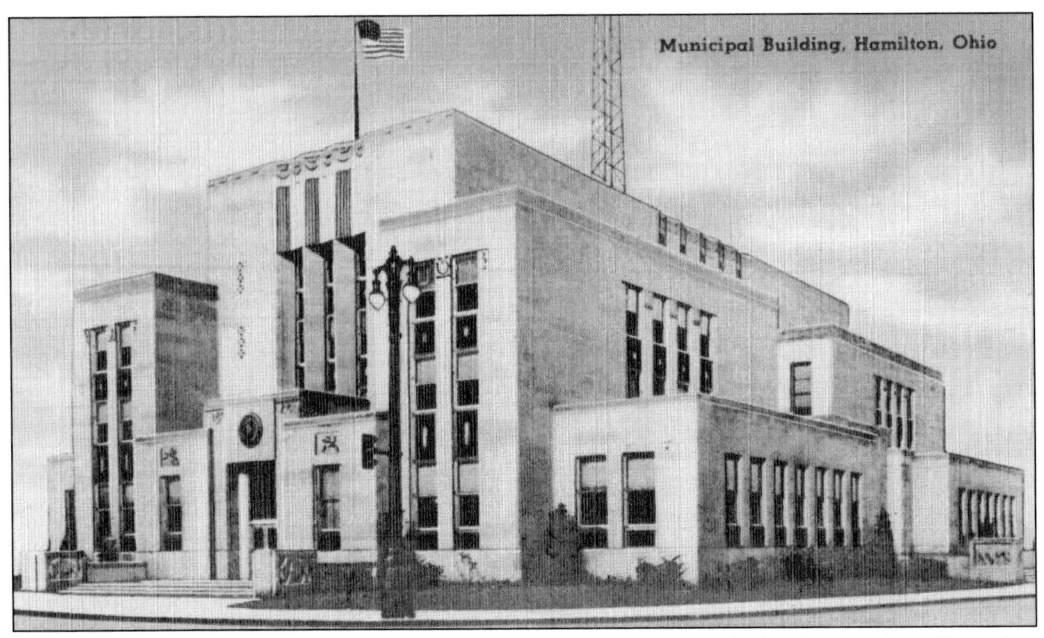

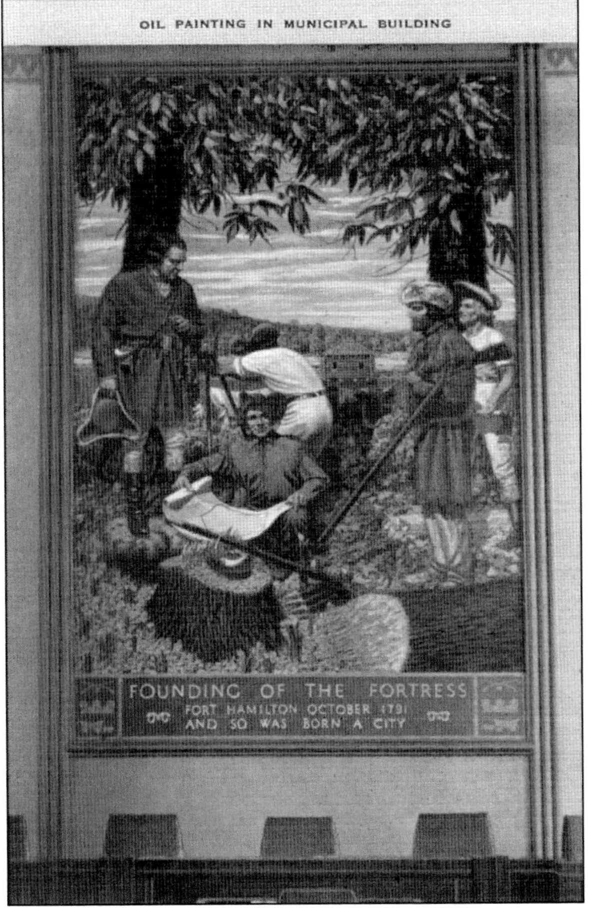

At its completion in October 1935, the new Hamilton Municipal Building was an architectural gem. The Public Works Administration, a federal program created during the Depression to provide employment, provided partial funding for the construction project, which totaled a little under $550,000. Designed through collaboration of the prominent local architects Frederick G. Mueller, George W. Barkman, and Robert E. Smith, the building was not only functionally unique but also an artistic and technological wonder as well. The Art Deco building includes exterior friezes designed by Hamilton native Robert McCloskey, and the council chambers house a painted mural by local artist Jack Willard depicting the founding of Fort Hamilton (left). The building provided the city with new state-of-the-art police and fire facilities, prompting the purchase of new vehicles for both departments. The city conducted business in the building until 2000, when the new One Renaissance Center was opened. The structure now houses the Hamilton Mill, a small-business incubator, the Heritage Hall Museum, and the Robert McCloskey Museum.

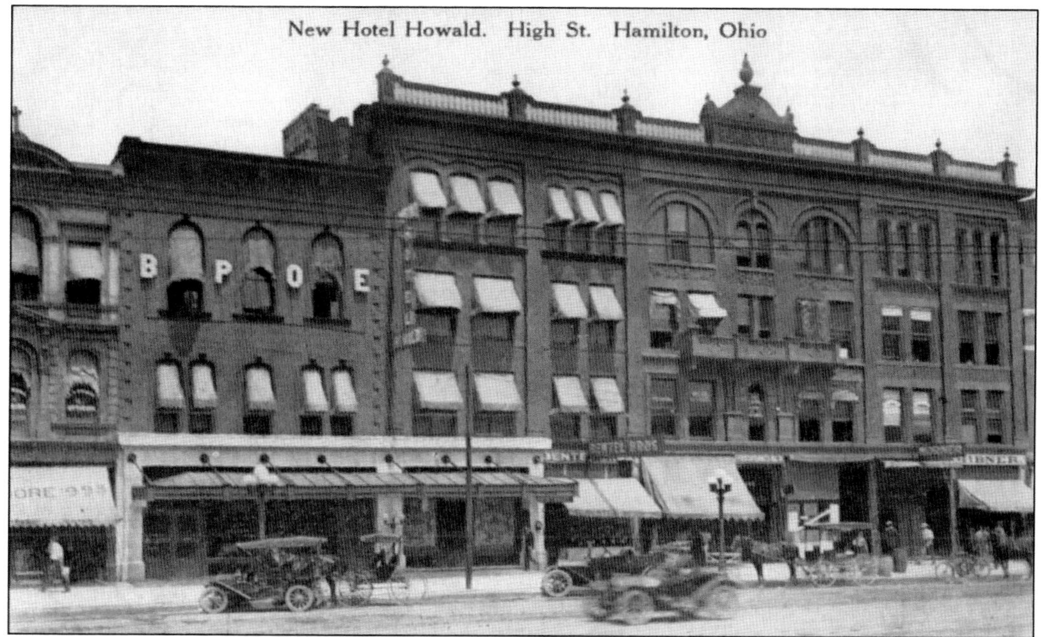

German immigrant Charles Howald came to Hamilton as an infant in 1862. In 1884, he opened the Hamilton House on the northwest corner of High and North Second Streets and gained a reputation as quite a congenial host. He opened the Howald Hotel, located at 140–144 High Street, in 1890. This card shows the hotel soon after an extensive remodeling and expansion project in 1912.

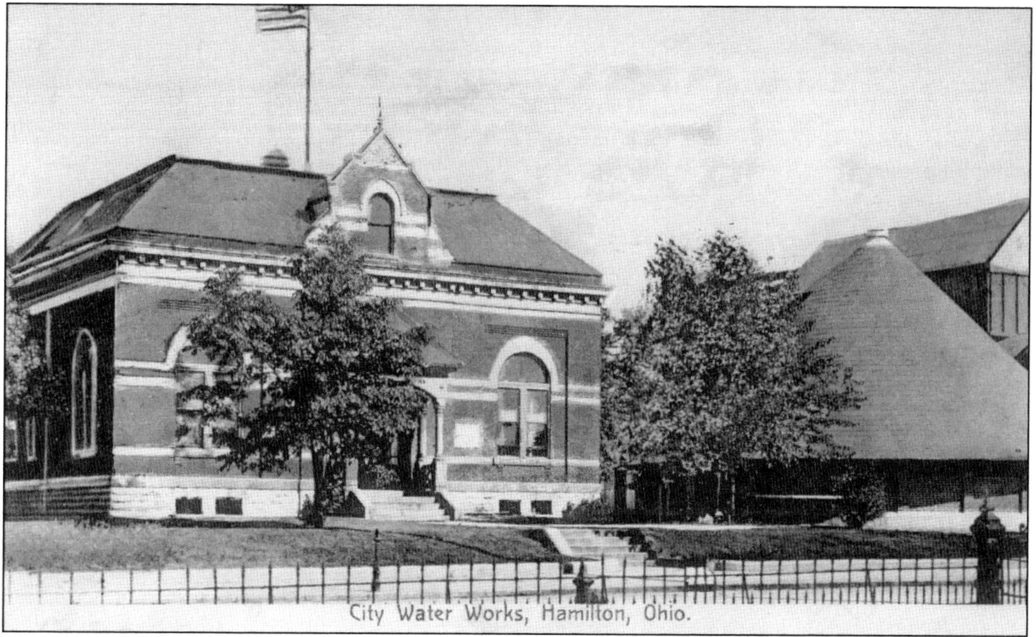

The original city waterworks plant was located on the east side of North Third Street across from where Second Street intersects it. Slipped in between the city gas works and the city electric plant, the facility was constructed in 1884 and consisted of a single well drilled at the riverbank and a six-million-gallon open concrete reservoir.

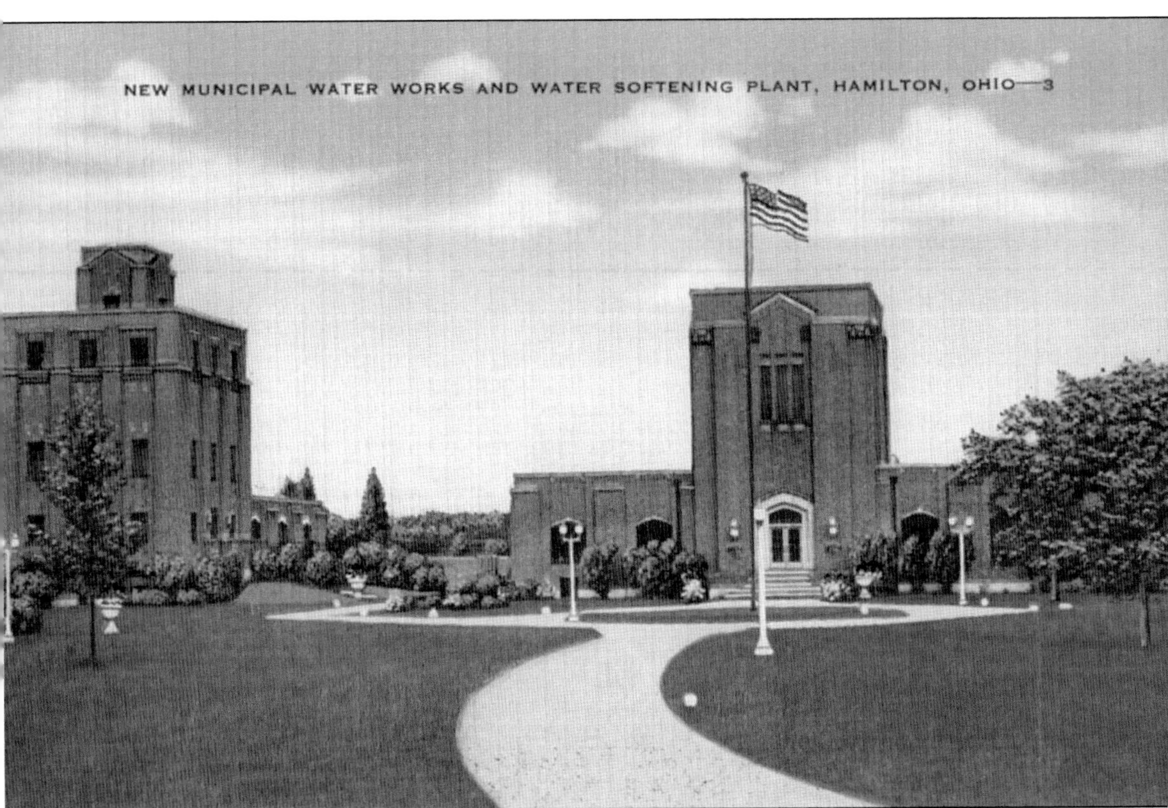

At its opening in October 1935, Hamilton's new municipal waterworks was capable of pumping 17 million gallons per day from six wells. Located one mile north of the city on the Third Street extension, the water-softening plant was not brought online until December of the same year, after chemists experimented in finding the perfect blend of chemicals. The following June, municipal pool manager Ray Tilton reported that due to the softer water, the swimming experience was "much improved."

Hamilton's first skyscraper was the Rentschler Building. Completed in 1906, local industrial magnate George A. Rentschler developed and constructed the eight-story office and retail building located on the southeast corner of High and South Second Streets. For over a century, the structure has been the address for some of Hamilton's most prominent professionals and businesses.

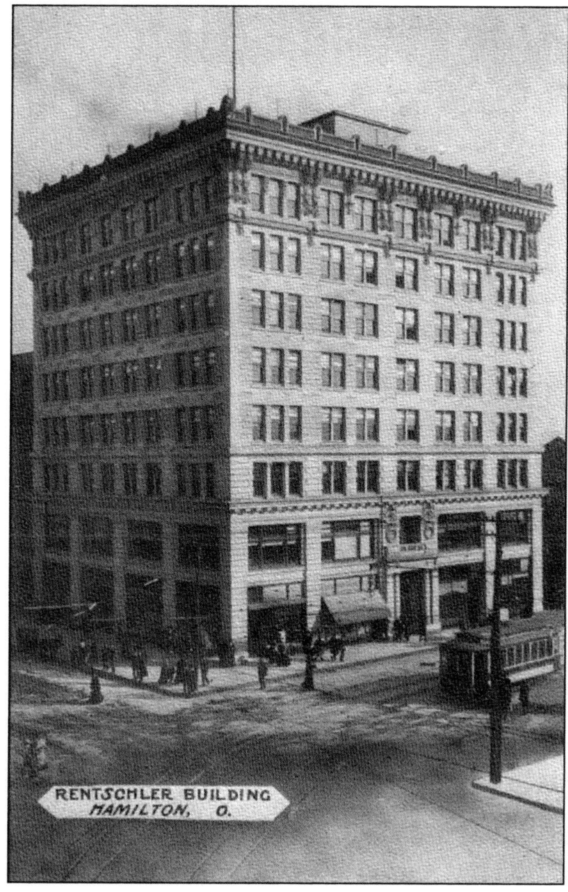
RENTSCHLER BUILDING
HAMILTON, O.

Alvin Seidensticker started his jewelry business in 1876, and for three generations, the Seidensticker name was trusted throughout the city in providing quality service and products. Alvin's son Arthur took over the family business, and this card shows the interior of the store at High Street and Journal Square as it looked around 1920. A family-owned business until the end, the store finally closed its doors in 1961.

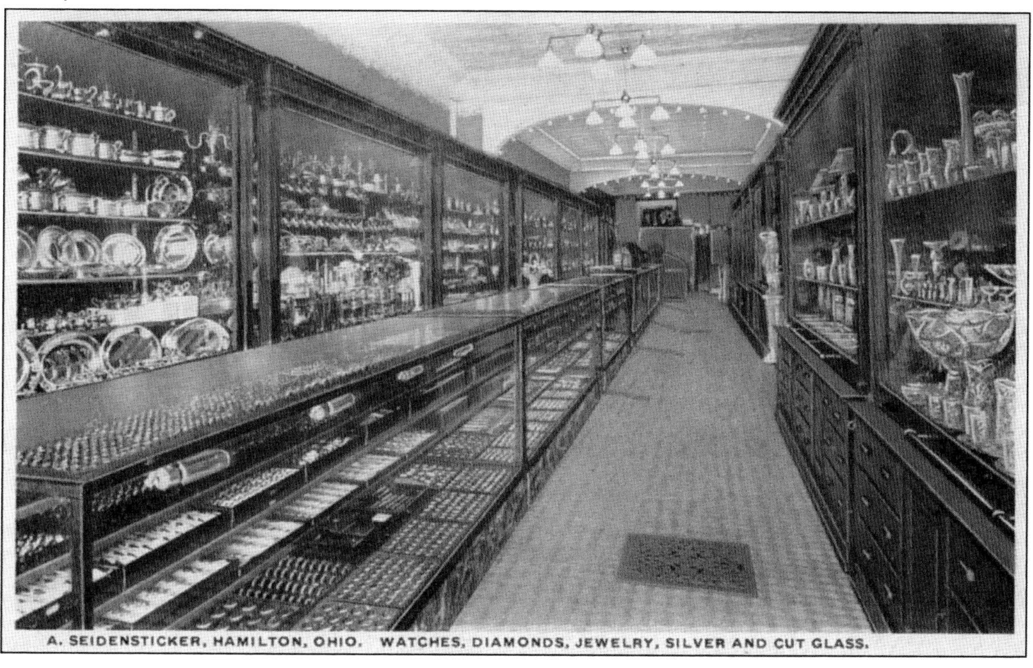
A. SEIDENSTICKER, HAMILTON, OHIO. WATCHES, DIAMONDS, JEWELRY, SILVER AND CUT GLASS.

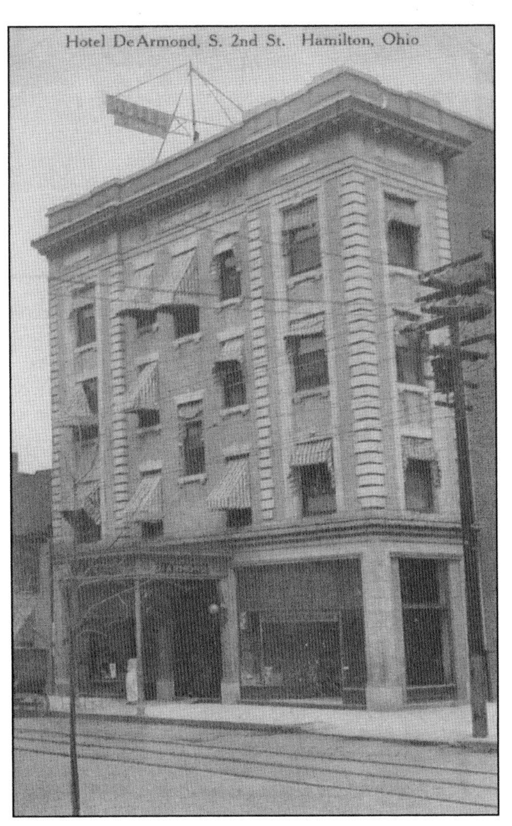

The building at 218 South Second Street has had a long and illustrious career in the hospitality business. In 1909, the building began as the Seville Hotel. In only a year, ownership changed and so did the name, becoming the Hotel Connor until 1912. In 1912, Clarence DeArmond purchased the building and it became known as the Hotel DeArmond. This name lasted until 1916, when former Hamilton mayor Charles Bosch bought the property and changed the name once again, this time to the Hotel Hamilton. The Hotel Hamilton survived until the 1960s. It consisted of 65 rooms and a full-service restaurant. Fire Company No. 2 captain Benjamin F. Evans sent the card below to an unknown recipient. It shows a firefighter rescuing someone from the second story of the hotel as smoke billows from the open window. Captain Evans wrote, "Hamilton, O. May 13, 1916 – 10:50 a.m. Compliments of Captain Ben F. Evans" on the back of the card.

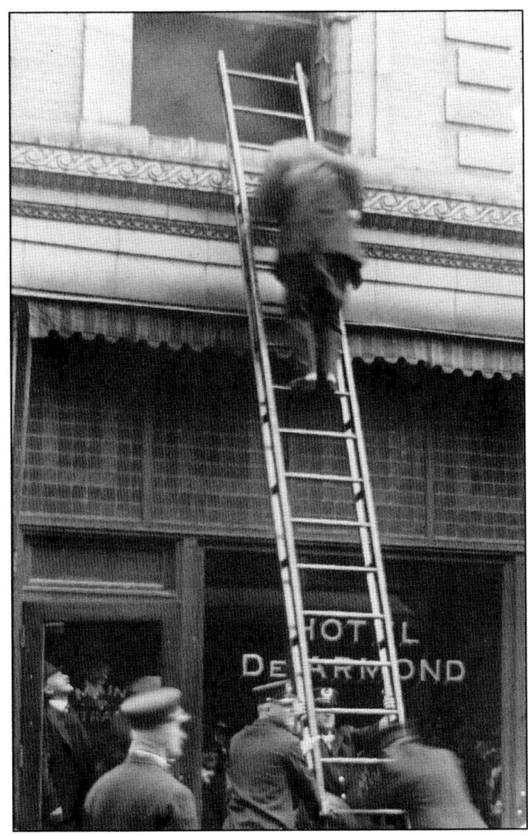

Six

Churches

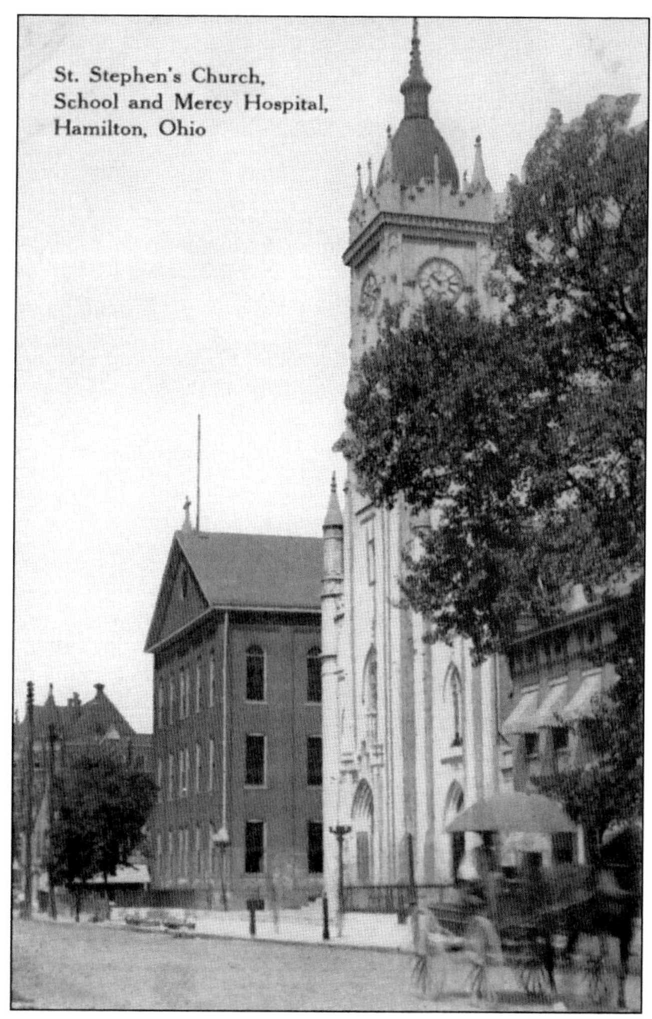

St. Stephen Church is the first Catholic church in Butler County. In 1829, there was reported to be only one Catholic residing in Hamilton and only about a dozen or more scattered throughout the county. Despite these low numbers, Bishop Edward D. Fenwick himself held services on several occasions in Hamilton at the courthouse. In 1830, land was purchased from James and Hannah McBride at the northeast corner of Dayton and Second Streets for $400, and in 1836 the first St. Stephen church was dedicated. The origins of the current structure date back to 1853. This view includes the new limestone facade and tower, which were added in 1912. The school building (left) was opened in 1889 and consisted of eight classrooms and an auditorium. After consolidation of local parishes in 1989, the name of the church became St. Julie Billiart.

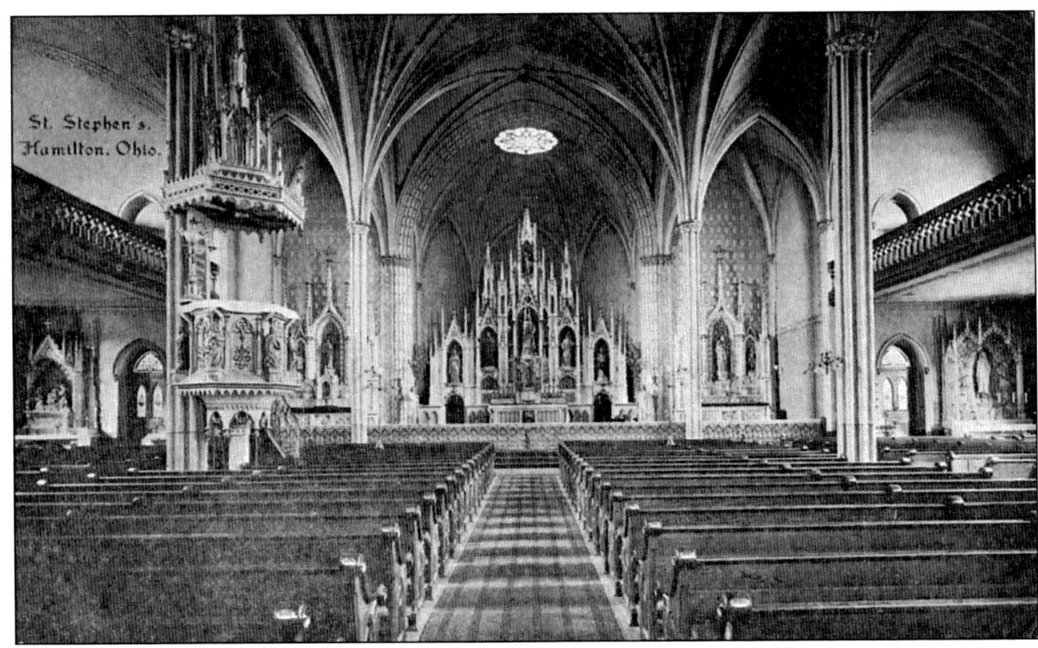

Pictured here is the interior of St. Stephen Church as it looked in 1907. Renovations to the church were underway in the late 1980s, and the church was to be rededicated in 1990. Just before the dedication event, a massive fire destroyed the ceiling and roof. It was not until 1992 that the structure again held services. The second-story balconies and interior columns are now gone, as is the elevated nave pulpit (left).

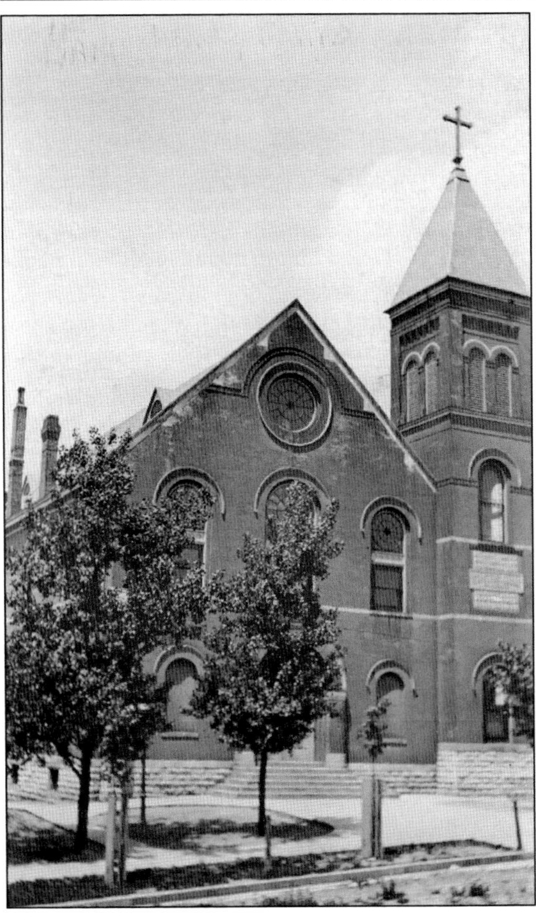

Catholics on the west side of the river wanted a church of their own, and in 1895 they got their wish when St. Peter in Chains was dedicated by Archbishop William H. Elder. This view from about 1905 shows the original building, which sat at the corner of Ridgelawn and Millville Avenues (now Liberty Avenue). Due to rapid growth on Hamilton's west side, a new facility was opened in 1938.

Due to language barriers and other cultural differences, English-speaking members of St. Stephen Church formed St. Mary Church on South Front and Court Streets in 1848, while the German members remained at St. Stephen. When St. Stephen could no longer adequately serve Hamilton's German Catholic community, St. Joseph Church was created. On July 23, 1865, the cornerstone was placed during a huge ceremony; a reported 3,000 people were in attendance. Construction of the church took two years, and on September 15, 1867, the formal dedication took place under the direction of Bishop Sylvester H. Rosecrans of the Archdiocese of Cincinnati. Located on South Second Street between Washington and Hanover Streets, the church includes a 175-foot steeple that can be seen from all directions. In 1877, parish priest Fr. Joseph Resch dedicated a new triple altar (below).

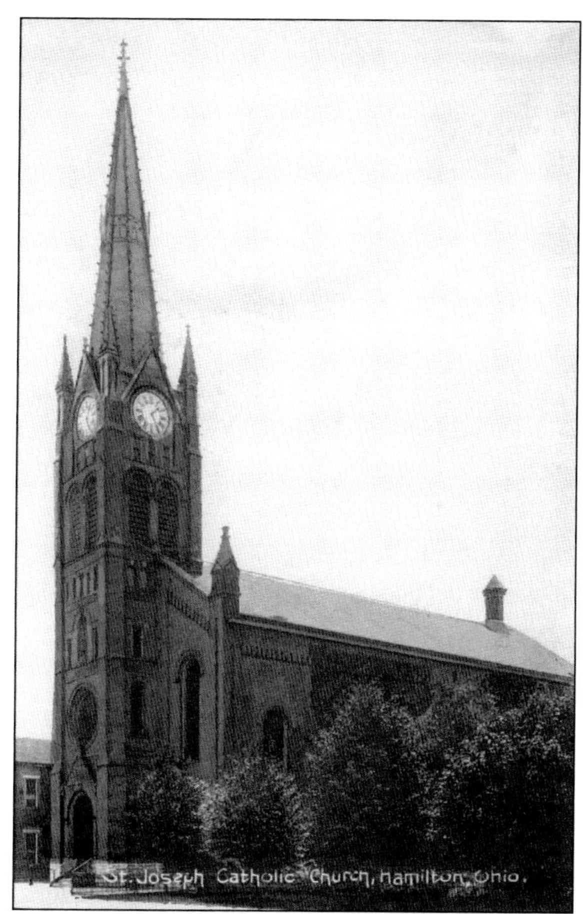

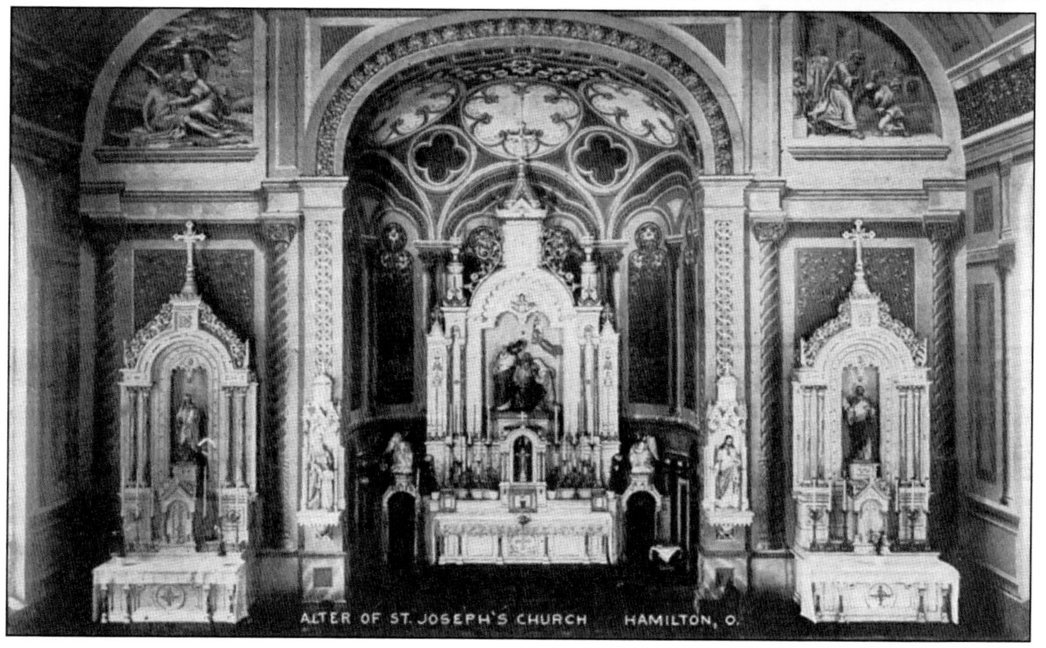

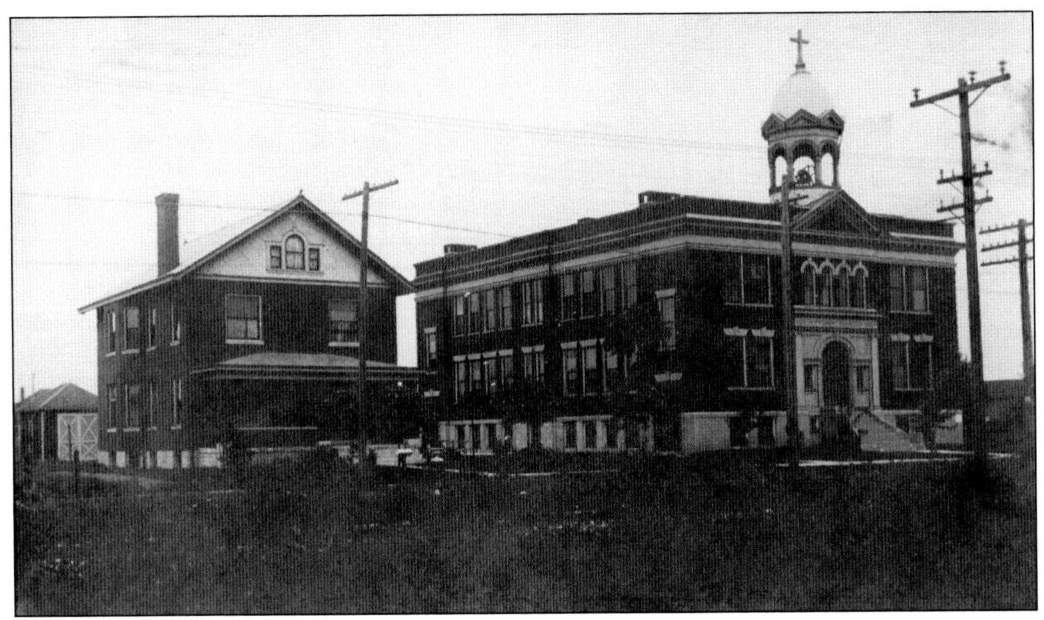

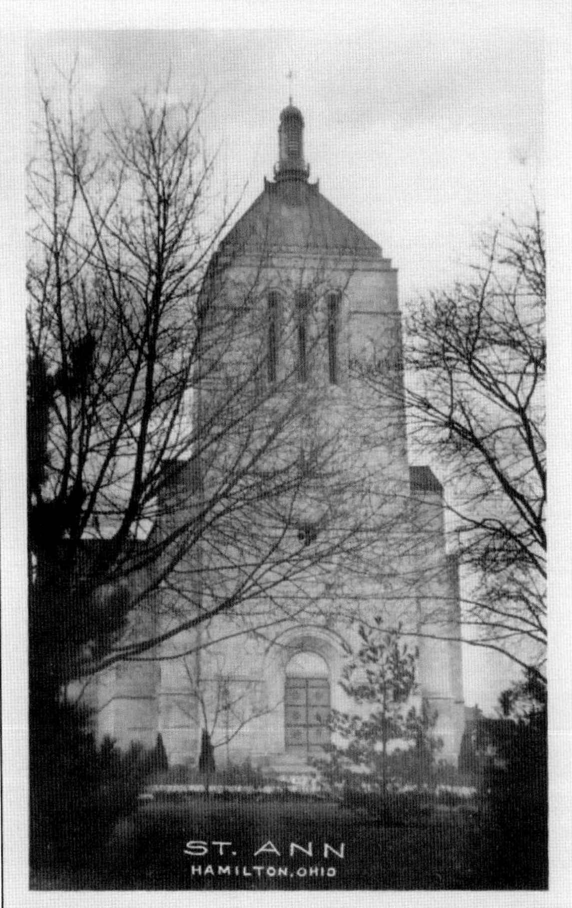

At the turn of the 20th century, Catholics in Lindenwald attended St. Joseph Church, a journey of over two miles on dirt roads. Bad weather often forced parishioners to miss services. In 1907, official talk of creating a new parish was underway. The above image shows the original St. Ann complex as it looked in 1914. The rectory (left) was less than two years old at the time, and the combination church and school (right) was dedicated in 1911. The message on the back of the card was signed by St. Ann's second resident pastor, Fr. Albert Van Den Bosch, and indicates that the school had over 150 students at the time. A convent was built in 1921. In the early 1930s, Father Van Den Bosch began collecting funds, and in June 1936, ground was broken for the new church. Unfortunately, Van Den Bosch died before the project was completed. The first services in the new church, shown at left, occurred on Christmas Day, 1937.

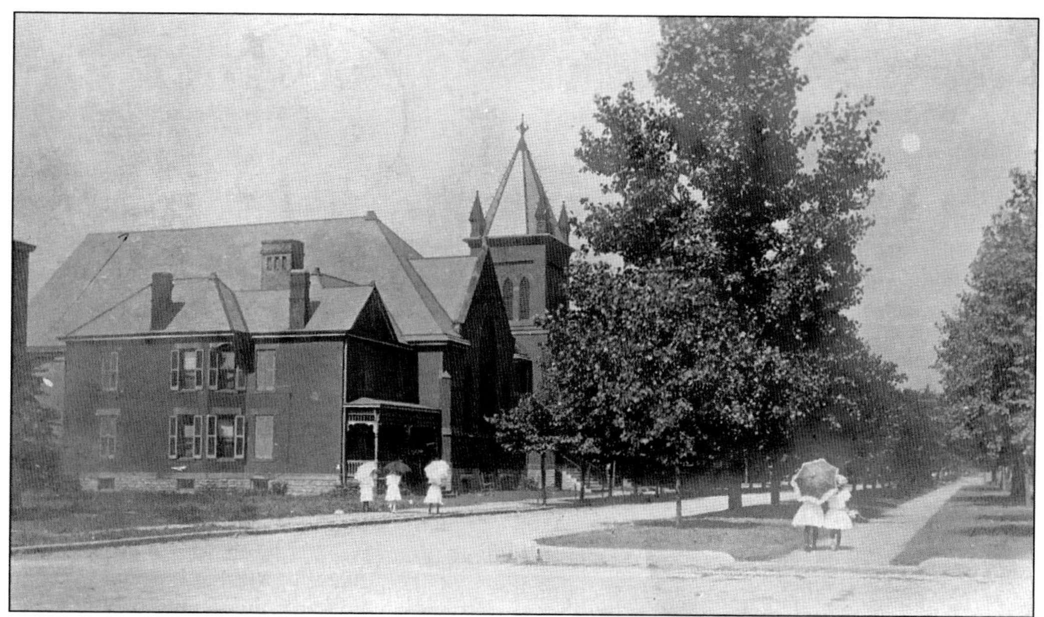

Located on Campbell Avenue and dedicated in 1894, the St. Paul Evangelical Church and parsonage are shown here. Steel magnate Andrew Carnegie donated funds in 1911 to assist in the building of a new pipe organ, and in 1921 the facility hosted over 160 ministers and delegates from the Indiana district of the German Evangelical Synod for five days. Today, the facility is the home of the Hamilton Dream Center.

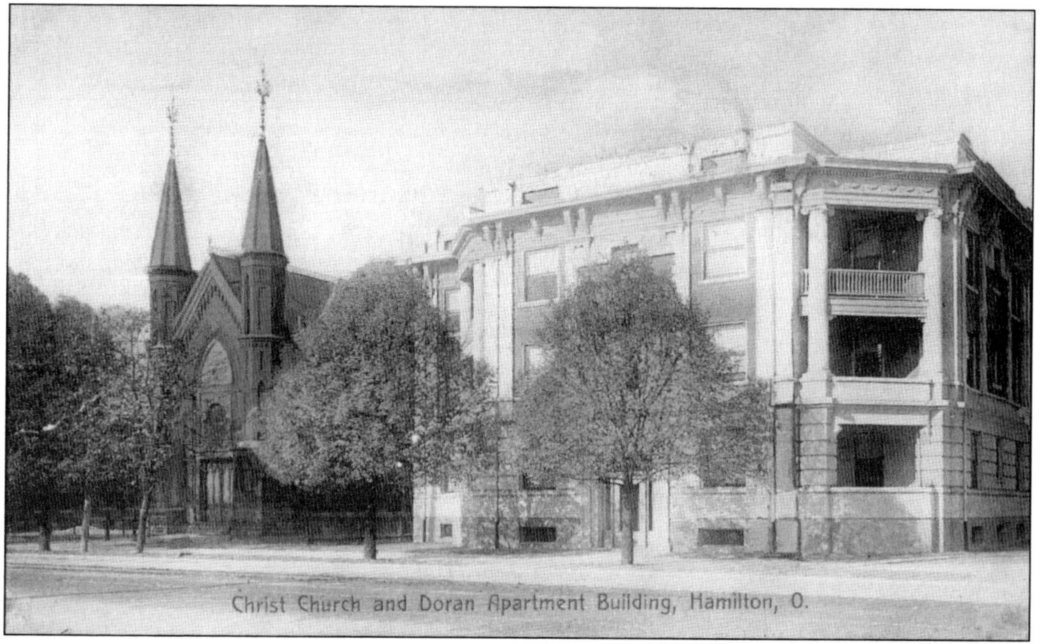

Prominent Hamilton businessman Asa Shuler was an important figure in the development of the High Street Church of Christ. His involvement with and financial contributions to the church early on led to the construction of Christ Church in 1883. The building sits at High and Center Streets between Fifth and Sixth Streets and now houses the New Hope Baptist Church.

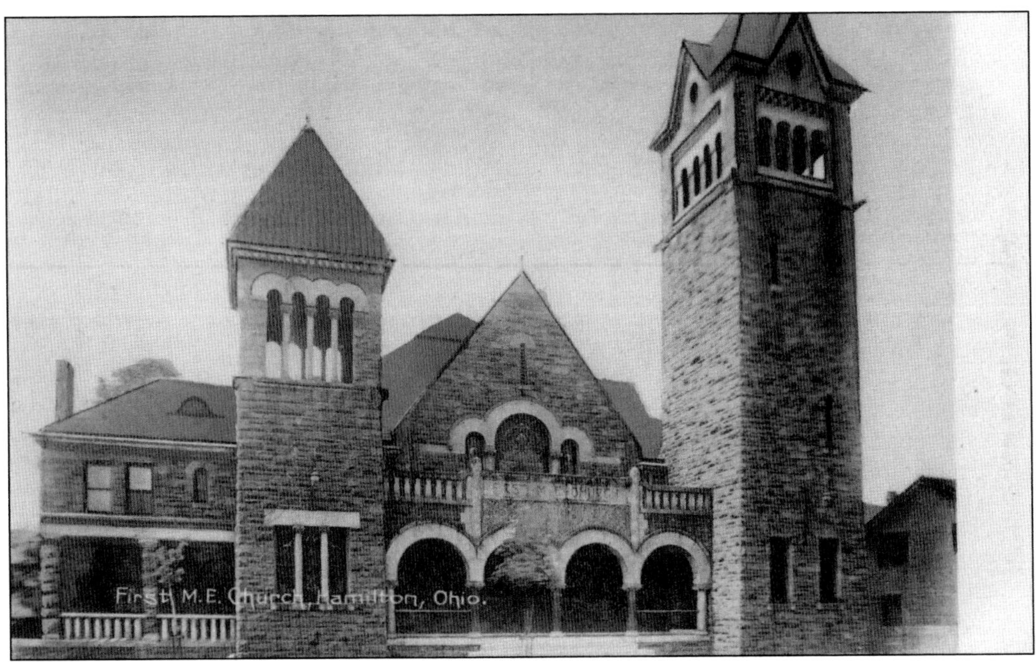

The Methodist influence in Hamilton stretches as far back as 1819, when a meetinghouse was constructed on Ludlow Street between Second and Third Streets through the beneficence of John Woods. This view from about 1908 shows the fourth Methodist Episcopal building to occupy the church's location on Ludlow Street. Built in 1894, this facility was completely destroyed by fire on February 24, 1924.

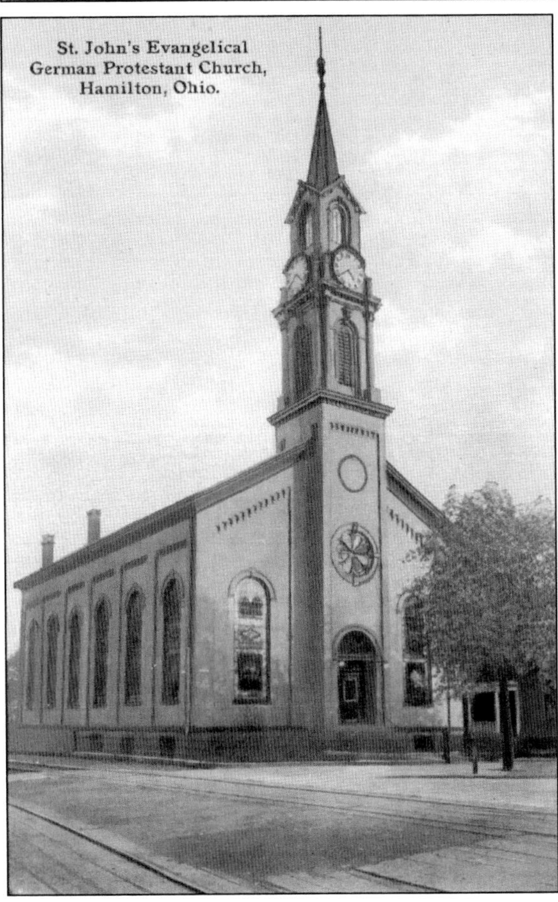

Organized in 1837 by German immigrants, this was the second church built by the St. John Evangelical German Protestant Church. Constructed in 1867, the church is seen here in 1911 complete with its original bell tower and steeple. Located on South Front Street, the building now houses the First St. John United Church of Christ.

In 1843, a few members and the pastor of St. John splintered off and founded the Evangelical Lutheran congregation at Hamilton and Rossville. By 1845, a church was built at Fourth and Ludlow Streets. For 20 years, the congregation thrived, so much so that a new building was needed at the close of the Civil War. Property on the northeast corner of Front and Ludlow Streets was purchased for $3,300, and plans for a new $27,000 church building were created. In 1904, the church association introduced services in English without the approval of pastor G.H. Trebel, and he resigned. Taking his place was Rev. C.F.W. Allwardt, who served Zion Lutheran for 30 years. In 1906, the church built a new parsonage, located at 212 South Front Street, for Allwardt and his family. The card below, showing the impressive home, was sent by the reverend's wife, Antonia, in 1908.

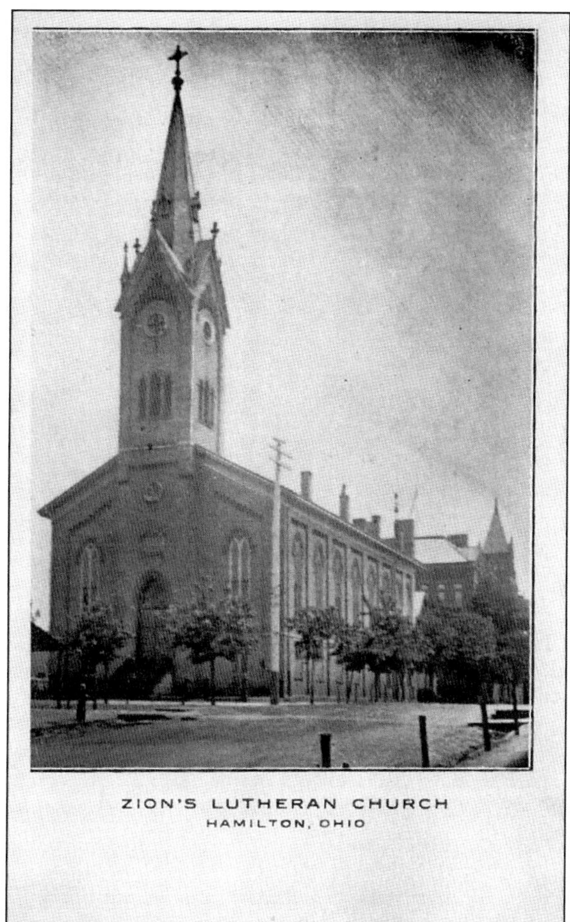

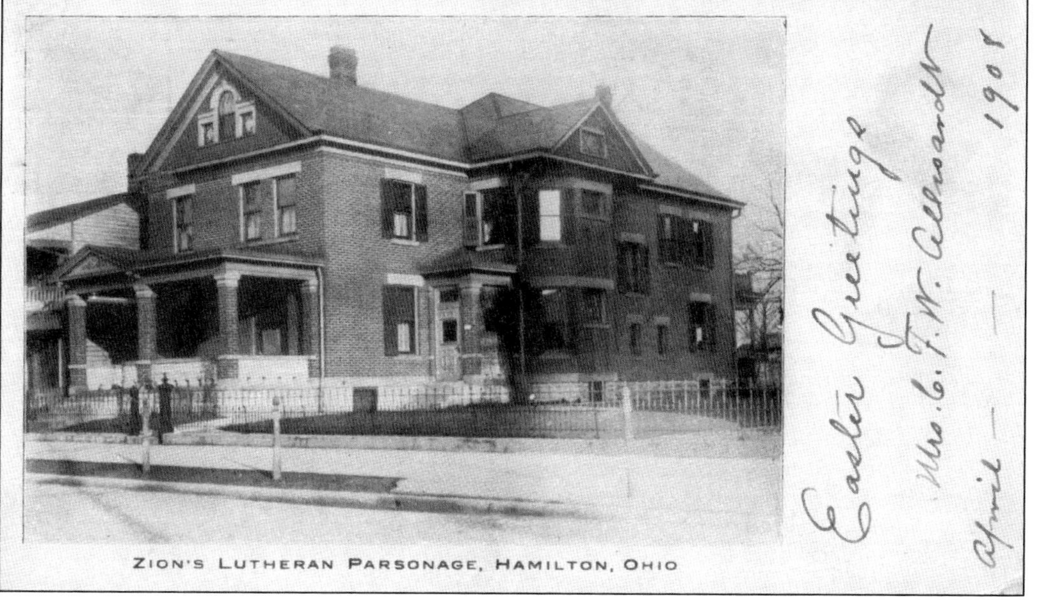

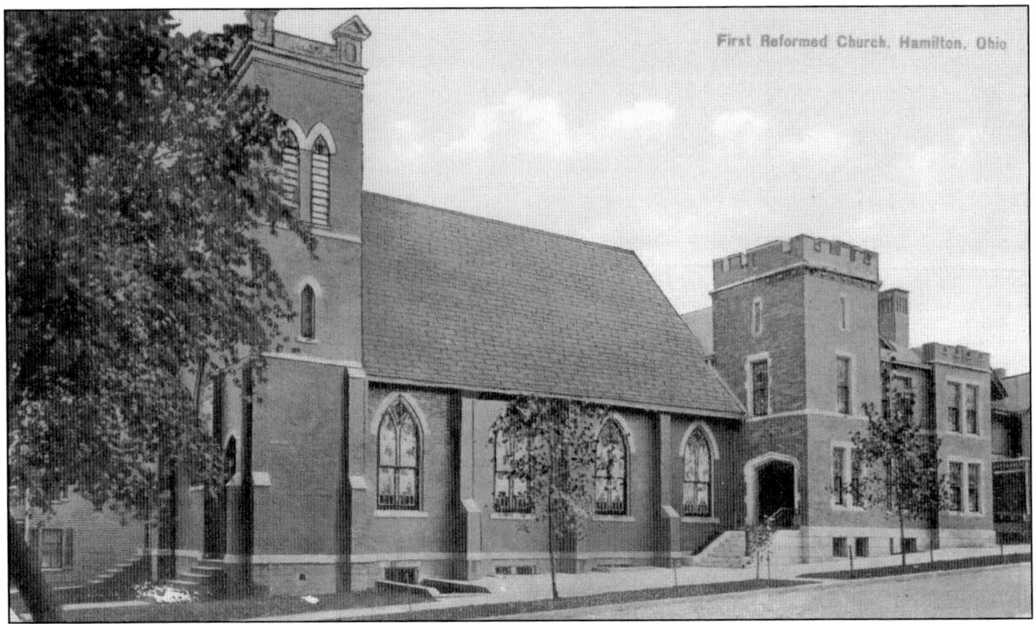

Originally constructed in 1869 with financial assistance from Reformed churches in Seven Mile, Millville, West Alexandria, Xenia, and as far away as Pennsylvania, the First Reformed Church sits on the southeast corner of Ross Avenue and South D Street. The parsonage, which still stands, was built on South D Street. The building has housed the Christ Tabernacle Apostolic Church since 1976.

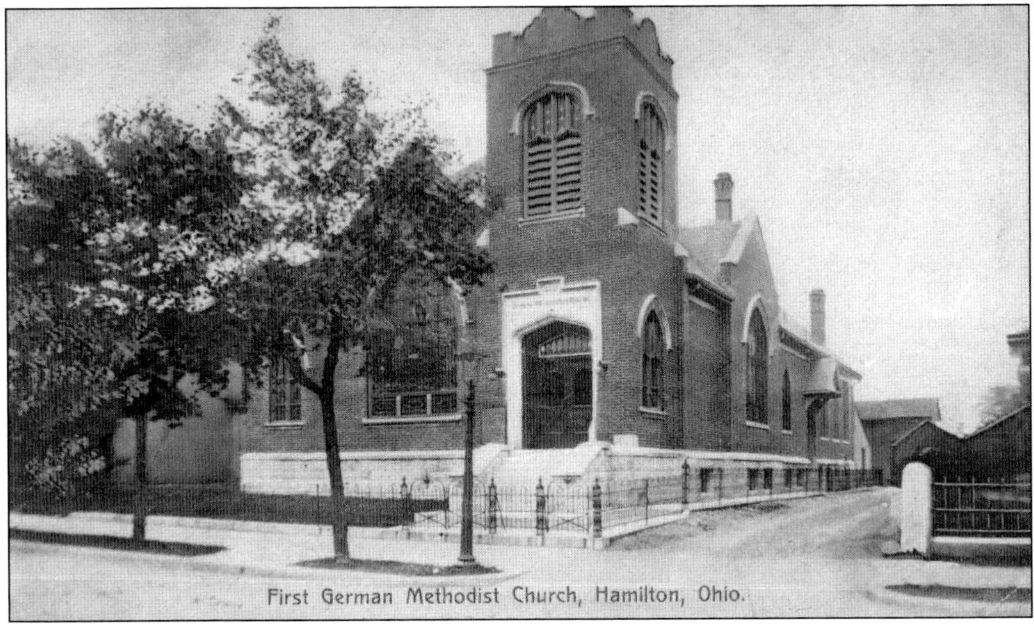

In 1854, three German Methodist preachers organized in Hamilton, and soon thereafter, converts appeared. By 1859, services were being held at a church on North C Street. This building, located on the east side of South Front Street between Ludlow and Sycamore Streets, was dedicated in May 1907. Later known as Grace Methodist Church, the building now serves as a portion of the Payne Chapel, an AME church.

This view from 1913 shows the Universalist church erected in 1893. It was the third building occupied by the sect. Located on North Seventh Street, the church was used by the Universalists until 1930, when the Universalist state convention decided to close the Hamilton location. After the closure, many Hamilton Universalists were forced to attend services in Cincinnati. Today, the building is home to the Fellowship Christian Center.

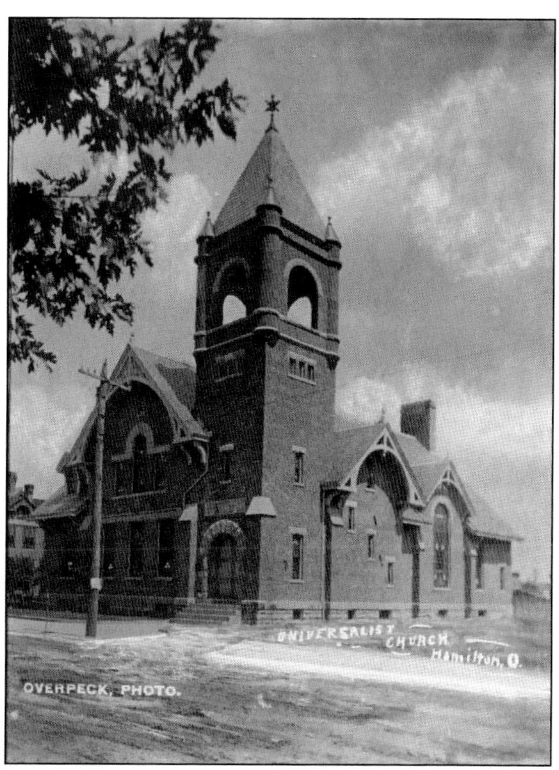

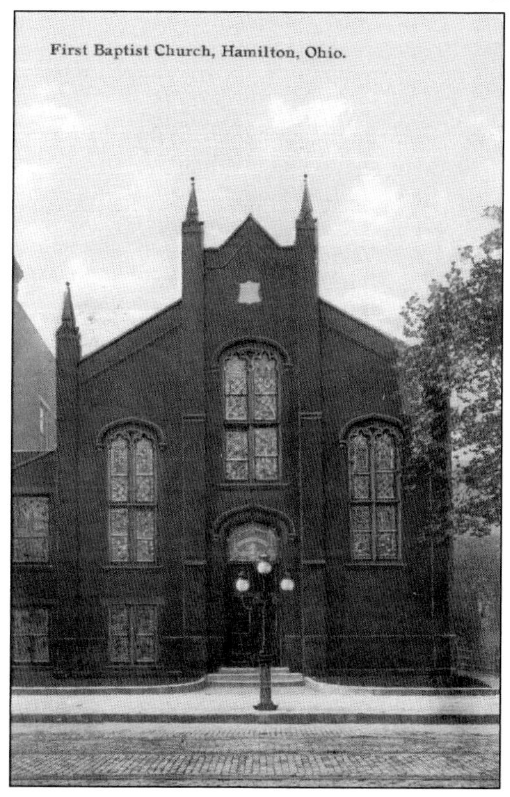

In 1844, Baptists worshipped in a small meetinghouse on North Third Street between Market and Dayton Streets, and in 1848 the First Baptist Church was organized by Pastor William Ashmore. A decade later, the congregation purchased land on the south side of Court Street and constructed the building pictured here in 1912.

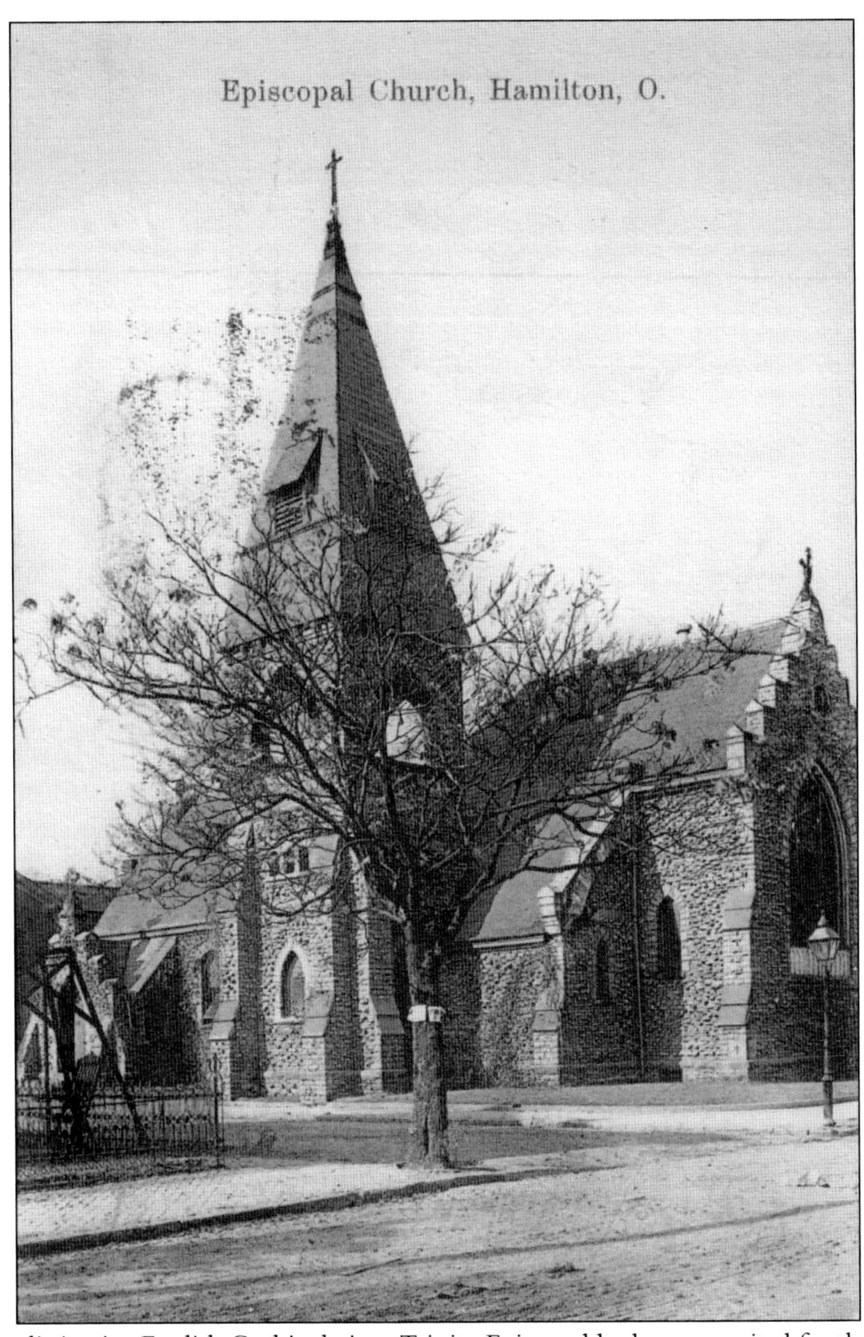

With its distinctive English Gothic design, Trinity Episcopal looks more suited for the rolling hills of Great Britain than downtown Hamilton. With the nave built in 1888, the church stood incomplete for four years until monies were provided by William A. Proctor, of Proctor & Gamble fame, and others. In 1892, the choir, chancel, and tower were completed. Finishing amenities were added, and by 1894 Trinity Episcopal was officially incorporated. In 1919, Trinity Episcopal was a key component in radio-broadcast history, as Hamilton radio pioneers Shuler and Joseph Doron aired, from inside the vestry of the church, one of the first church service broadcasts in the nation on their Hamilton-based station, WRK.

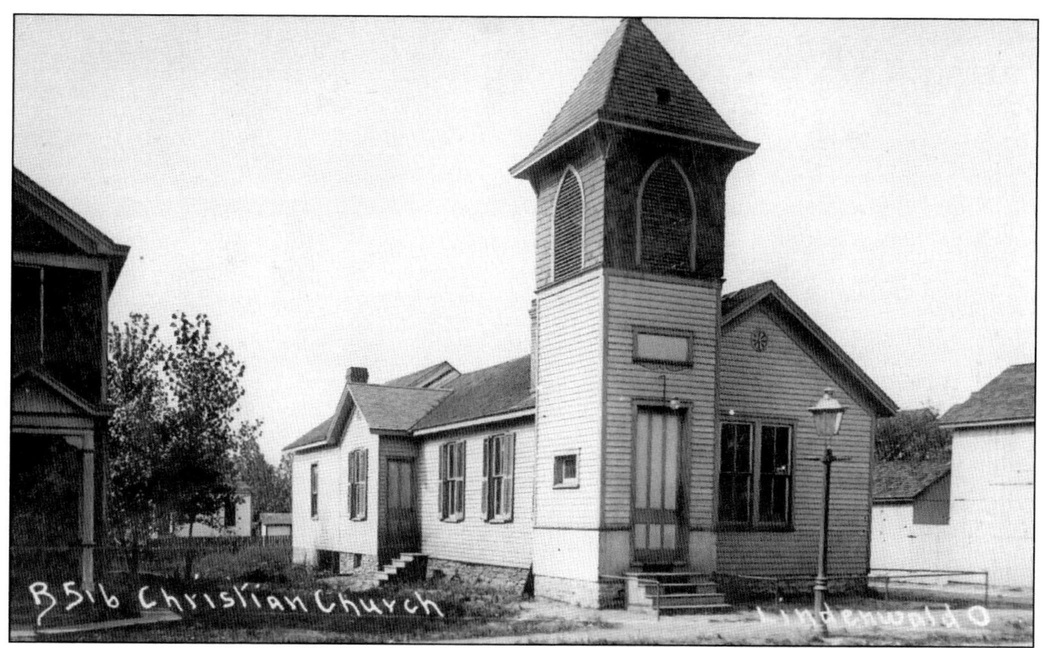

This card shows the Lindenwald Christian Church prior to 1910 after additions and renovations. Organized from a mission Sunday school in 1898, this chapel was dedicated in 1902 and lasted until 1912, when a new brick building was constructed on an adjacent site. Located near the northwest corner of Forest and Benninghofen Avenues, this structure no longer exists.

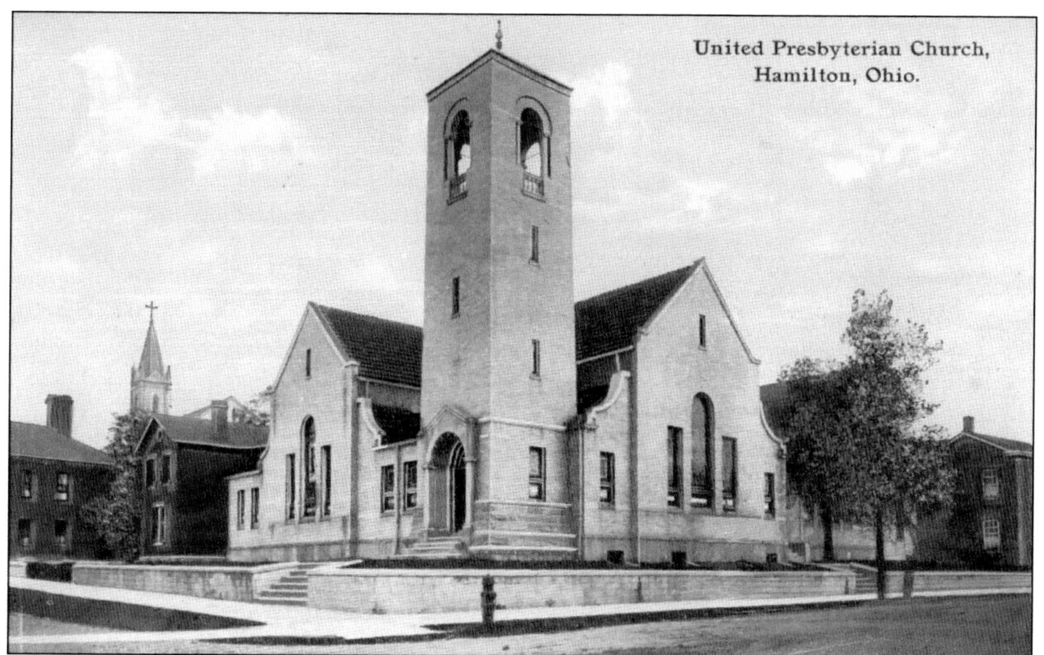

The history of the United Presbyterian Church stretches as far back as 1818. Located on the southeast corner of Court and Monument Streets, this was the third building in the history of the church. Dedicated in 1908, it was destroyed by fire on March 12, 1934. When the flames were extinguished, only the tower was left standing.

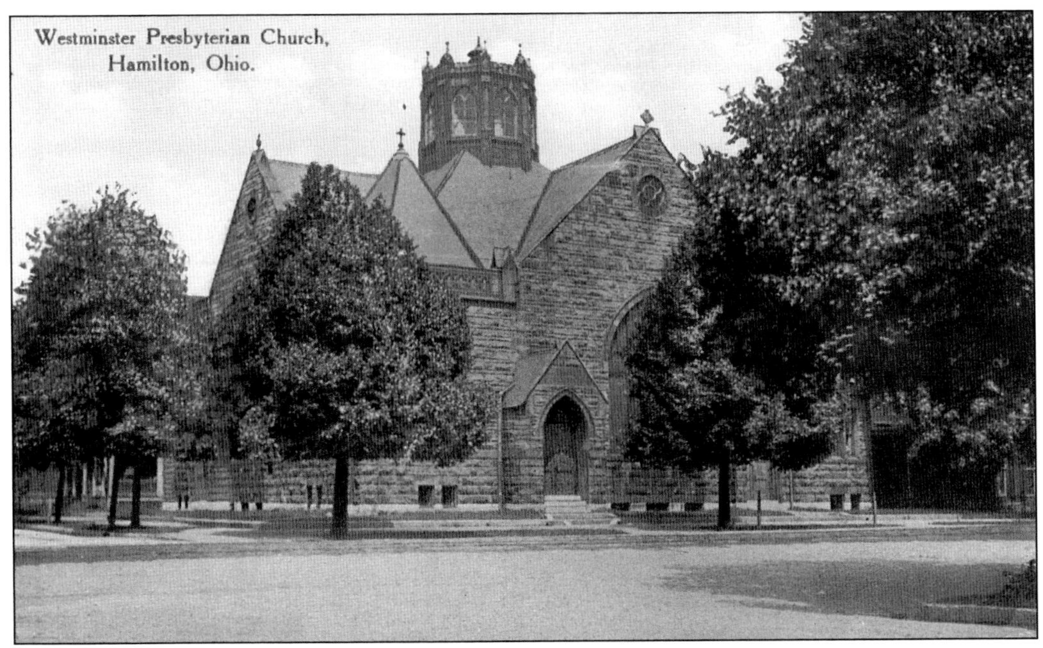

In 1893, division took place at the First Presbyterian Church, and 90 members petitioned national church leaders to form a new church. After receiving permission, the Westminster Presbyterian Church was born. The building, located at the northeast corner of Seventh and High Streets, was constructed in 1895. The life of the church was relatively short-lived, as it reunited with First Presbyterian in 1917. The building now houses the Calvary Church.

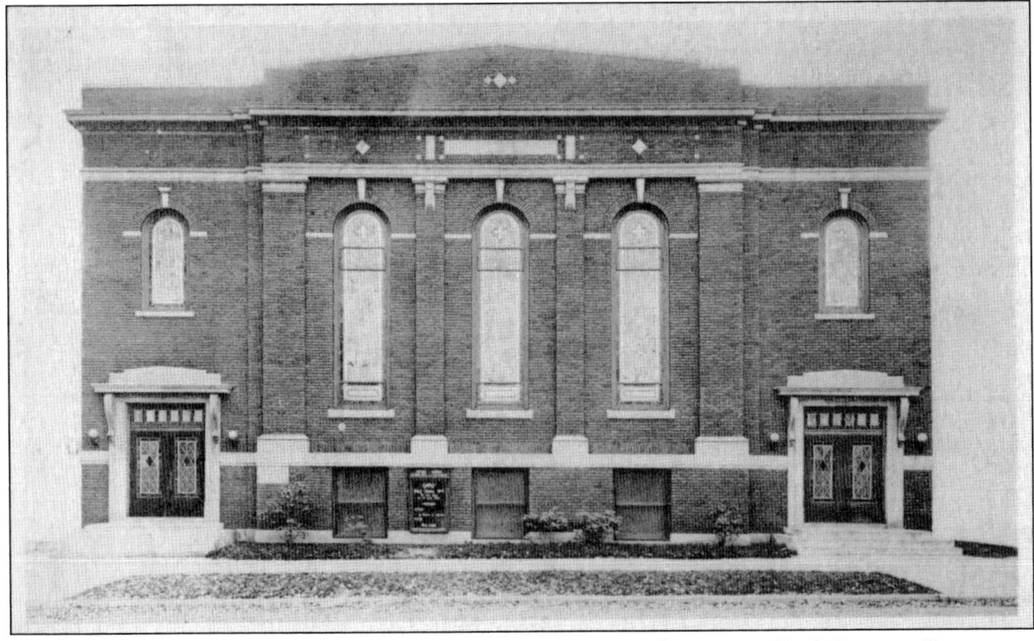

Organized by members who had decided to leave the St. John Evangelical German Protestant Church in 1910, Bethel Church found a home in the old residence of the Woodrough family on the west side of North B Street between Park Avenue and Main Street. This view shows the second Bethel Church, built on the site of its predecessor and dedicated in June 1920.

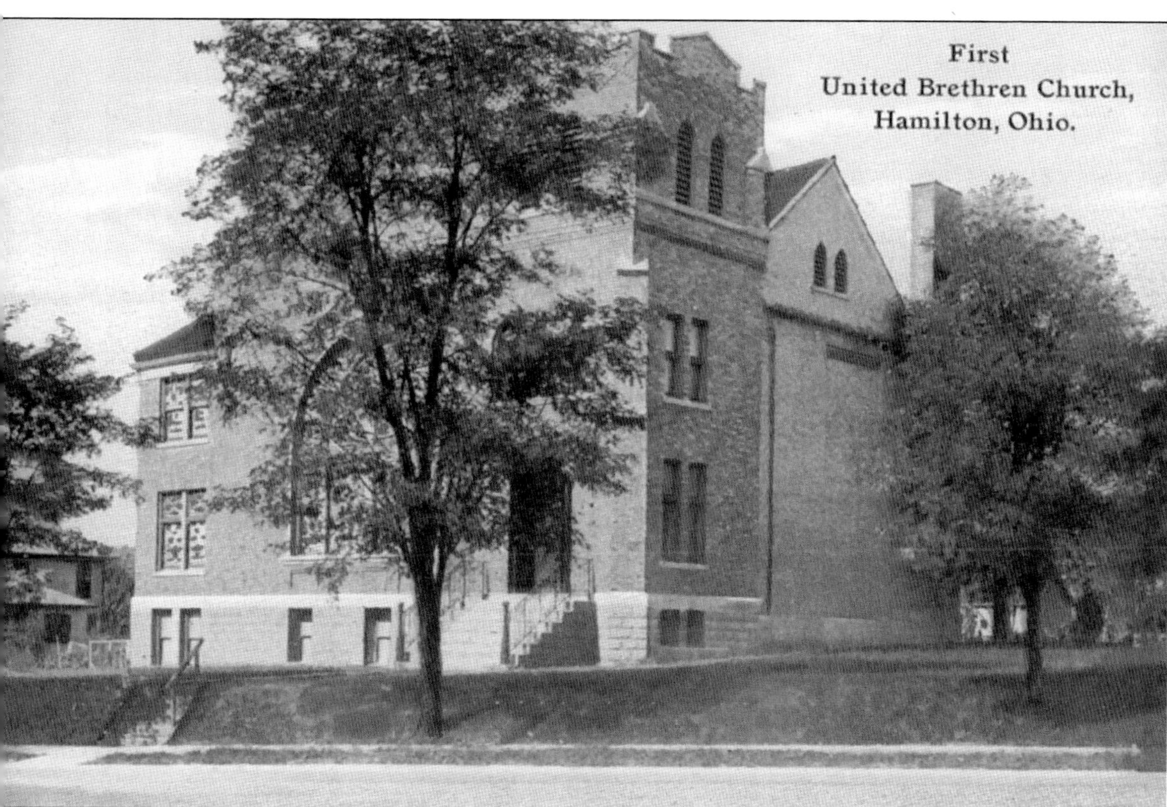

Organized in 1906, the First United Brethren Church did not have its own complete facility until 1908, when local architect George Barkman designed the structure standing at Park and Dick Avenues as shown on this card from 1911. Though a very small congregation at the start, church leaders predicted a population boom for the city's west side and built the church larger than its current need at the time.

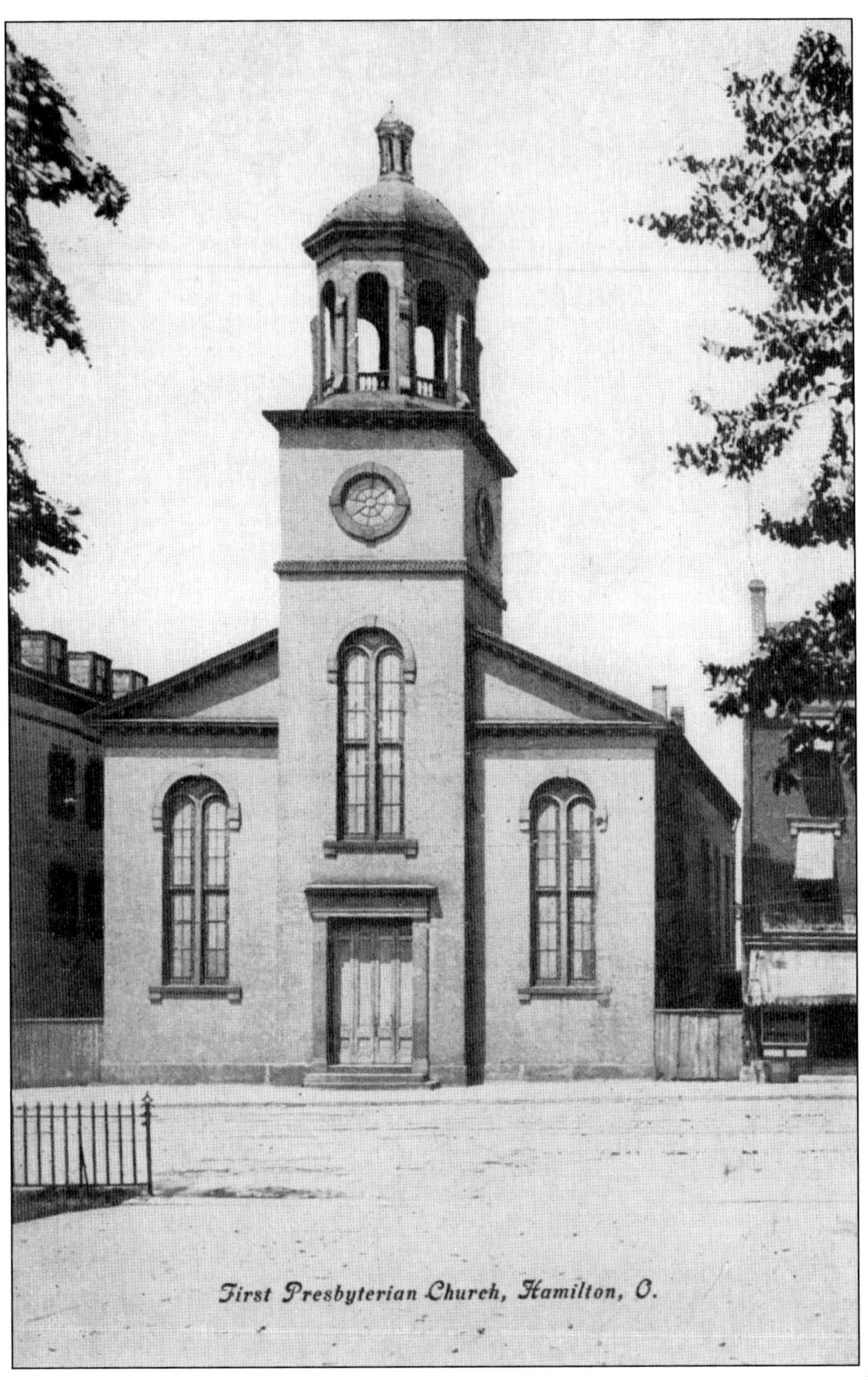

One of the oldest church buildings still surviving in the city is the First Presbyterian Church, which dates back to 1854. Twice the congregation has divided due to differences among its members, once in 1832 and again in 1893, but each time a reunification eventually took place. Located on South Front Street, this view of the church from 1907 illustrates the building's original cupola, which was replaced in 1940.

Seven

Schools

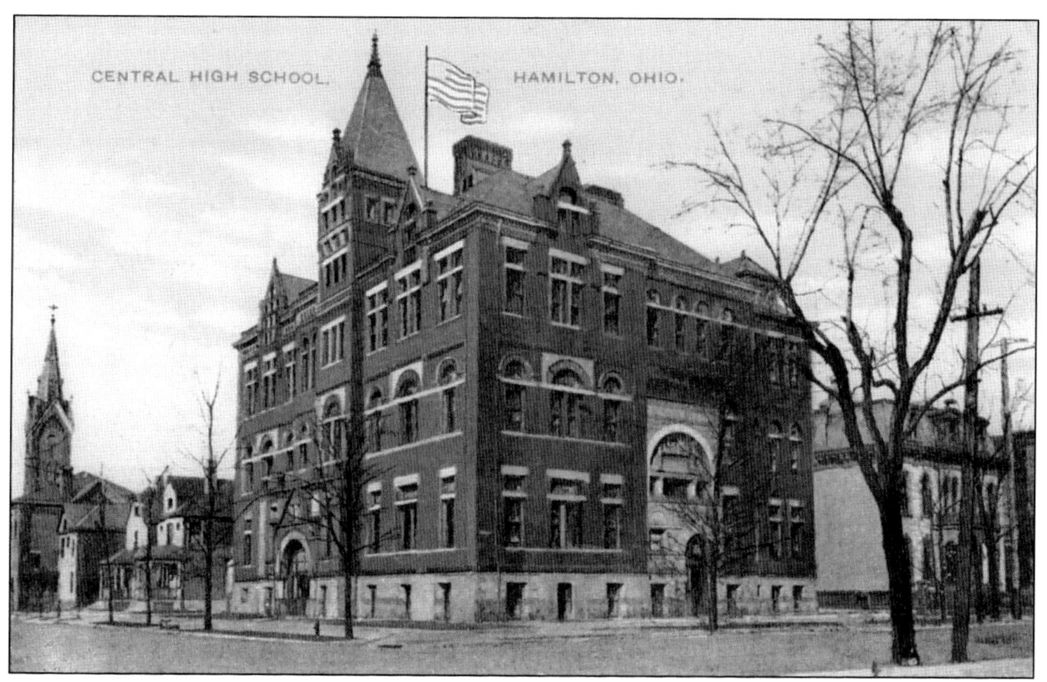

Completed in June 1892 on the northeast corner of South Second and Ludlow Streets, the Central High School building finally realized the city's desires for a centrally located secondary school; a desire reaching as far back as the mid-1870s. The building was closed in 1915, but reopened a short time later and served as a junior high until 1934 and was then demolished in 1940. Hamilton's rapid growth in the early 1900s caused serious overcrowding at the Central High School, so much so that in 1908, the adjoining home of local dry goods purveyor and grocer, the late W.C. Frechtling (right) was purchased from his widow and became known as the High School Annex. Zion Lutheran Church can be seen in the background (left).

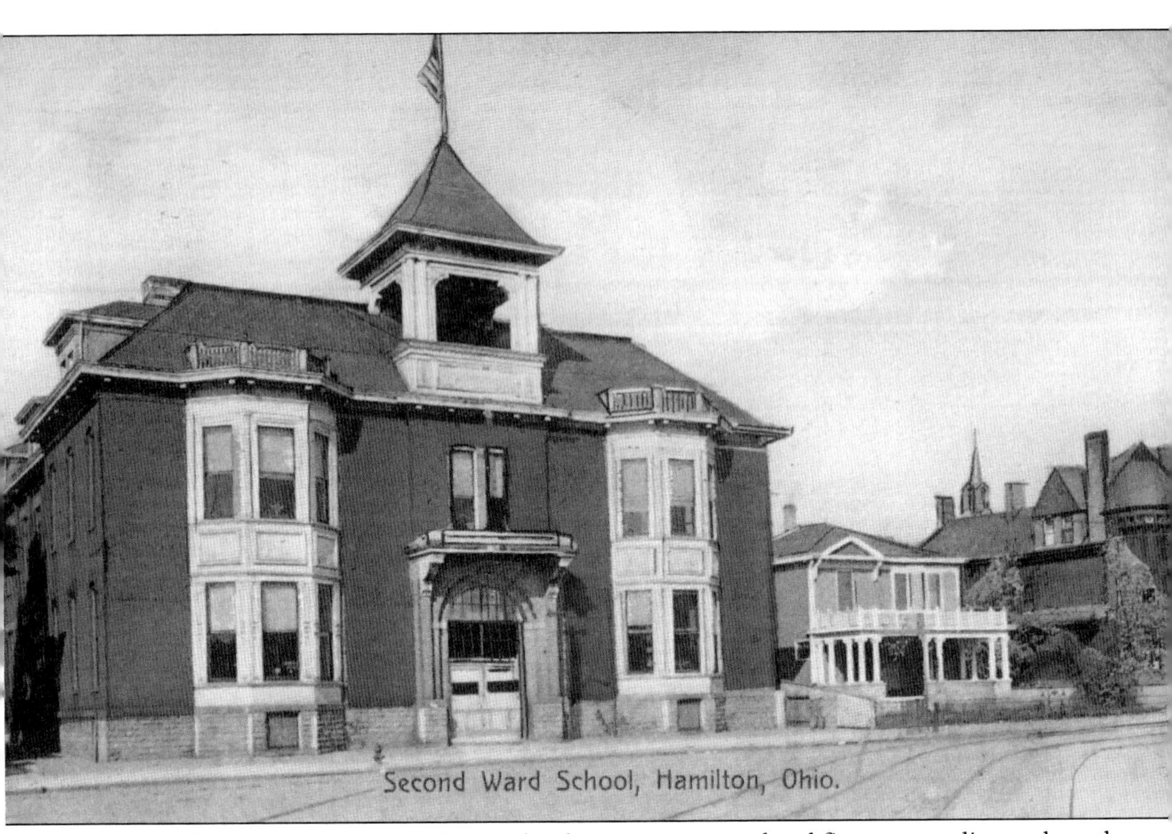

By 1899, the Second Ward had two schools—one was completed five years earlier, and another, built in 1838, was a constant maintenance headache for the district. After nearly two years of political finger pointing, rumored bid coercion, perceived architectural fee improprieties, and court injunctions, the Straub School was finally opened on Long Street in 1894. The original Second Ward School, located on Front Street across from the Cincinnati Brewing Company, had long become a liability. It was decided that instead of building a replacement, the newest school in the ward would be the result of the renovation of an existing building. Situated on South Second Street, the old United German Society's Music Hall was selected. This view from 1909 shows the school just before its name change to Harrison School. The building ceased educational functions in 1952 and was demolished in 1999.

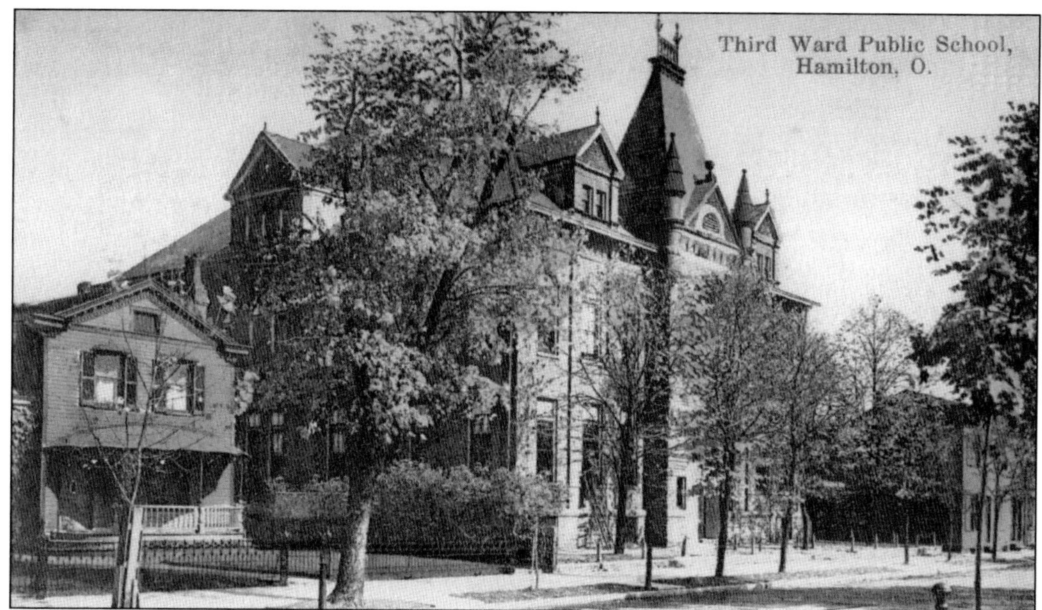

One of the few remaining old school buildings within the city stands on the north side of Dayton Street between Third Street and Martin Luther King Boulevard. Originally known as the Third Ward School, the building was constructed in 1889. In 1909, the school's name was changed to the Washington School, and the facility continued to matriculate students until the building became the administrative offices for Hamilton City Schools in 1947. The building is currently occupied by Community Development Professionals LLC.

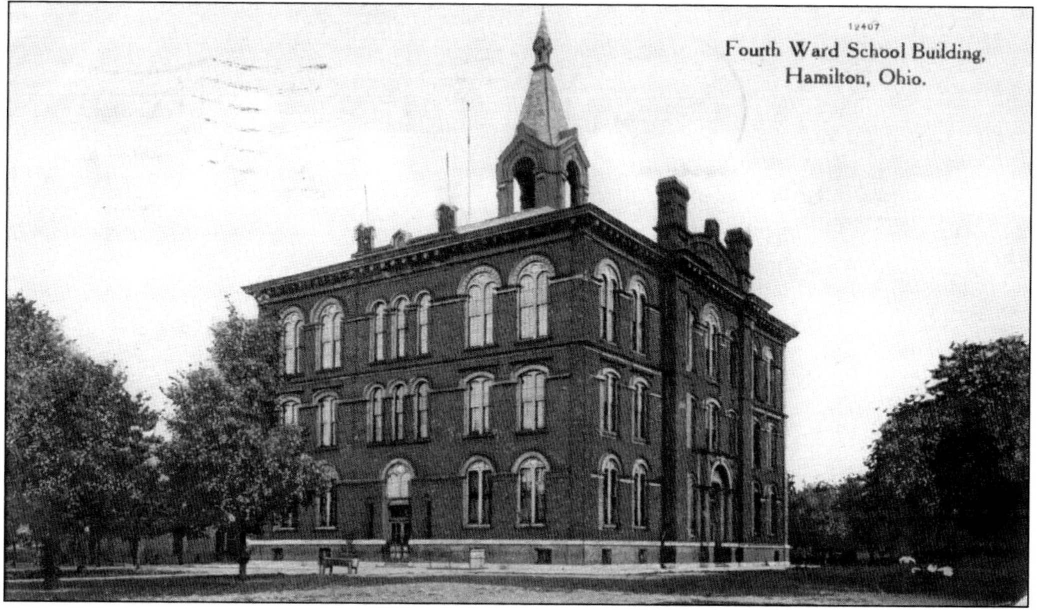

The Fourth Ward School was located between South Eighth and Ninth Streets to the east and west and Rigdon and Chestnut Streets to the north and south. Completed in 1874, the building gained a reputation as a money pit, as the construction costs nearly tripled from the original $38,000 to over $91,000. Serving as a high school from 1880 to 1892 and renamed Jefferson School in 1909, the building was in service until its demise in 1952.

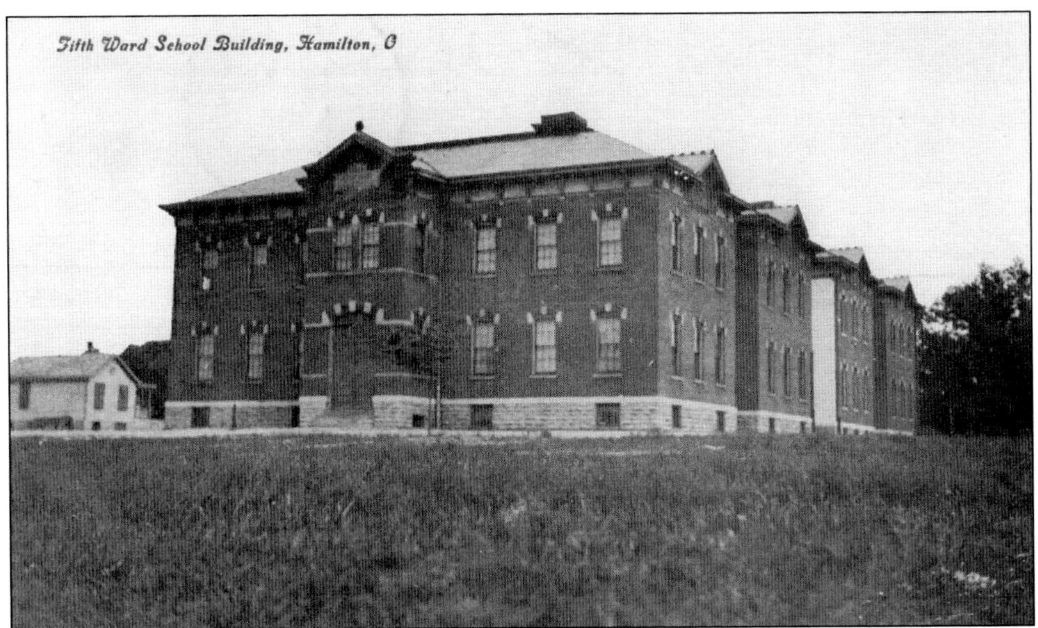

When completed in 1884, the Fifth Ward School sat between North Ninth and Tenth Streets on Shillito Street (current-day Buckeye Street). Becoming Madison School in the 1909 district-wide name change, this school also met its fate during the 1950s. This view shows the school after its 1898 expansion to meet the needs of a growing Hamilton eastside.

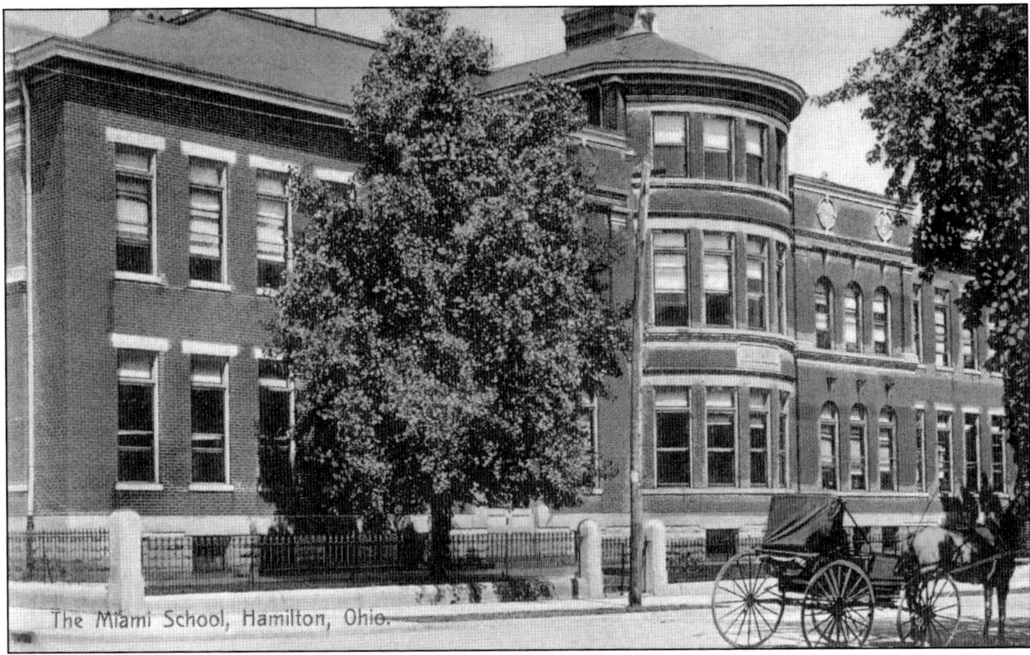

The Miami School was constructed in 1902 on the site of the First Ward School built in 1857, at Ross Avenue and C Street. In 1957, William Murstein, operator of Wilmer's Department Store, orchestrated the building's transformation into a senior citizen's center. This saved the building from suffering the demolition that nearly all of the city's school buildings have faced. Today, the Miami School building operates as Partners in Prime.

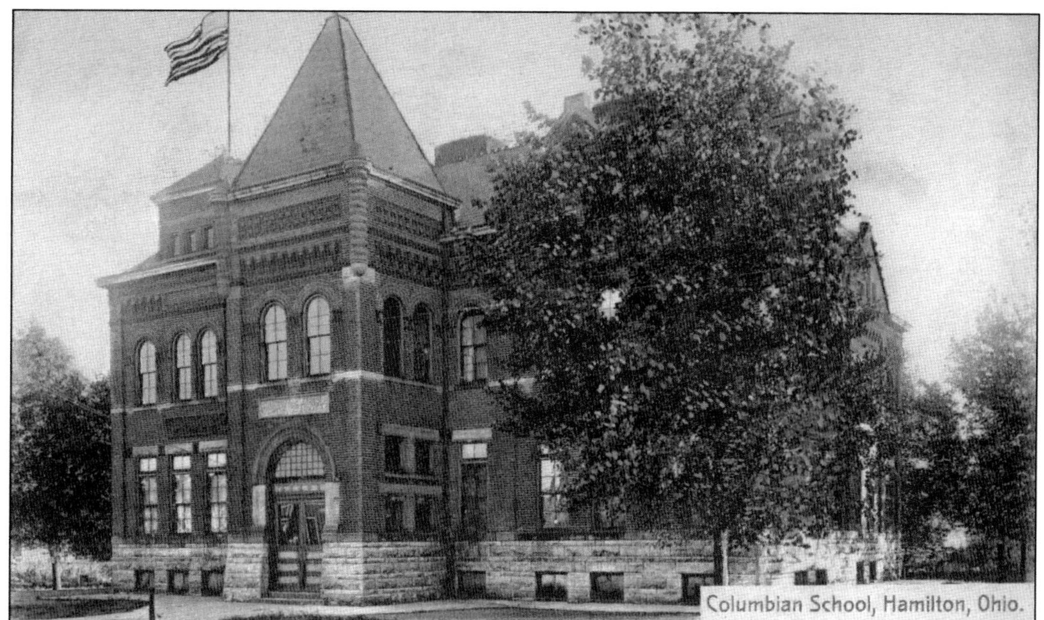

One of the last 19th-century city schools to remain standing, the Columbian School, also known as Jackson School, survived from 1892 to 1973. Located on Park Avenue across from Sherman Avenue, the school was named in honor of the 400th anniversary of Columbus's discovery of the New World. Designed by local architect Max Ruetti, the school's basic design was also used for the new Second Ward Straub School, which opened in 1893.

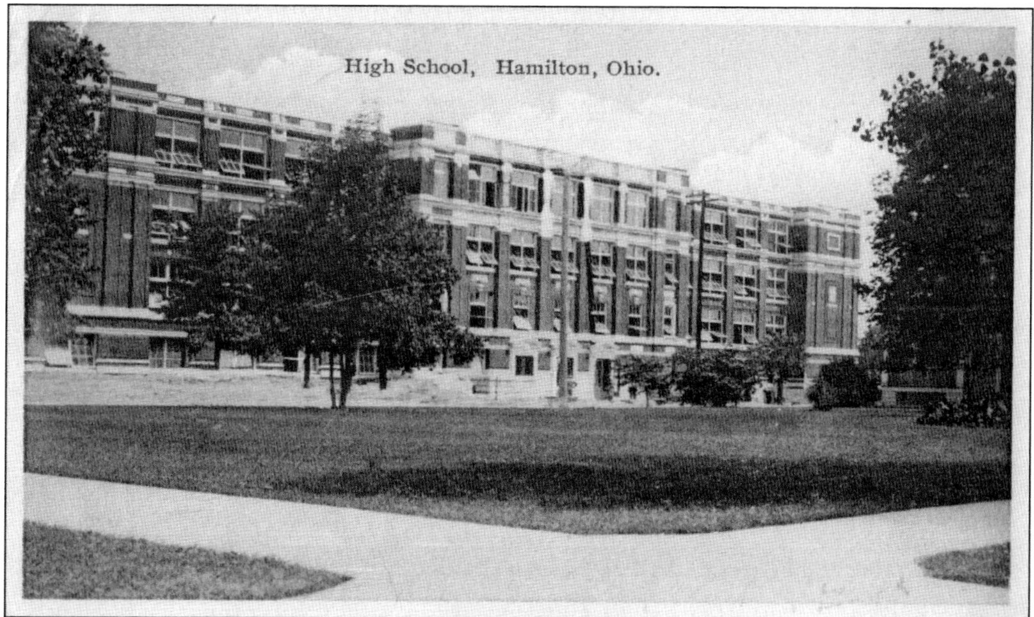

Completed in 1915 for a cost of nearly $214,000, the new Hamilton High School building brought the city into the modern age of both academic and vocational education. Located on North Sixth Street between Dayton and Butler Streets, the building served high school students until 1959, when Garfield and Taft High Schools were opened. Renamed Harding Junior High, the facility continued operation until 1980. The school fell to the wrecking ball in 1982.

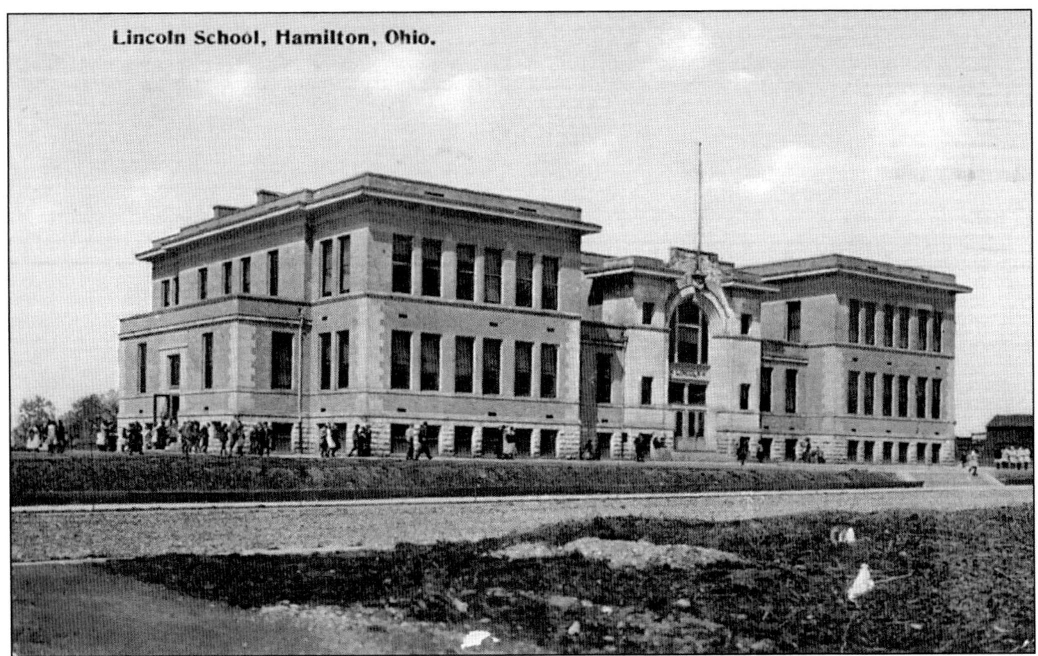

The opening of Lincoln School in 1909 coincided with the renaming of existing ward schools with the names of presidents. Situated on North E Street between Gray and Webster Avenues, Lincoln School served the residents of the Rheadon Park subdivision and surrounding areas in the First Ward with distinction for over a century. The building was finally razed in 2010.

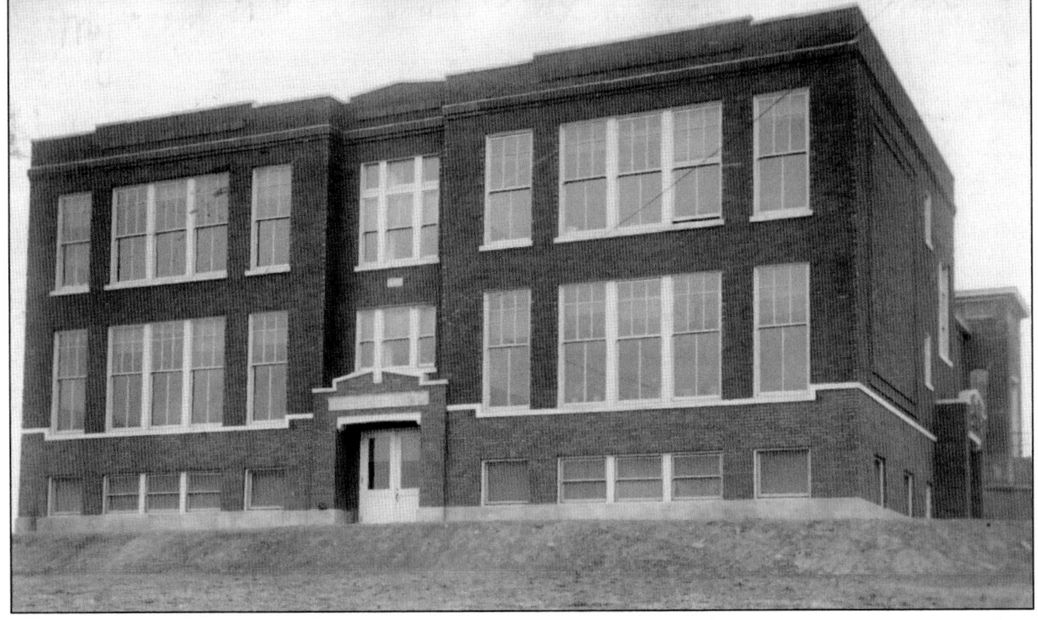

This real-photo postcard from 1915 shows the Van Buren School during expansion construction. The original Van Buren, known as Mosler School or the Fourth Ward Annex when it opened in 1900, was woefully undersized to meet the growing eastside population. Located on Grand Avenue, the school saw two major expansion projects and a name change to the Coolidge School during its lifetime, which lasted into the 1960s.

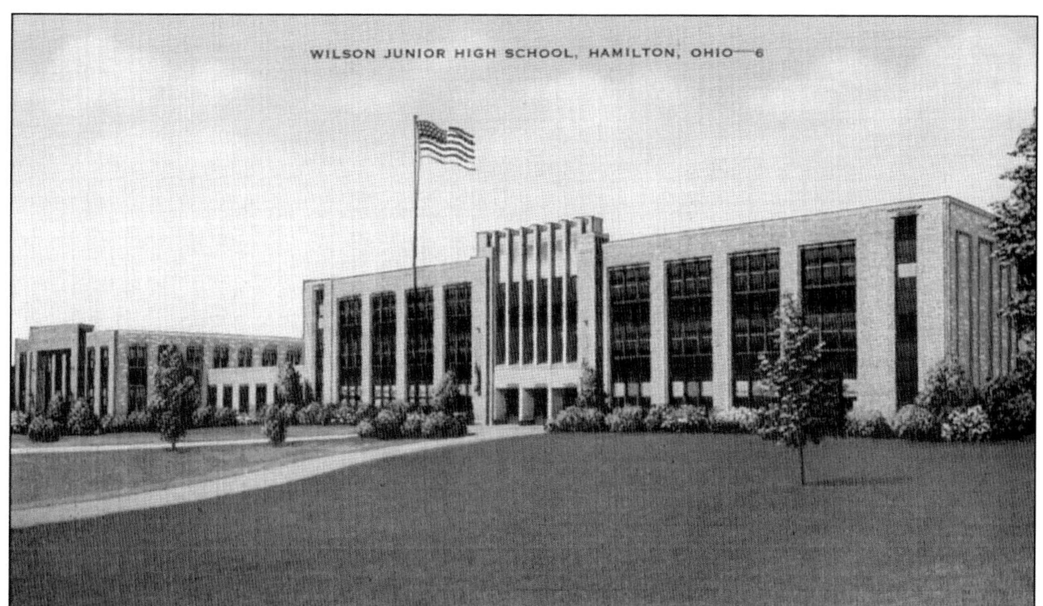

The 1930s marked the rise of the junior high school in the city. Roosevelt Junior High School was completed in 1930, and the construction of Wilson Junior High in 1934 brought the city its first Art Deco school design. Located on Eaton Avenue, the building housed grades seven to nine until 2004 with the opening of the freshman school. Except for the fine-arts wing, the facility was demolished and rebuilt in 2011 as Wilson Middle School.

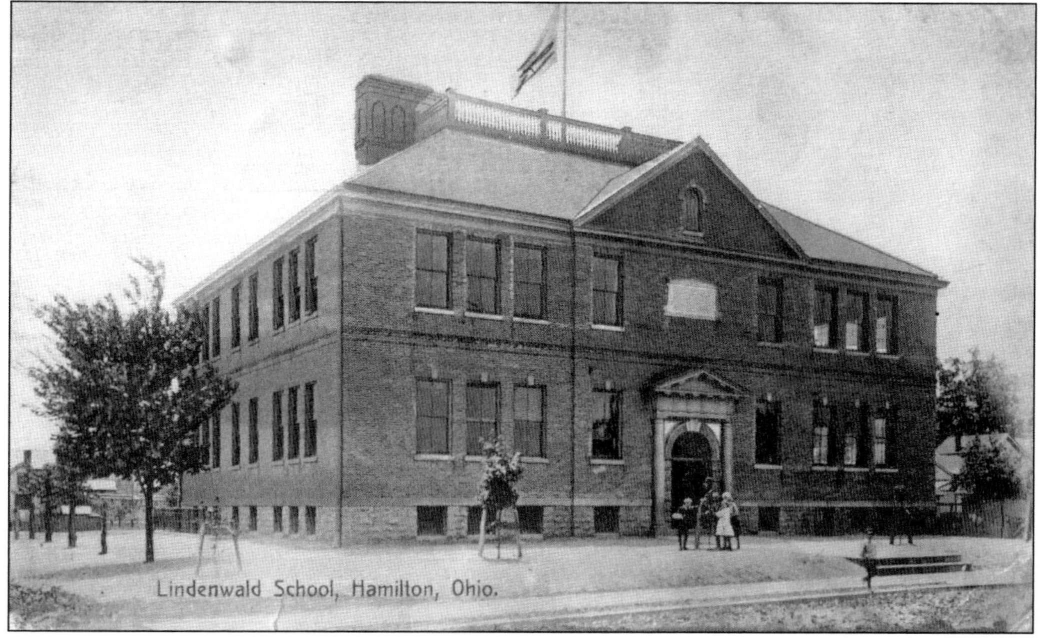

When the city of Hamilton annexed the residential area of Lindenwald in 1908, the existing Lindenwald School fell under the auspices of the Hamilton City School District. The building was located on Woodlawn Avenue and had been constructed in 1895 with funding provided by the local residents. A year after the annexation, the facility became Polk School and served students until 1973.

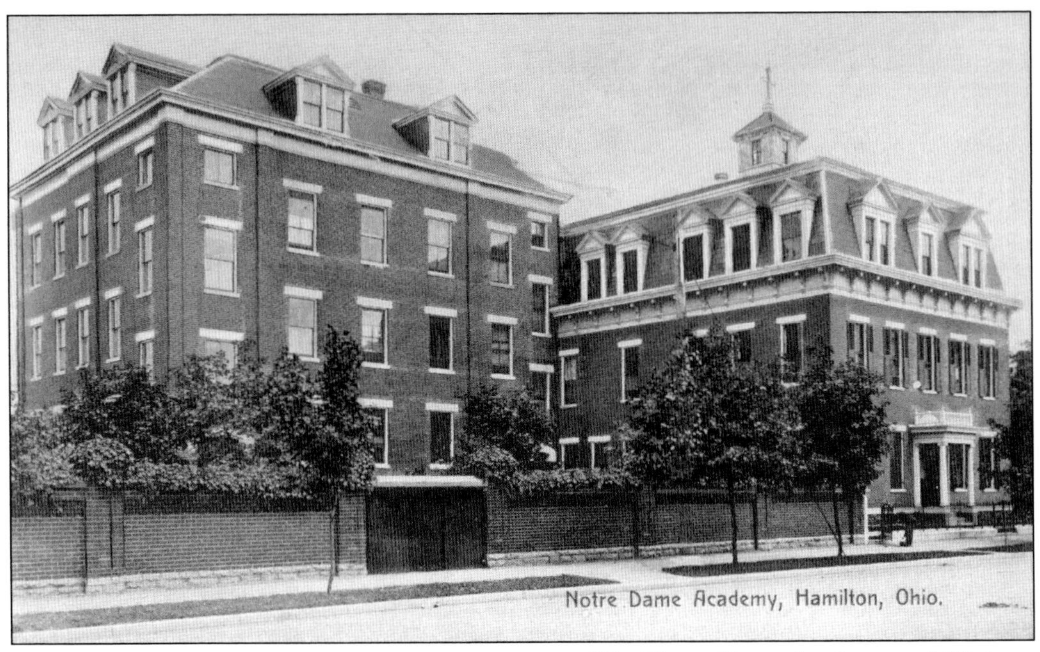
Notre Dame Academy, Hamilton, Ohio.

The Notre Dame Academy and High School educated Hamilton's Catholic girls from 1887 to 1966. The school, located at Second and Hanover Streets, is pictured here. The original structure (right) was designed in 1873 as a residence for nuns teaching at parochial schools throughout the city. Growing demand for higher schooling of Catholic girls forced the sisters to open their property up to educational purposes. In 1902, an expansion was completed (left).

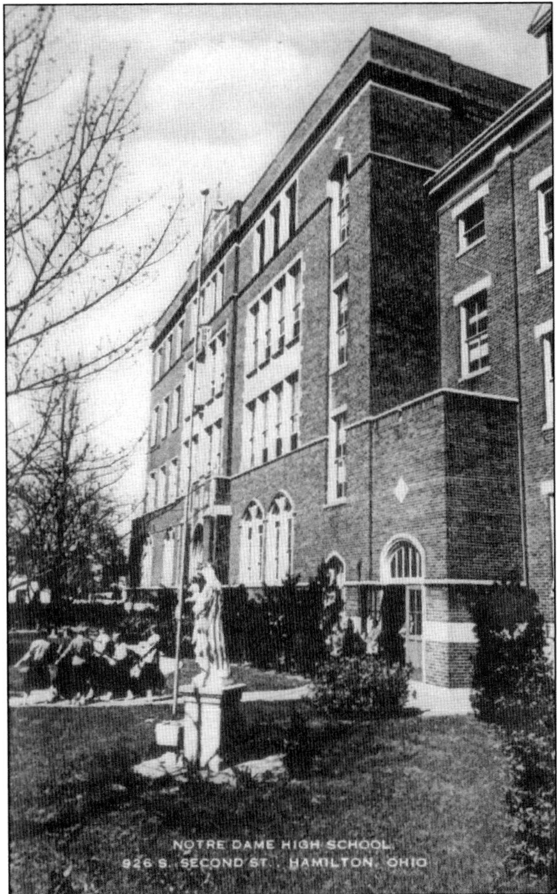
NOTRE DAME HIGH SCHOOL.
926 S. SECOND ST., HAMILTON, OHIO

Continued rise in enrollment created the need for further expansion of Notre Dame Academy. In 1924, funds were raised to construct a new school building, causing the Second Street complex to stretch the entire block between Hanover and Washington Streets. With the project completed, the institution became a free school for girls, with local parishes paying the tuition, and the name was changed to Notre Dame High School.

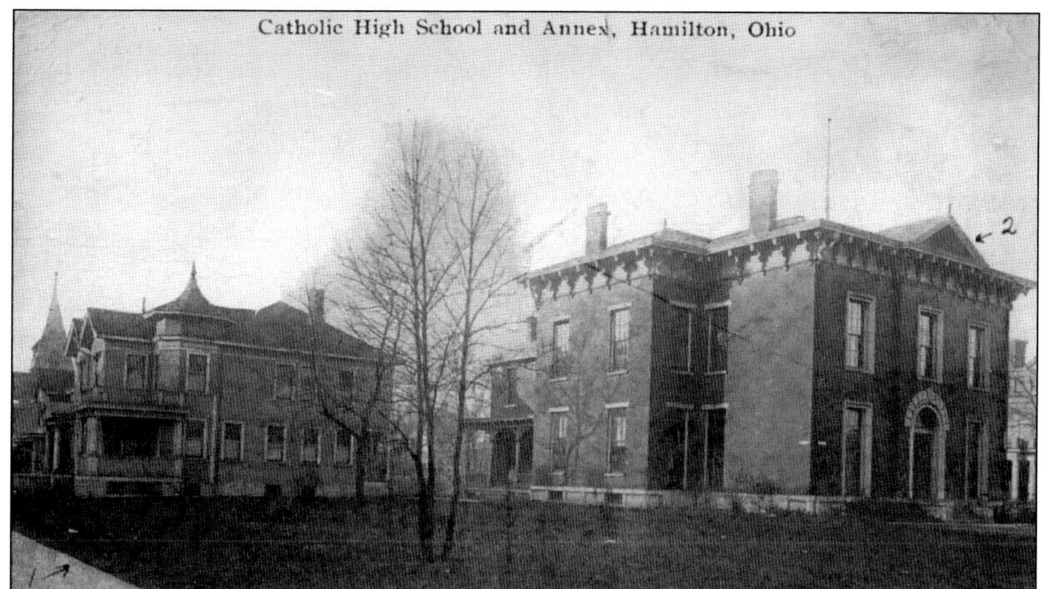

In 1909, through the efforts of Rev. F. Solanus Schaeffer, the Morey home on the southwest corner of Sixth and Dayton Streets was purchased and converted into Hamilton's first Catholic high school for boys. Enrollment at the opening of the school totaled 53 students. Within a few years, an additional home was purchased on Sixth Street to serve as an annex to meet growing student numbers. (Courtesy of BCHS.)

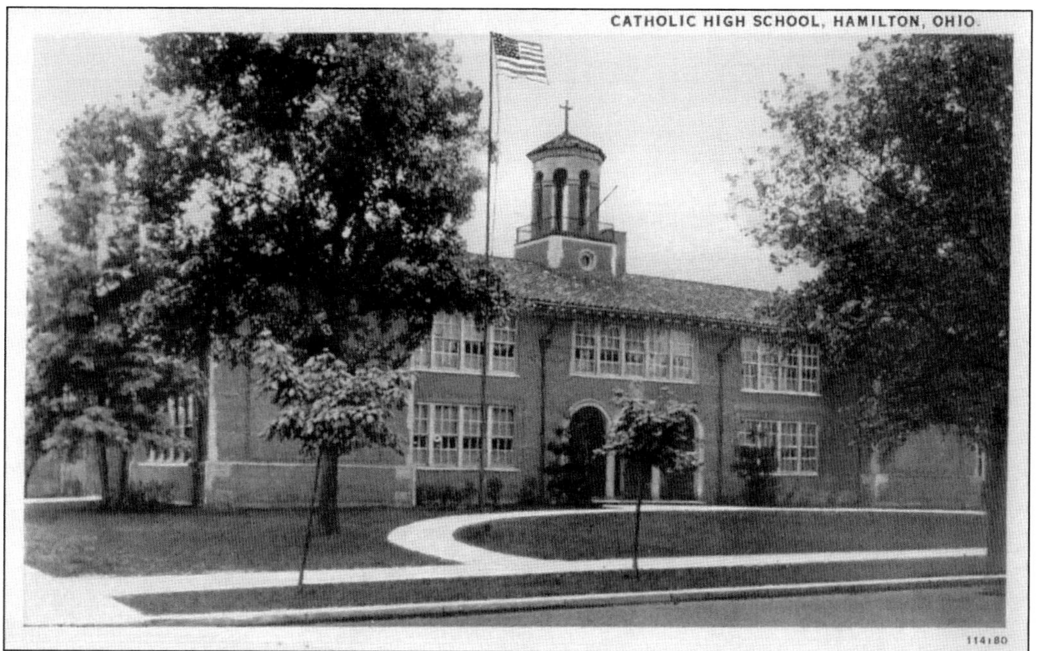

By the 1920s, the original Catholic high school building was insufficient to meet enrollment demands. On November 1, 1922, ground was broken for a new building on the same site. This facility is one of the few school buildings that has survived the wrecking ball. The school ceased operations in 1966 with the opening of Stephen T. Badin High School. The building now houses the board of education and administrative offices for the Hamilton City Schools.

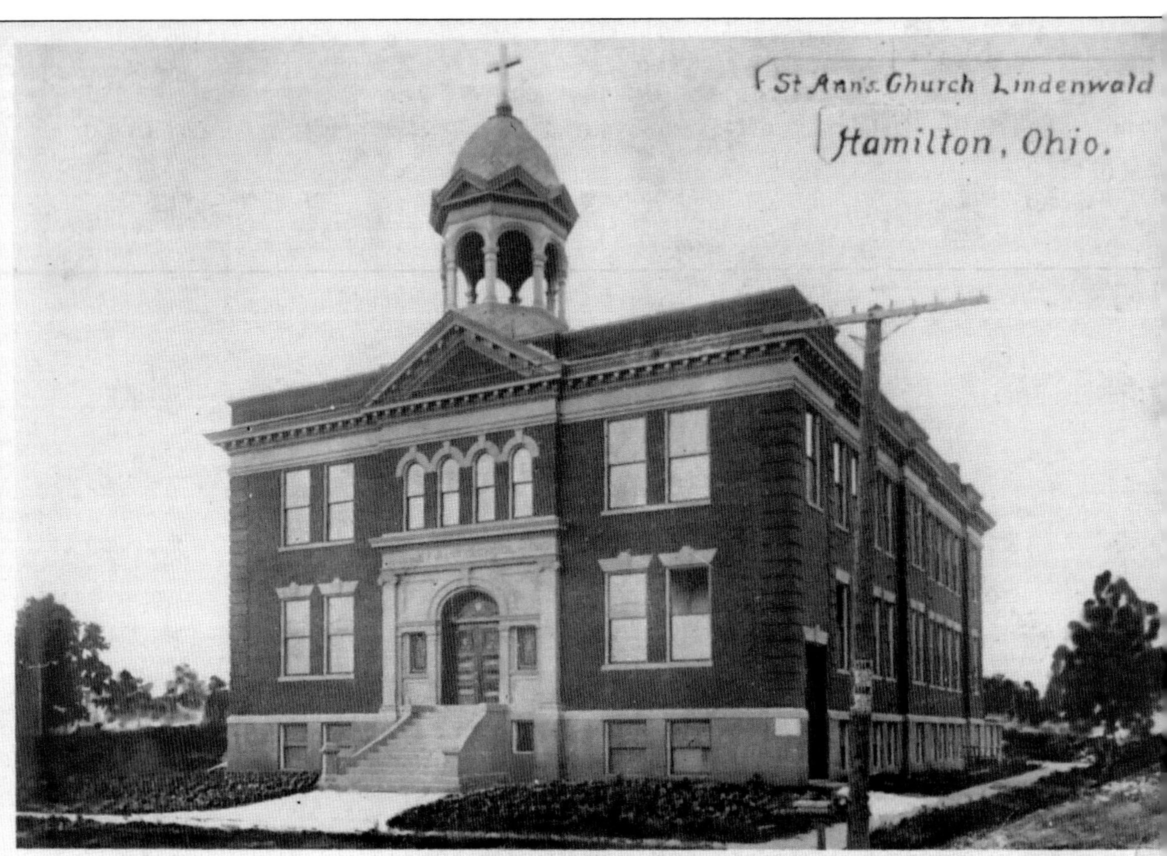

Still in operation today, the facility housing St. Ann's School was officially dedicated on June 25, 1911. Located on Pleasant and Hooven Avenues, the building pictured here housed both the parish school on the upper floors and the church in the basement. The first classes in the new school found three sisters from Oldenburg convent instructing approximately 50 students in five grades. The building served these dual purposes until 1937.

Eight

Neighborhoods

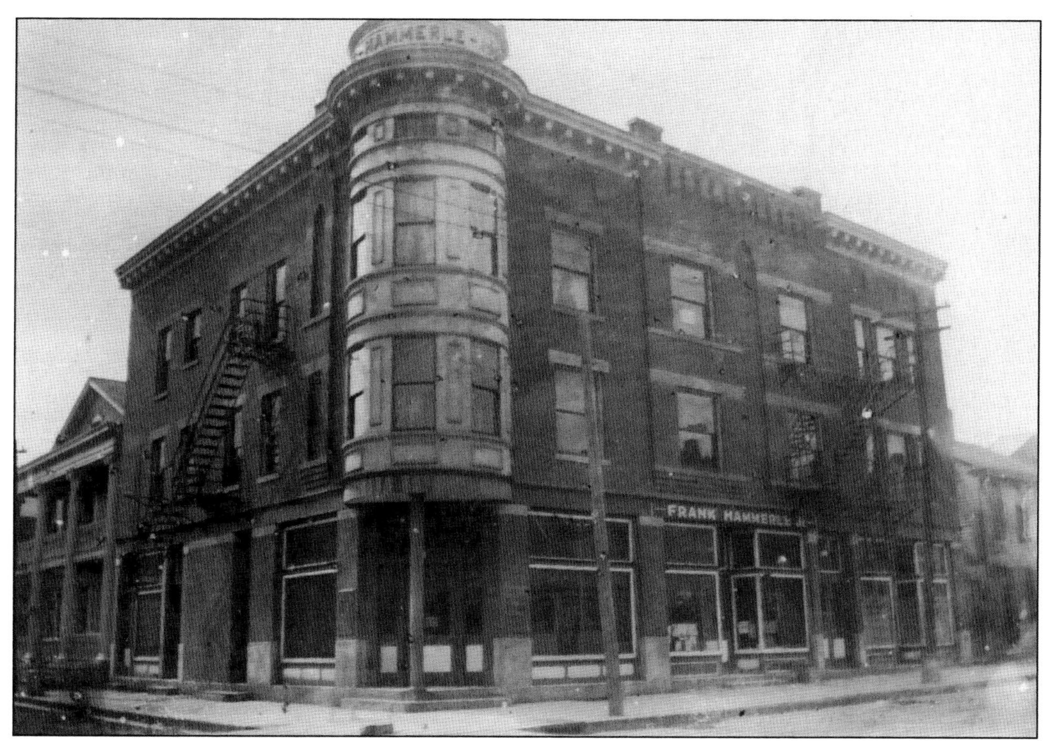

Constructed in 1906, the Hammerle Building has seen many uses over the decades. While the upper floors consisted of living apartments, the ground floor of the building has housed a wide variety of stores and businesses. Its original builder and owner, Frank Hammerle Jr., operated a combination confectionery, gun shop, and bee shop in the building on the southwest corner of C and Main Streets. In fact, Hammerle was the county's first licensed bee inspector. The West Side Building and Loan Association was also a tenant when the building first opened.

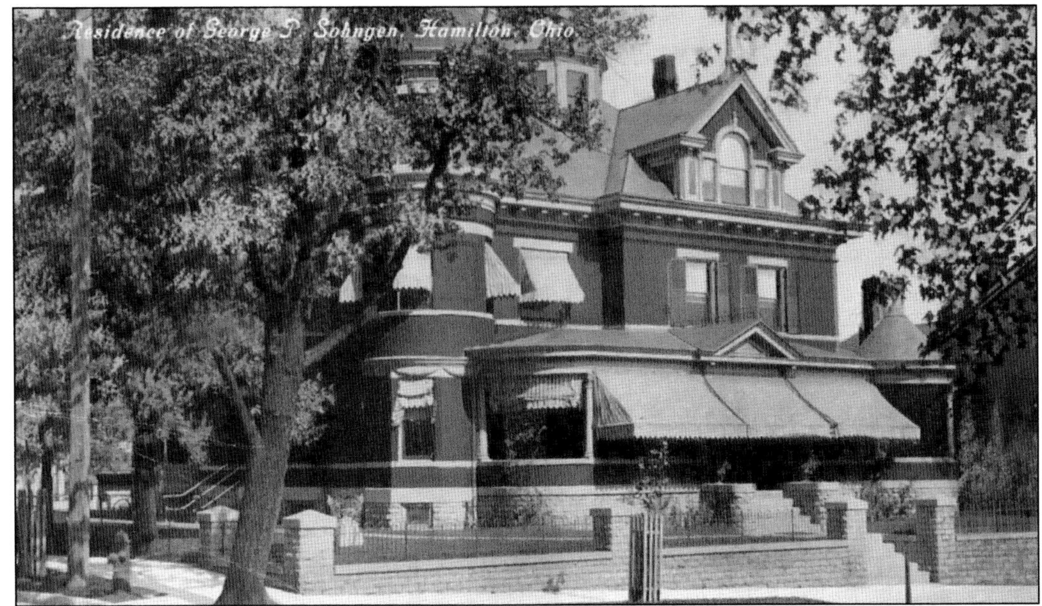

The home of George P. Sohngen, built in 1900, is situated on the northeast corner of Ross Avenue and South D Street. The Sohngen family made their wealth selling hops to local brewers. By the 1870s, the family's American Malting Company was the largest malting business in southern Ohio. Sohngen was also president of the Hamilton Dime Savings Bank and the Mathes Dry Goods Company, and vice president of the Second National Bank.

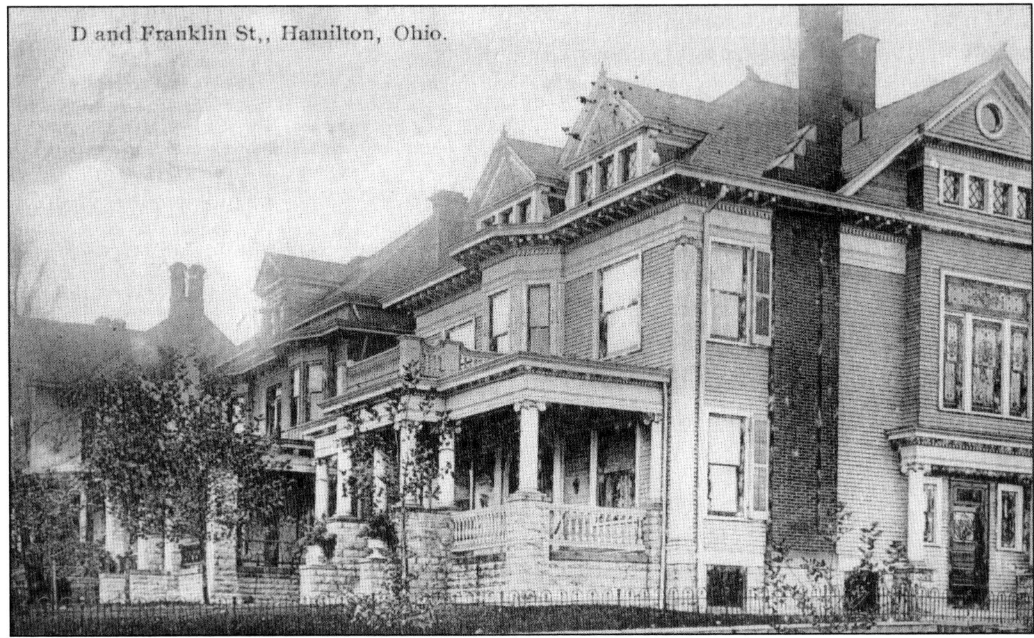

Prominent Hamilton businessman Edward C. Sohngen made his home at 203 South D Street. Following in his father Louis's footsteps, he opened his own malt company at High and Fourth Streets in 1897, quickly developing an impressive list of clients who sought his high-quality product. In 1919, he became half owner of the Miami Motor Car Company on South Second Street, which was known to have the finest garage in town.

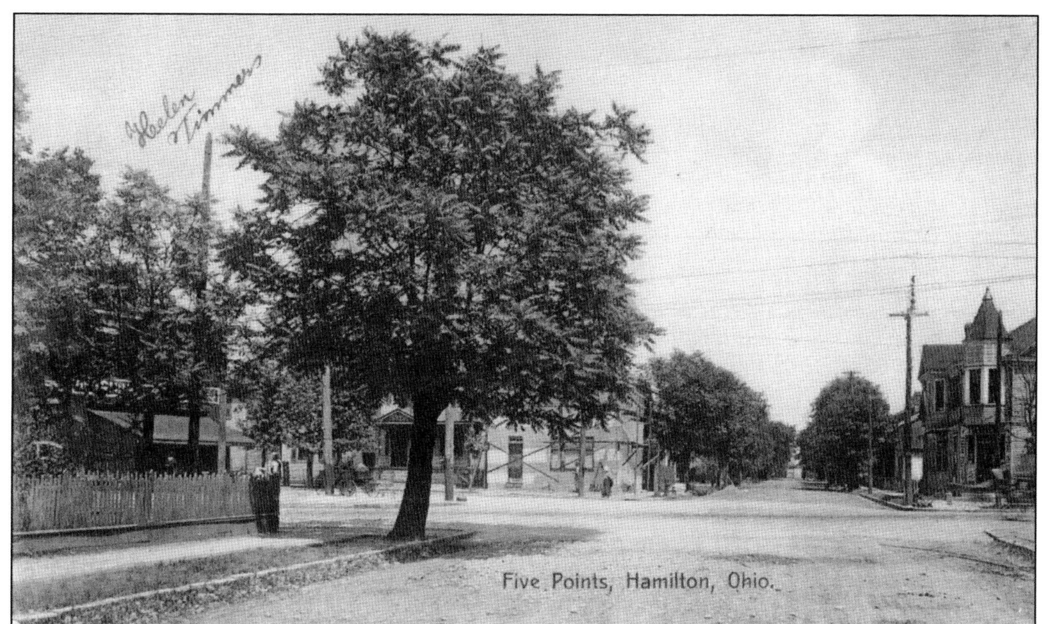

This is a view from Wood Street (Pershing Avenue) looking east at the Five Points intersection on the border of Second and Fourth Wards. South Third Street intersects from north (left) while Central Avenue crosses Wood at a southeast angle. The spired residence and shop (right) at 602 Central Avenue belongs to Frank J. Schliesman, grinder of and dealer in razors, scissors, knives, surgical supplies, lawn mowers, and barber supplies.

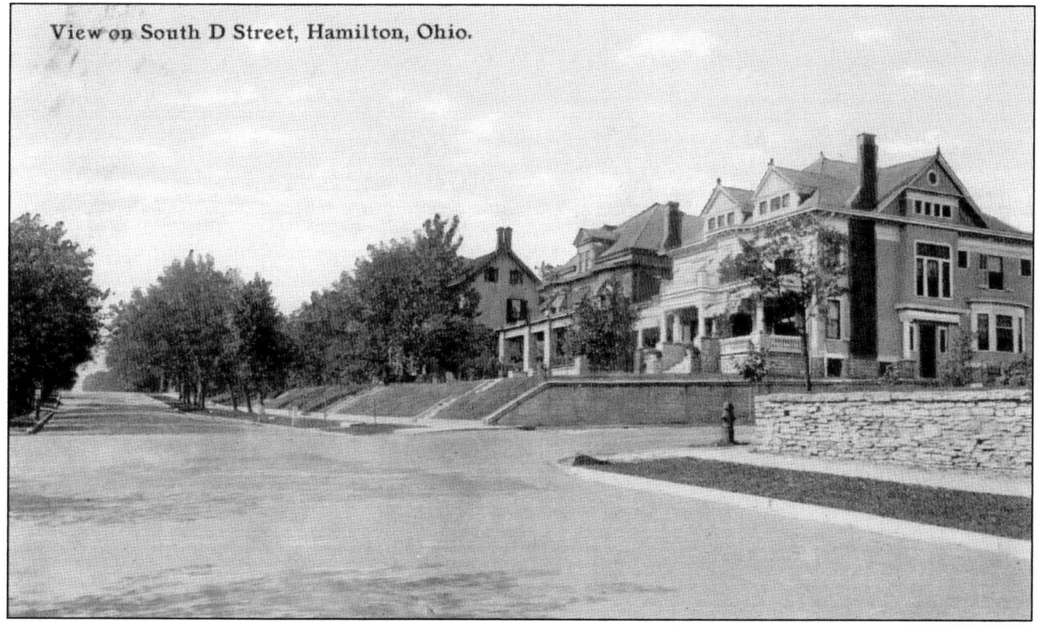

This card from 1912 shows the corner of South D and Franklin Streets, looking south. The homes of successful malt dealer Edward C. Sohngen (right) and millinery, notions, and fancy goods merchant Charles D. Mathes (center) sit prominently overlooking the city to the east across the river. The farthest visible house was originally constructed in 1862 by attorney Isaac Robertson.

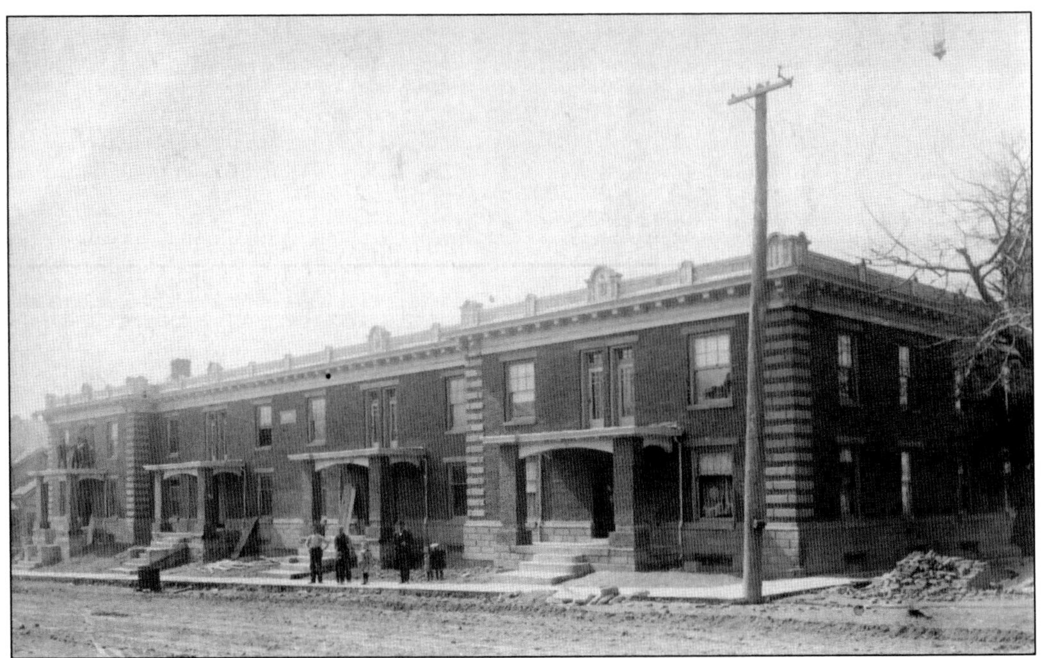

When completed in summer 1907, the Park Terrace Flats boasted the finest of modern conveniences. A listing in the October 1907 ***Hamilton Daily Republican News*** advertised a six-room apartment with steam heat, hot and cold running water, and janitor service all provided by the owner. Interested applicants were to contact Howard D. Stevenson, Flat 7, with references. No rent cost was listed. The image above shows the building while under construction in June 1907. The image below was published by the Kraemer Art Company of Cincinnati and is postmarked 1910. The building, located on the southeast corner of Park Avenue and C Street, still stands and still provides apartment living space to Hamiltonians today.

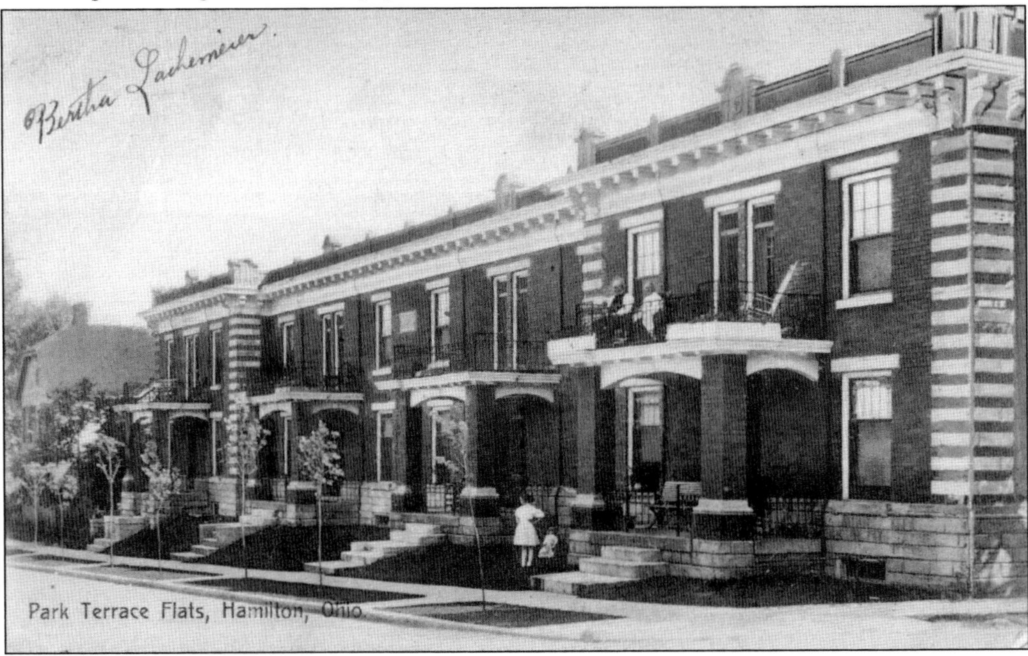

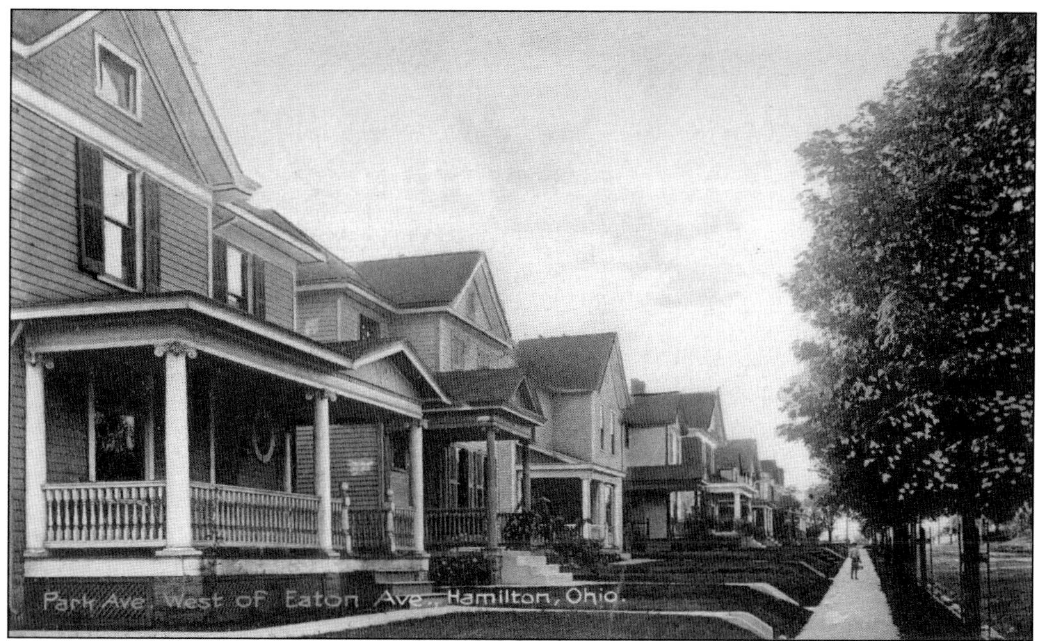

The epitome of sturdy middle-class living on Hamilton's west side was the Lawn View Subdivision. The triangular neighborhood was bounded by Eaton Road to the west, Main Street to the south and east, and Webster Avenue to the north, with Park Avenue splitting the middle. Except for the smaller trees, this view of Park Avenue from 1910 does not look very different than today.

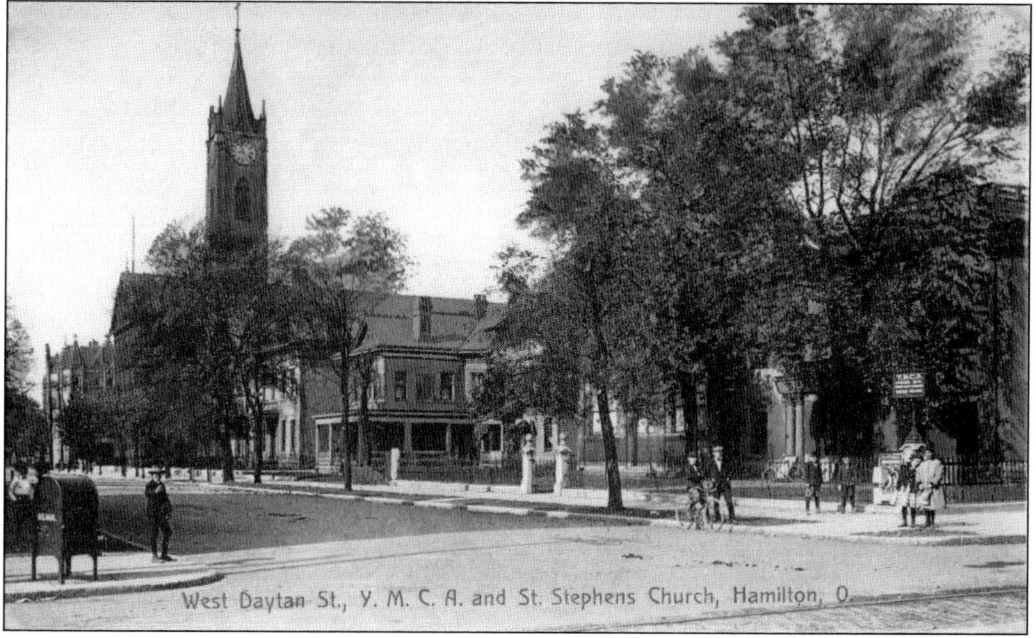

Dayton Street was split at Fifth Street by the Hamilton Hydraulic and at Fourth Street by the CH&D railroad. The residential section of Dayton Street to the west of these breaks is practically nonexistent today. Since the 1940s, expansions, including Mercy Hospital and Ohio Casualty Corporation, both now gone, eradicated dozens of stately homes. Recently, exciting redevelopment has come to the area with the RiversEdge Amphitheater and Marcum Park.

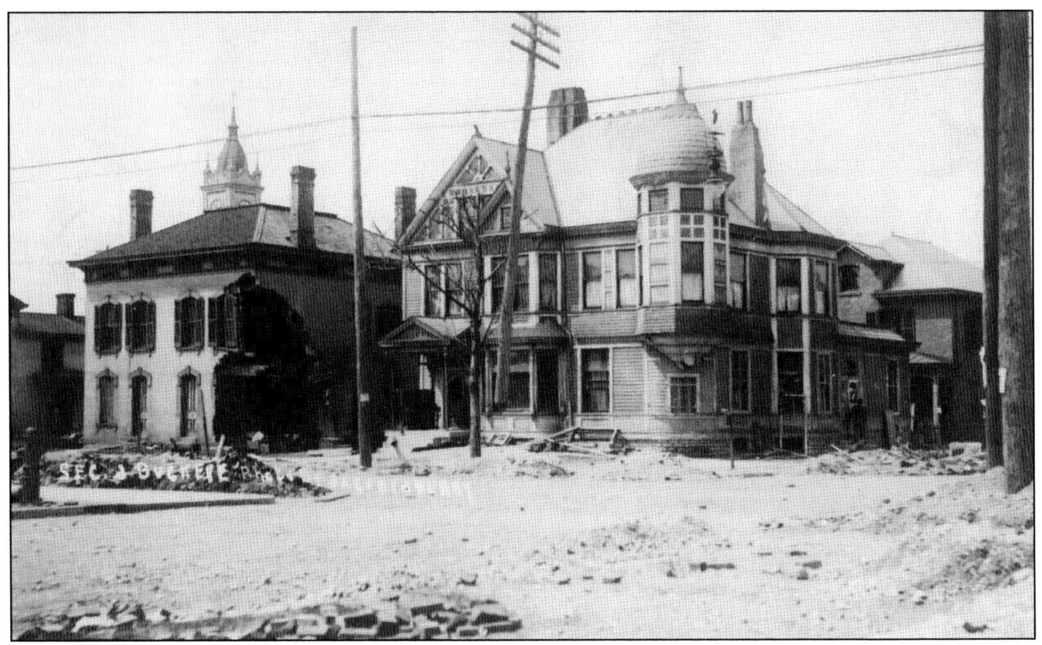

Dr. George C. Skinner, at his retirement in 1924, was the oldest practicing physician in Hamilton. A most beloved and respected citizen, he tended to the ill of the city for 44 years. In 1889, Dr. Skinner built his residence and office on the southwest corner of Third and Buckeye Streets. The home resisted the ravages of the 1913 flood fairly well, unlike its neighbor to the west.

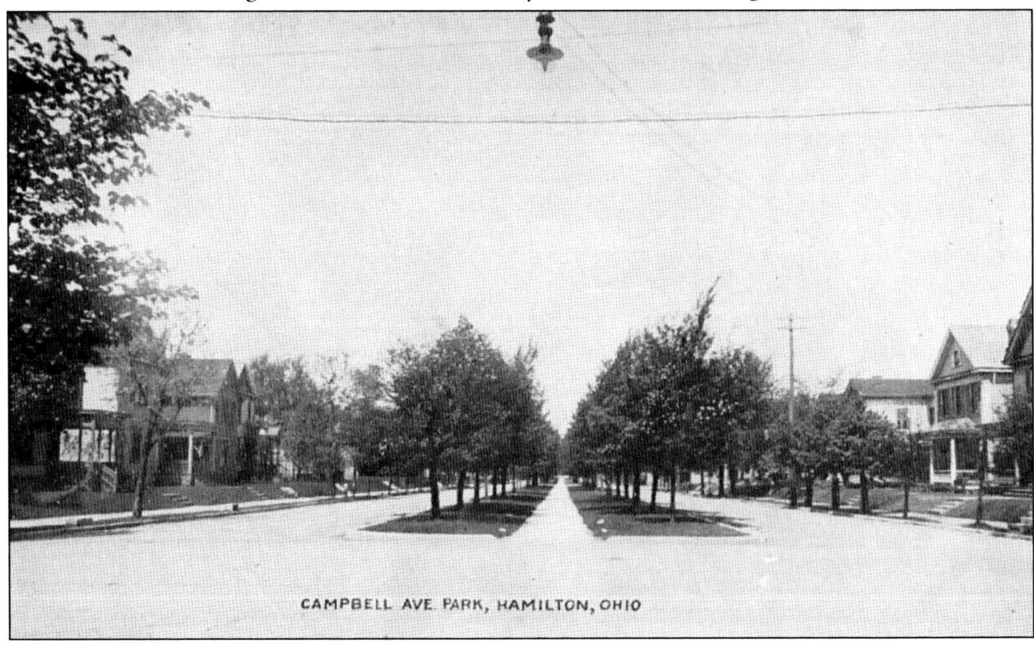

During the 1870s and 1880s, Hamilton spread east. The area from Fifth Street to Tenth Street and High Street to Buckeye Street became the area of choice for many of Hamilton's elite. Campbell Avenue, with its tree-lined center promenade and park, served as an address for many prominent city leaders and upper-middle-class families. The street and its architecture are part of the Dayton-Campbell Historic District.

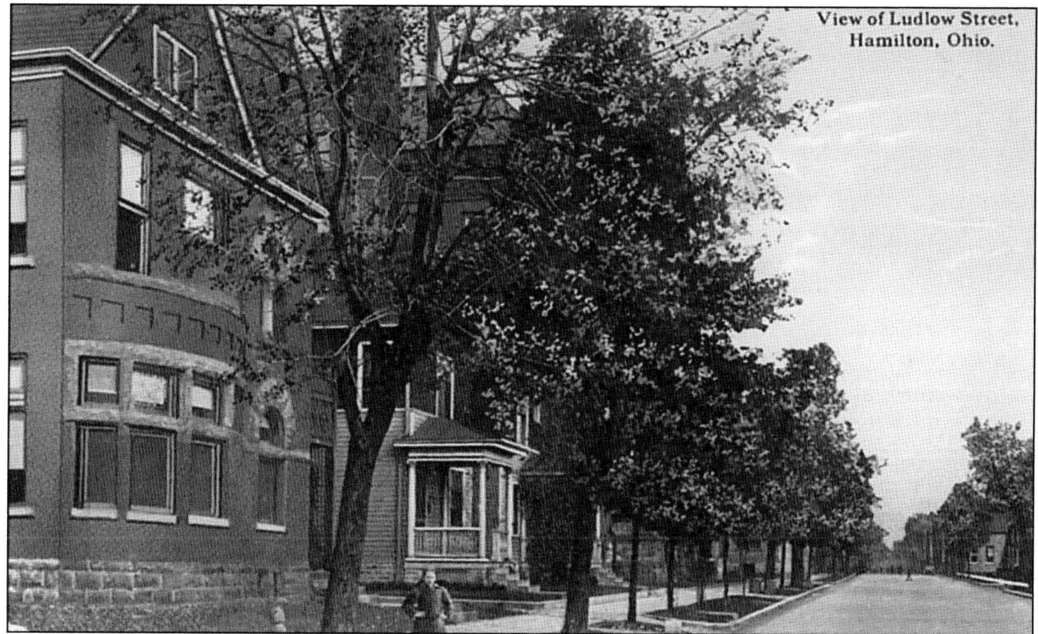

Once a living testimony of the American Dream and Hamilton's prosperous possibilities, Ludlow Street was the heart of the Fourth Ward. The tree-lined street boasted handsome brick and wood-siding homes, neighborhood watering holes, family-owned corner stores, and thriving local businesses. Unfortunately, the passing of time and the city's loss of industrial prominence have taken their toll on the area and the once-vibrant neighborhood is struggling.

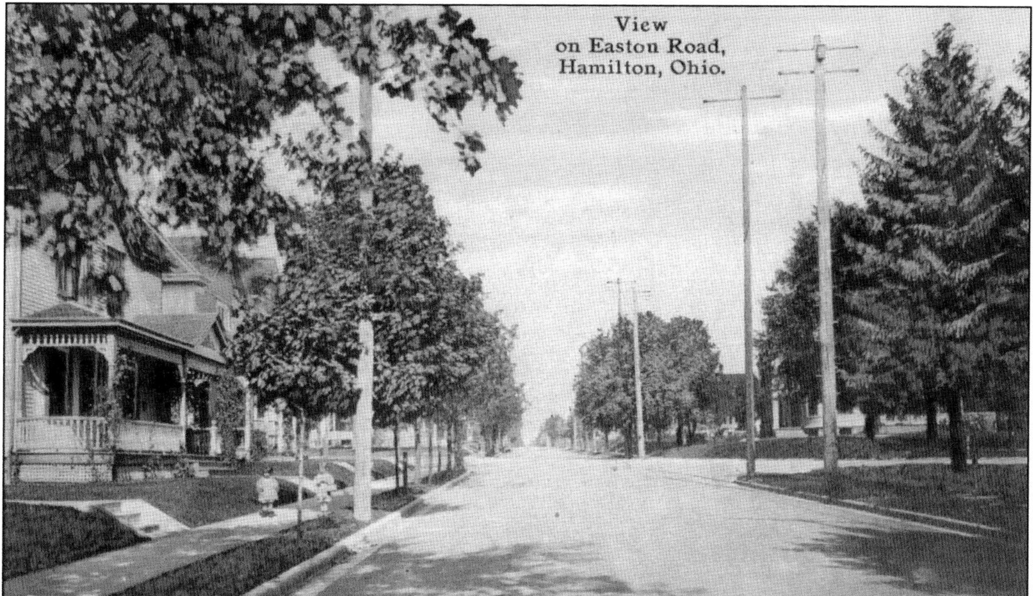

This view of Eaton Avenue looking north, complete with typographical error, was postmarked in August 1912. Seven months later, on a cold night in March, hundreds of Rossville residents trudged up this road, many in their nightclothes and weighted down with all the prized possessions they could carry. They were all searching for higher ground as the rising flood waters of the Great Miami filled the neighborhood below.

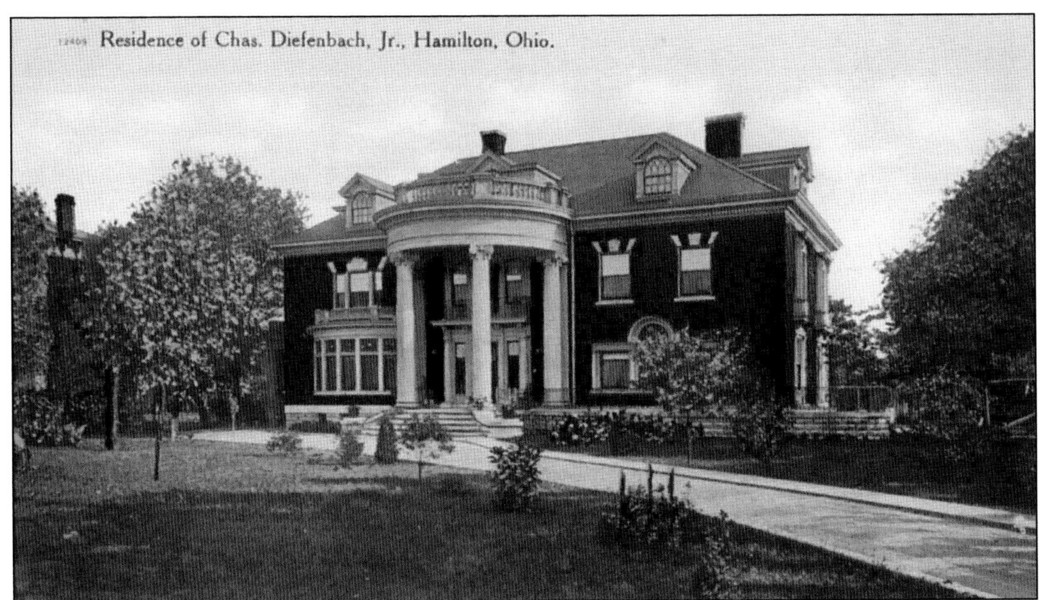

Known as Colonade by its residents, Charles and Maggie Diefenbach, this impressive residence at 515 Dayton Street was built in 1905. Charles owned and operated his jewelry, watch, clock and silver goods store at 124 High Street for over 46 years. His routine from 5:00 to 7:00 a.m. every morning involved winding close to 200 clocks on display at the store. Sojourner House now occupies the building.

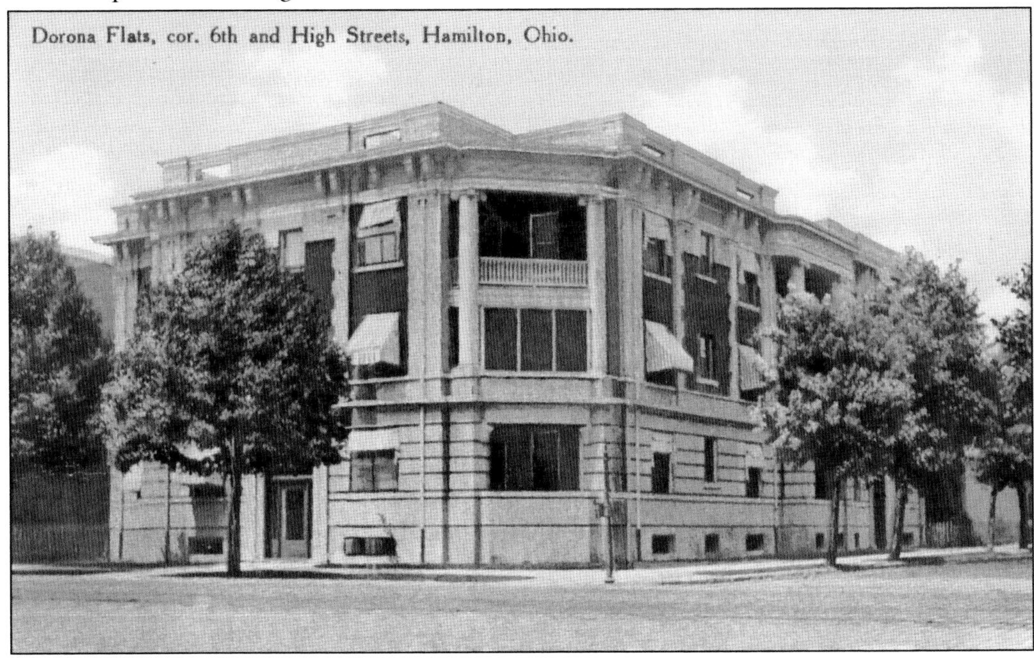

New York salesman Joseph W. Doron married Ellen Shuler, daughter of Asa Shuler of Shuler and Benninghofen Woolen Mills fame, in 1889. They settled in Hamilton and built a house on North C Street atop Prospect Hill. In 1906, at a cost of $30,000, Doron developed the three-story Dorona Flats on the northwest corner of Sixth and High Streets. Today, the building serves as the Haven House emergency shelter.

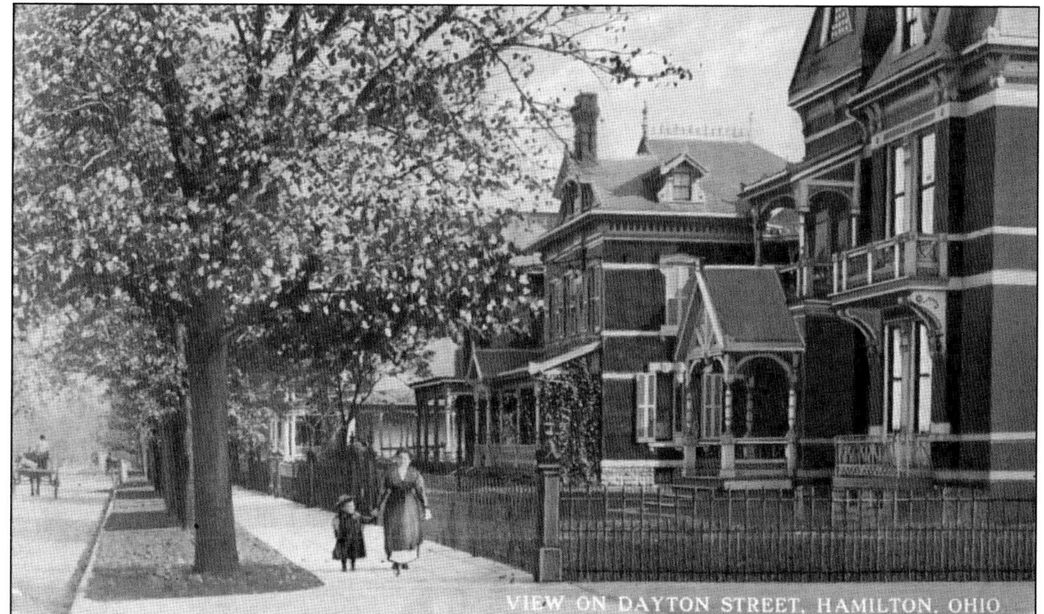

Listed in the National Register of Historic Places in 1985, the Dayton Lane area is part of the Dayton-Campbell Historic District. The area is a prime example of the opulence that came along with Hamilton's industrial boom in the late 19th century. Many of Hamilton's biggest industrialists settled in the area. Today, the Historic Dayton Lane Area Inc. conducts several educational and entertaining events focused on the neighborhood's history.

Travelling west on Main Street, past Eaton and Millville Avenues and through Highland Park to the north, various architectural styles abound. These neighborhoods are a symbol of the city's diverse citizenship that originally lived in these fine homes, the skilled local craftsmen who constructed them, and the proud current owners who keep them in such fine condition. This image from 1909 could have been taken yesterday.

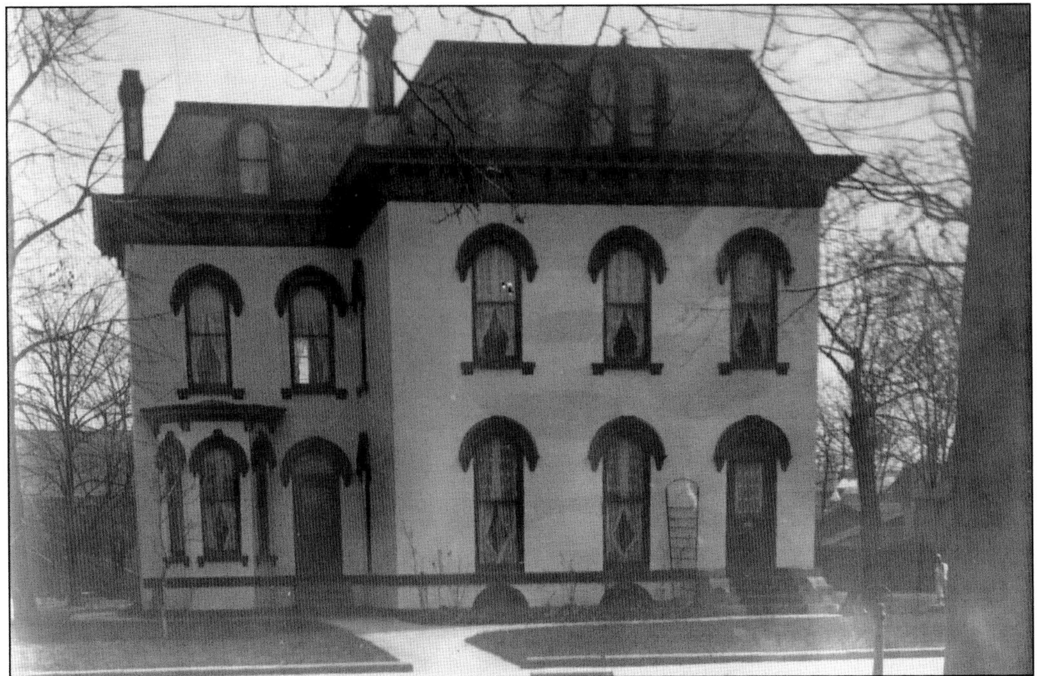

Shown here is the residence of the honorable James E. Neal and his wife, May. Neal was a prominent Hamilton attorney, the first president of the Butler County Bar Association, and an Ohio legislator. Located at 442 South Second Street, the home no longer stands, and the property is now the site of the former Butler County Resolutions Jail. (Courtesy of BCHS.)

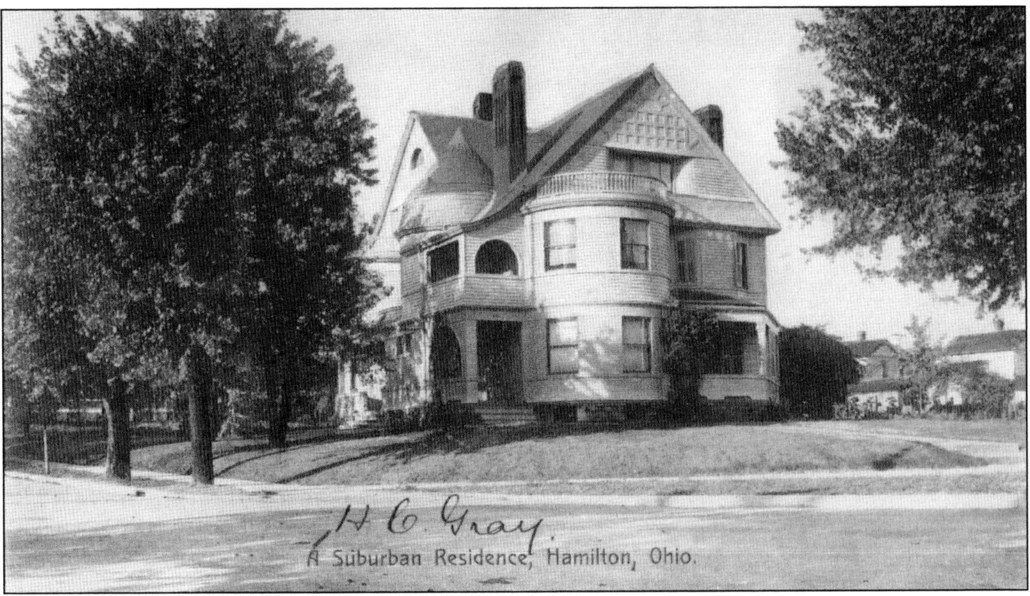

Built sometime in the 1890s, the home of Henry C. Gray stands on the corner of Park and Eaton Avenues. Gray began his professional career at his family's mercantile store in Reily. He later became an important political figure in the county, serving as both the recorder and auditor. When James Cox became governor, Gray was selected as state oil inspector and later as agent for veterans' payroll.

Nine

Parks and Recreation

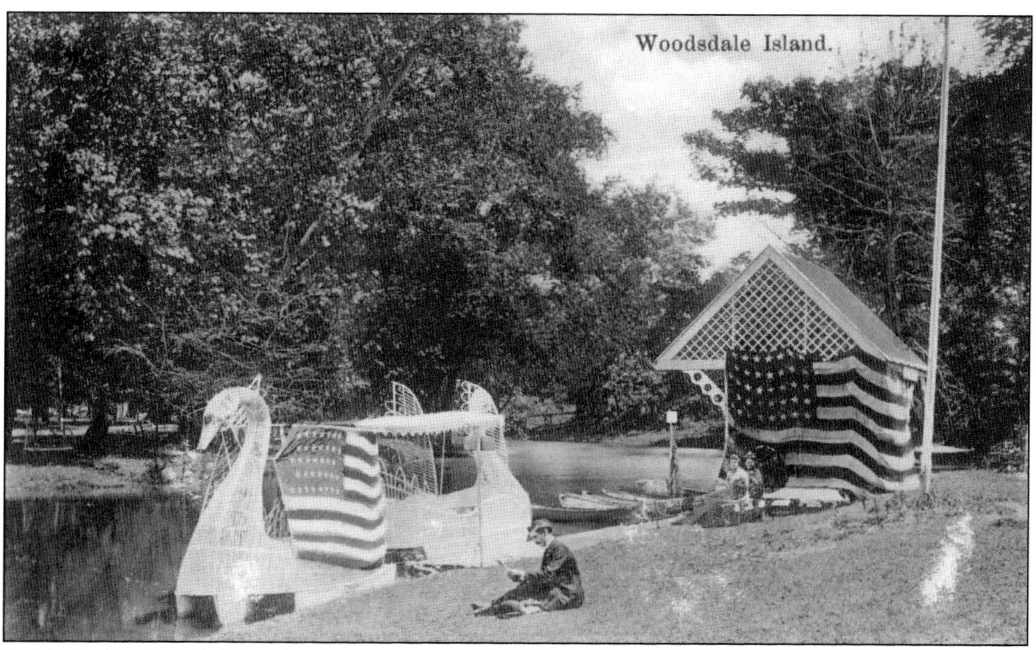

In 1891, the Woodsdale Island Amusement Park, northeast of town on the Great Miami River, was the self-proclaimed "playground of Southwest Ohio." Designed for day excursions by Cincinnatians and locals, the park included all the necessary amenities to serve over 5,000 people. Located on the CH&D rail line and adjacent to the Miami and Erie Canal, the park totaled 34 acres. At its peak, it included a dance hall, restaurant, amusement rides, lemonade and ice-cream pavilions, bathhouse facilities, baseball fields, tennis courts, a bowling alley, and numerous midway-type games and shooting galleries. One of the special attractions of the park were the swan boats as shown here. Powered by a naphtha engine, the larger boats could seat up to 20. The 1898 flood began the decline of the park, though it managed to survive; however, the 1913 flood wiped any last remnants of the park away, and it was never rebuilt.

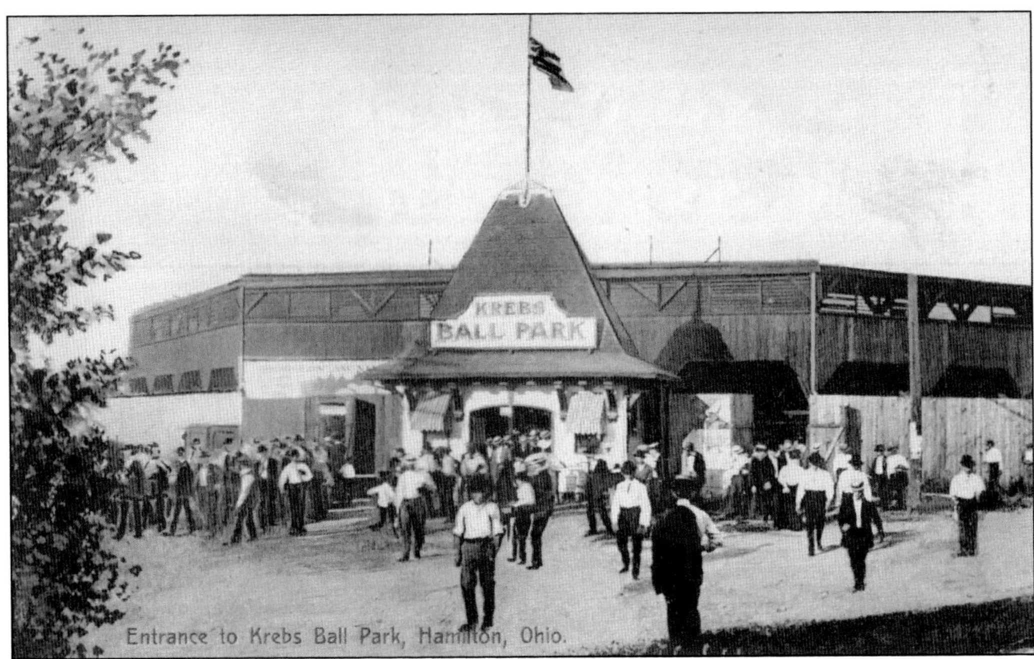

In the early 1900s, amateur and semiprofessional baseball reigned supreme, as local businesses and even neighborhoods fielded their own teams. Since the late 1800s, baseball in Hamilton was played at Lindenwald Park, but by 1908, the city's love for the game had grown too large for the aging four-acre field. Hamilton business owner George Krebs proposed a new facility to house his beloved team, the Hamilton Krebs. Managed by local sports enthusiast and entrepreneur Jacob Milders, the team moved into Krebs Park in the summer of 1908. Located at High Street and Lockwood Avenue east of the Miami and Erie Canal, and built at a cost of just over $10,000, the new park boasted general seating for up to 1,500 spectators, 30 luxury boxes, and reserved seating for 800. The field was razed in the early 1920s.

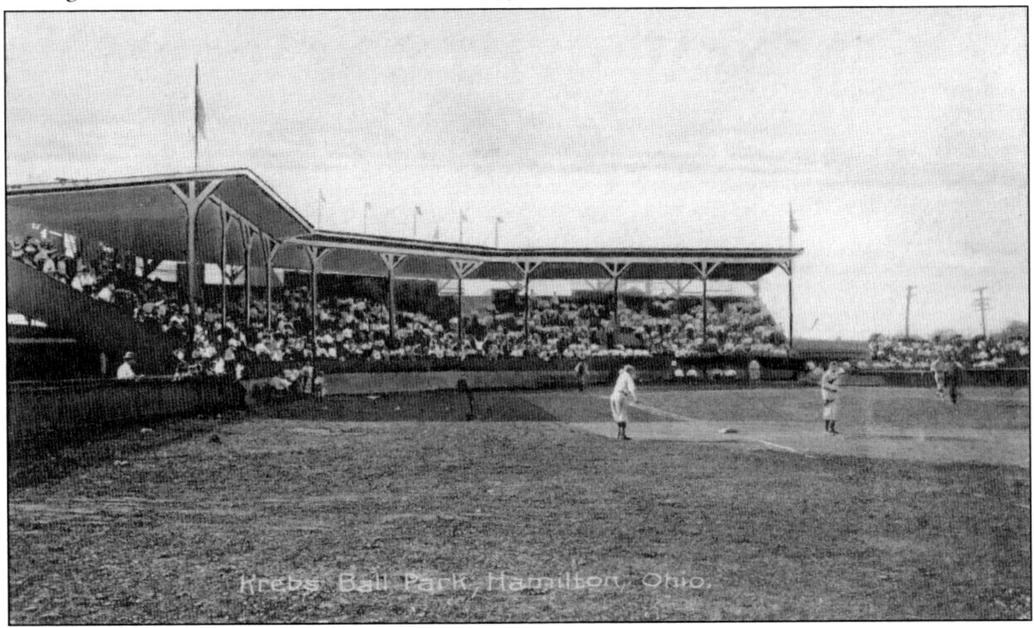

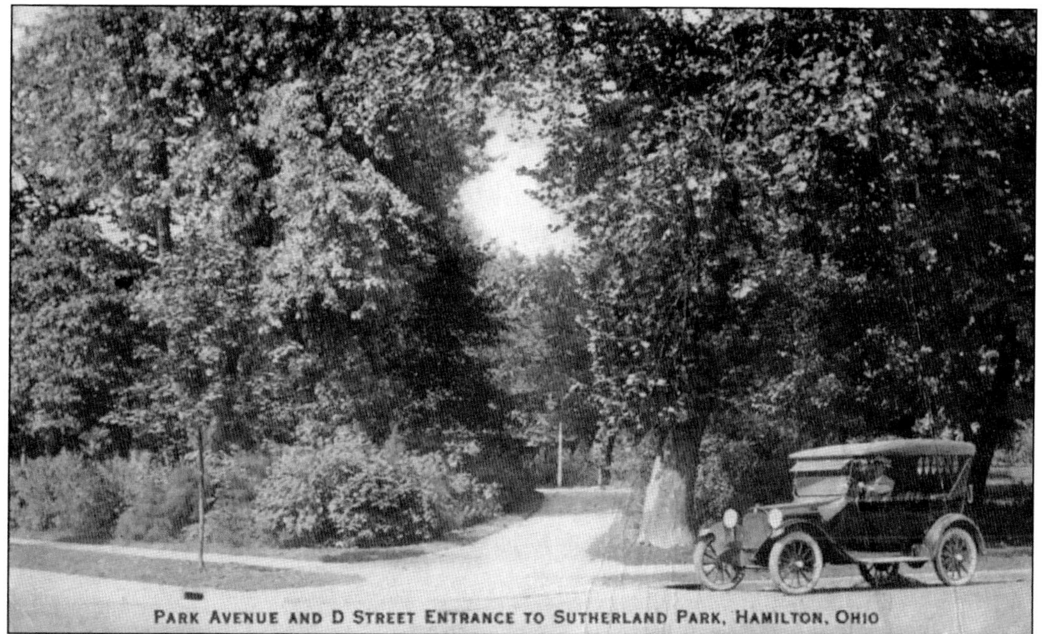
PARK AVENUE AND D STREET ENTRANCE TO SUTHERLAND PARK, HAMILTON, OHIO

Sutherland Park, also known as First Ward Park, began accepting bodies in 1804 when it was known as the Rossville Burying Grounds. By 1865, it was declared illegal to bury bodies there, as previous internments had been relocated to the new Greenwood Cemetery beginning in 1848. Named after John Sutherland, a soldier in Gen. Anthony Wayne's army and an early Rossville settler, the park was dedicated in 1890.

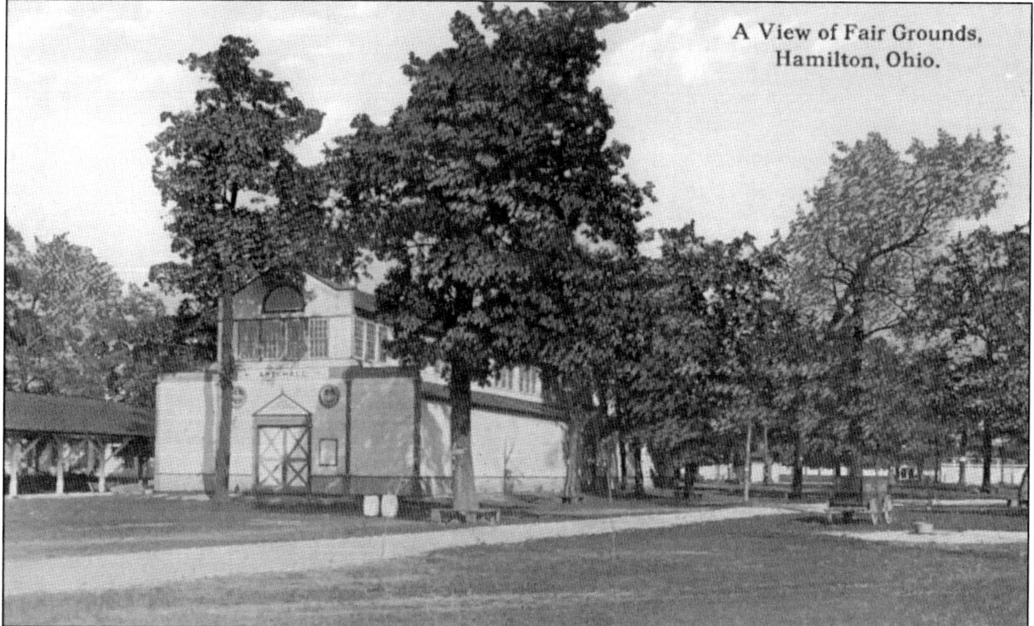
A View of Fair Grounds, Hamilton, Ohio.

Opening at its present location in 1856, The Butler County Fairgrounds has provided Hamiltonians and county residents nearly 160 years of entertainment and agricultural experiences. This 1907 view shows the new art hall, which was constructed in 1904. The hall housed displays for goods and services of local merchants as well as the craft, floral, and art creations of individual residents.

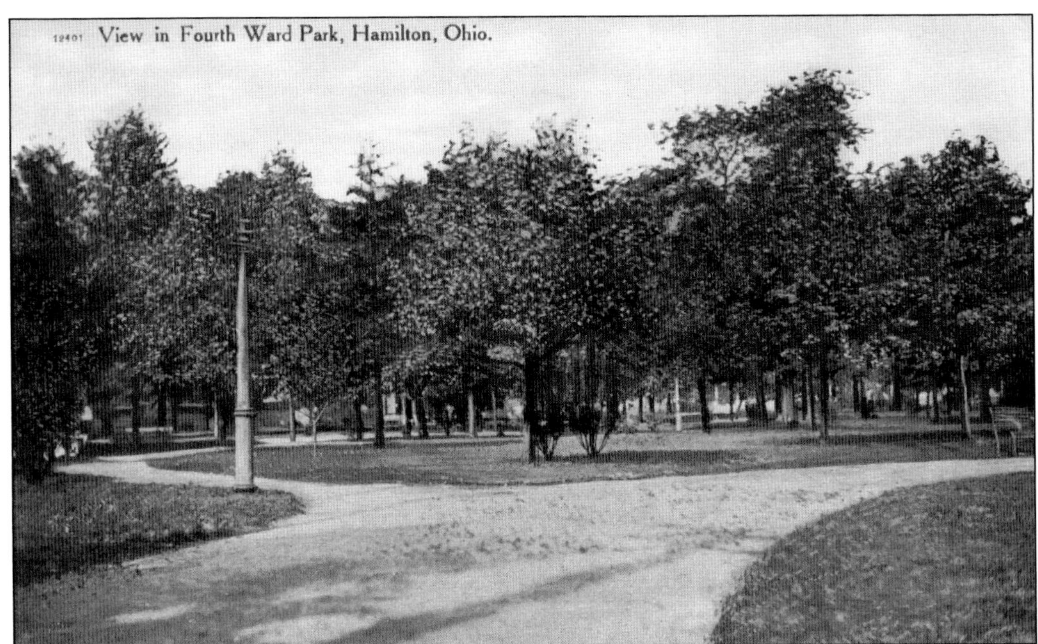

Named Ludlow Park in 1890, the land bounded by Third and Fourth Streets to the east and west and Sycamore and Williams Streets to the north and south offered residents shaded walks and quiet repast just across the street from their fine homes. Formerly a pioneer cemetery, many of the remains buried on the site were relocated to Greenwood Cemetery after it opened in 1848.

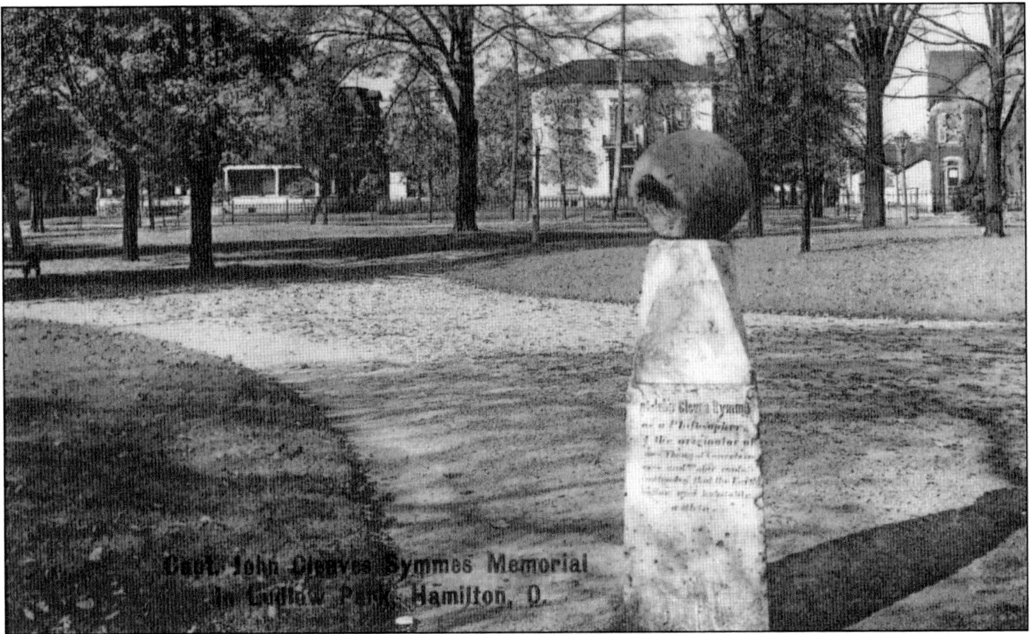

Erected by his son Americus in the 1840s, this monument to Capt. John Cleves Symmes still stands in Ludlow (now Symmes) Park. Symmes was a proponent of the Hollow Earth Theory, stating in 1818, "I declare the earth is hollow and habitable within." Symmes became a Hamilton resident and lectured fervently on his theory during the 1820s. He died in 1829, and the monument is said to mark his grave.

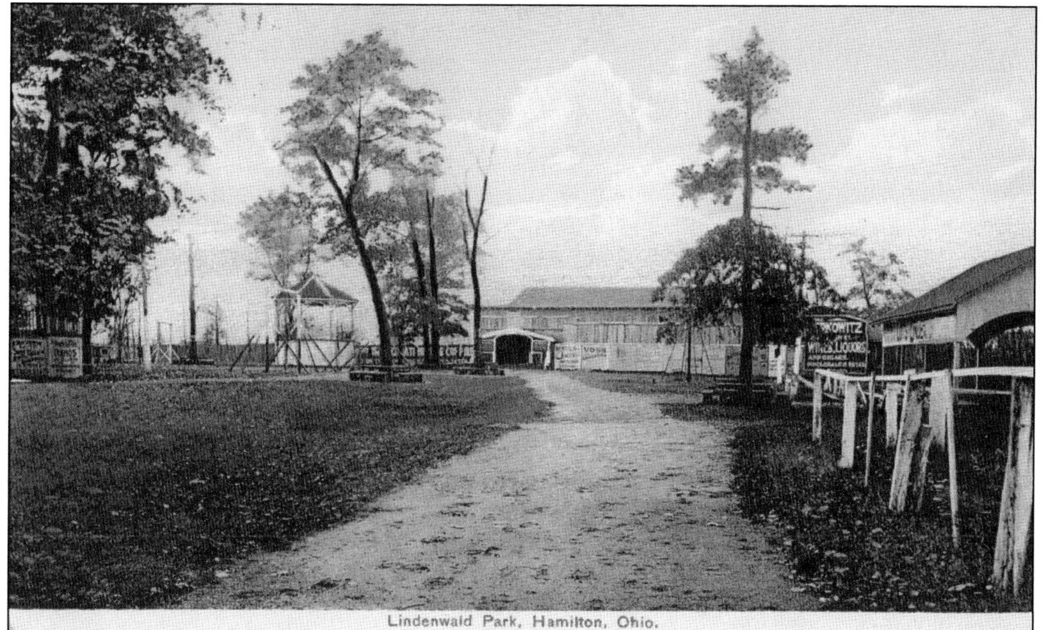

When this card was sent in 1907, Lindenwald was not yet part of Hamilton, but Hamiltonians had spent many a day and night at Lindenwald Park. Hamilton's first and only amusement park, the site opened in 1892 and eventually included athletic fields, picnic grounds, a 2,000-seat open-air theater, covered shelters, concessions, and gazebos. The park was located on the southeast corner of Benninghofen and Laurel Avenues.

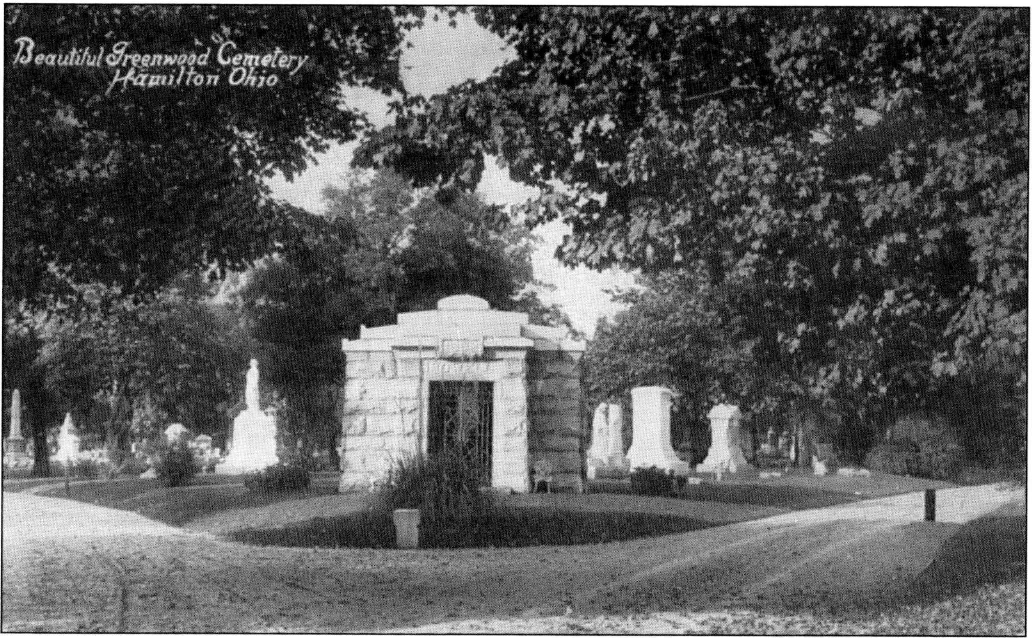

Greenwood Cemetery trustees hired a Professor McFarland of Miami University in Oxford and a Mr. Earnshaw of Cincinnati to plot out the land for the cemetery, which opened in the fall of 1848. The two men were given advice and consultation by famed landscape architect Adolph Strauch, designer of Spring Grove Cemetery, Eden Park, and Burnett Woods in Cincinnati.

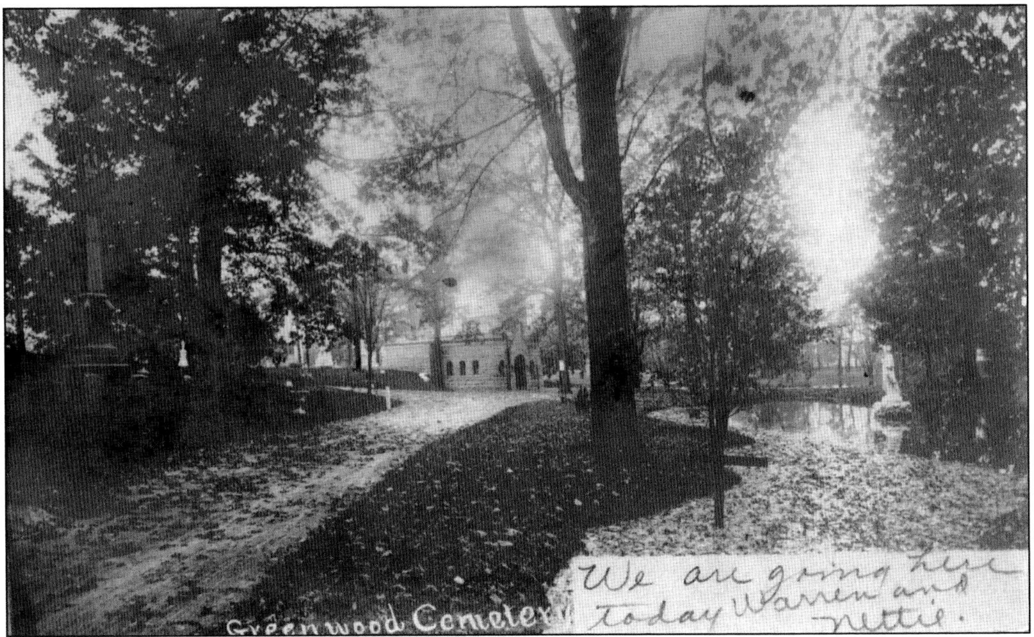

This view of Greenwood Cemetery from 1906, looking west, shows features that are still present on the grounds as well as others that are not. The public receiving vault (center), built to house bodies over the long winter months, was constructed in 1892 and is still the architectural jewel of the cemetery. However, the pond features and statues (right) have been removed.

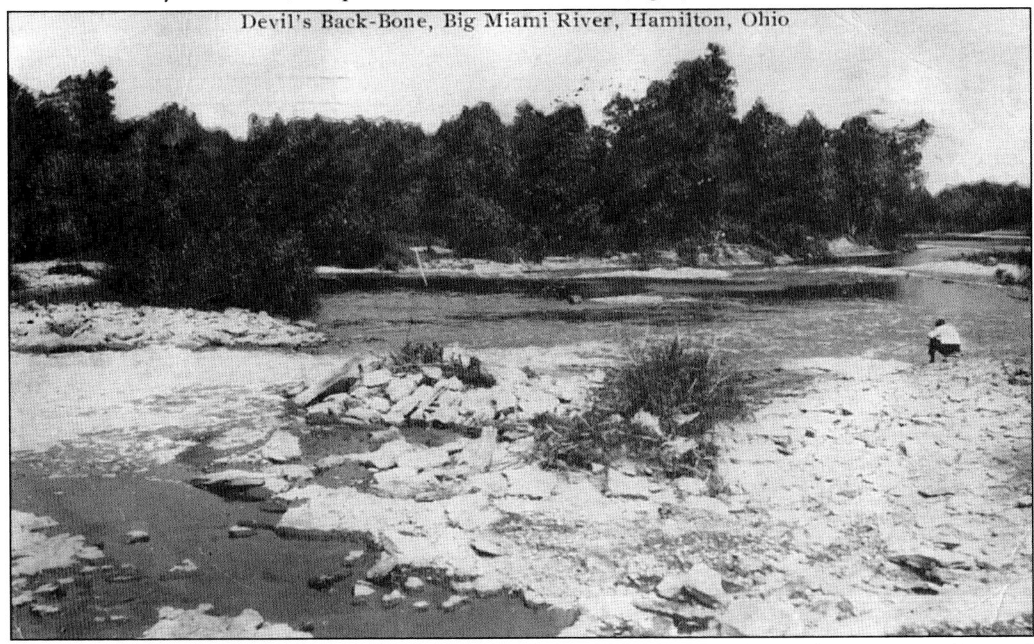

Believed to be part of an old mound-builder fortification, Devil's Back Bone was located north of the city above the old river bridge near Campbell's Island and the end of North Third Street. Noted as one of the best fishing spots on the river, the site was almost the location of a new city garbage plant in 1926, but the site was moved to Riley's Island below the Columbia Bridge instead.

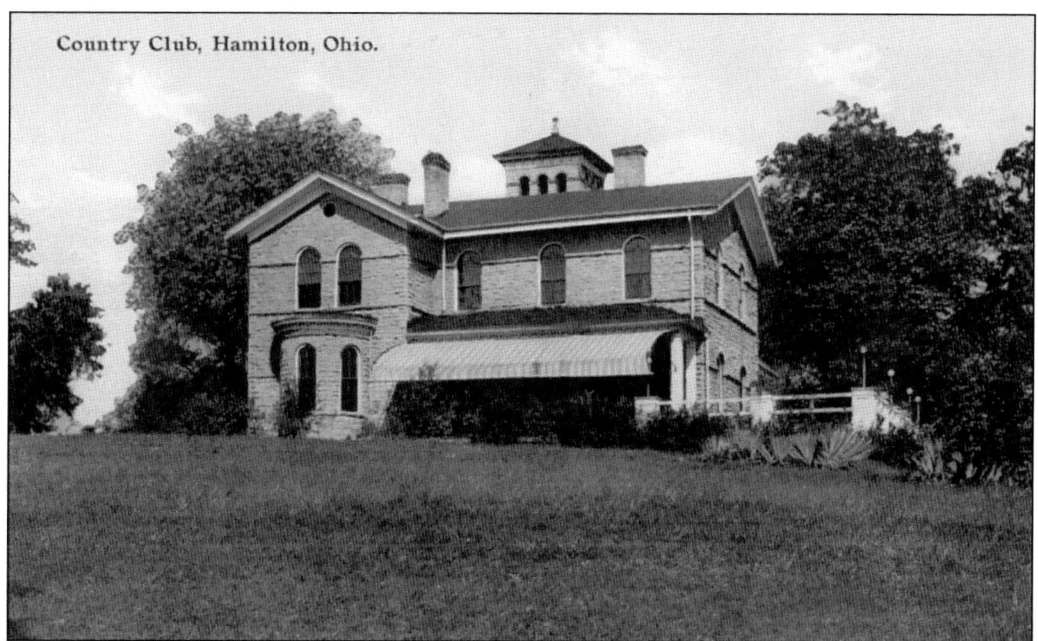

Hamilton's first country club, constructed in the late 1800s, was the site for countless society gatherings among Hamilton's turn of the century elite. Located high atop the hills of the west side and overlooking the city, the club was used as a shelter for Rossville flood victims in 1913. The entrance to the club was located on the west side of D Street south of Millikin Avenue, while the building was situated near the current Oakwood Drive area.

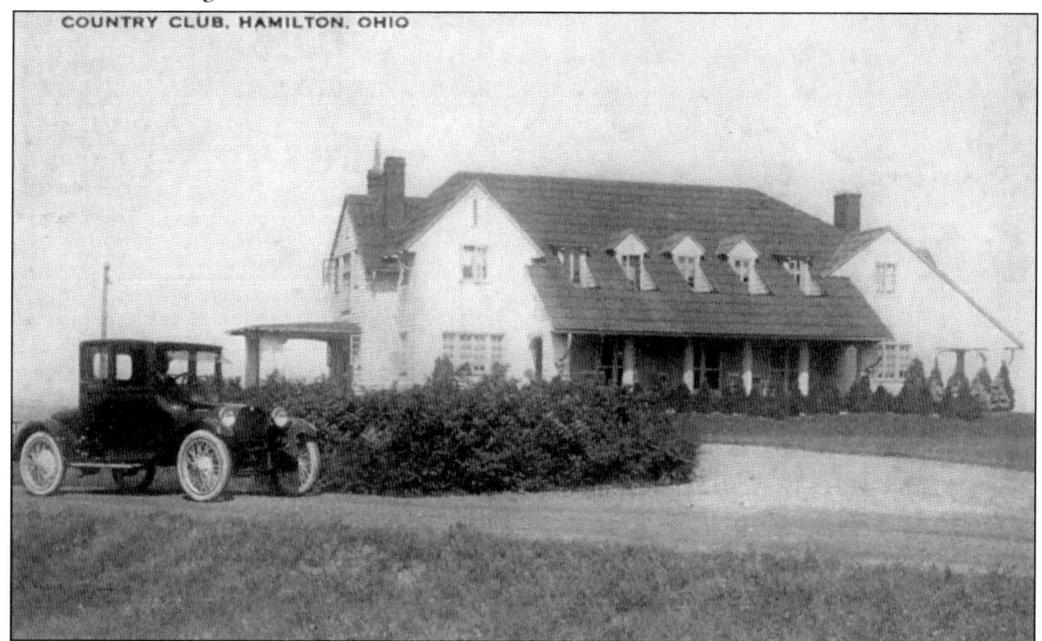

Opening on July 4, 1915, the Butler County Country Club was located on Middletown Pike, where the current Elks Golf Course is now located. Private members from Hamilton and Middletown utilized the club for a multitude of social gatherings, dances, and wedding receptions. The Elks lodge purchased the property in 1932.

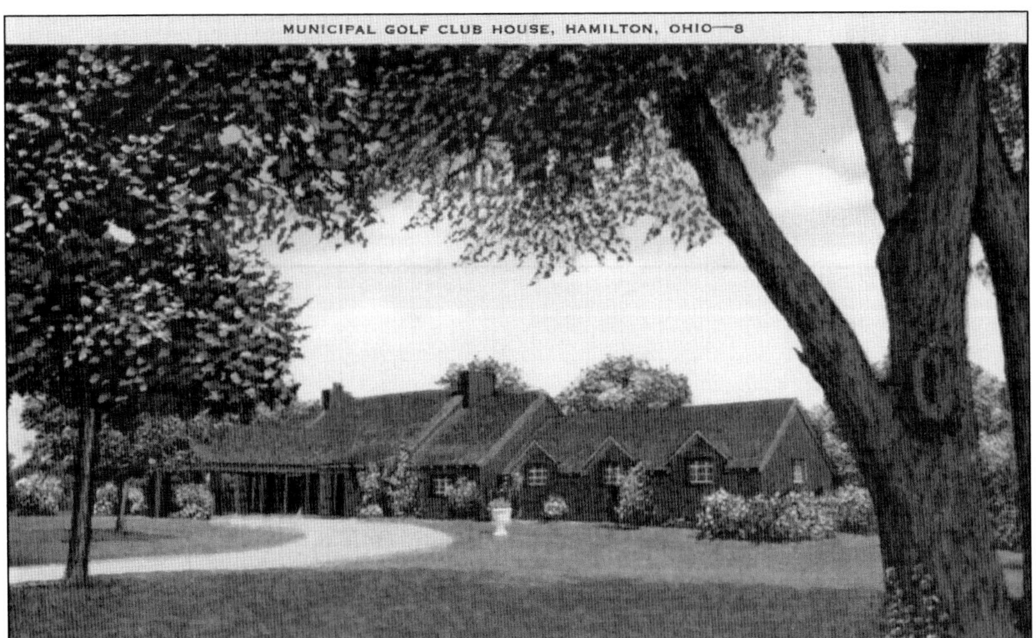

Named after Hamilton native, businessman, and philanthropist Ellis M. Potter, Potter Park Golf Course was created on land owned by Potter's grandfather. Previous gift offers of land from Ellis to the city had been refused for lack of city funding to maintain the projects. Potter offered the land again for the creation of a municipal course, if the city could promise development. Enough private monies were raised, and in 1927 the course opened to the public.

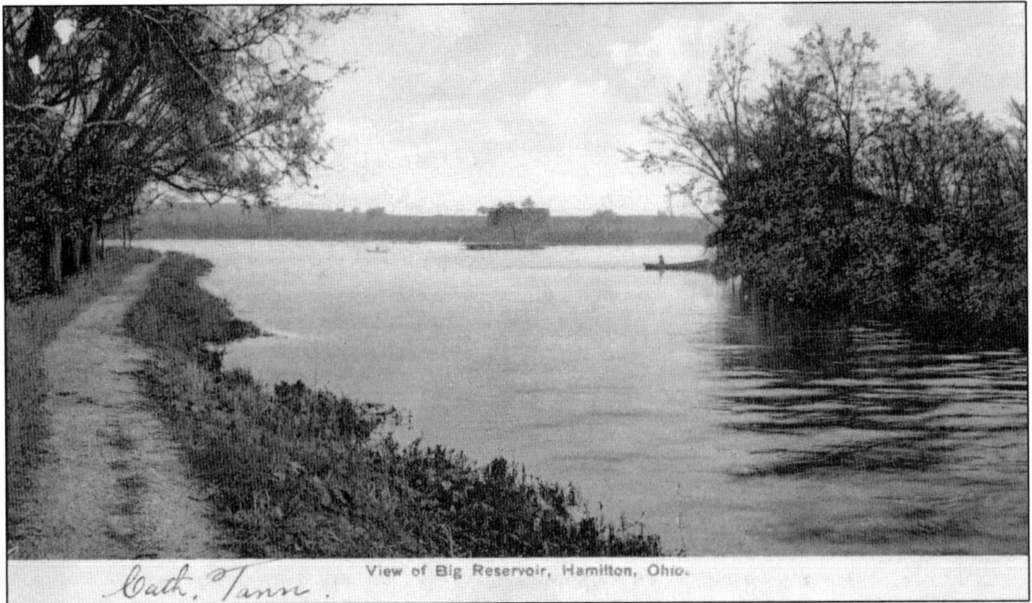

The birth of the Hamilton Hydraulic in 1845, whose purpose was to harness water power to run business and industry, created two reservoirs outside of the city. The larger, shown here, was located just to the northeast of Greenwood Cemetery. A smaller reservoir was located north of the city at the end of North Fifth, Sixth, and Seventh Streets. The hydraulic canal and reservoir system provided ample leisure, boating, and fishing opportunities.

Ten

PEOPLE AND EVENTS

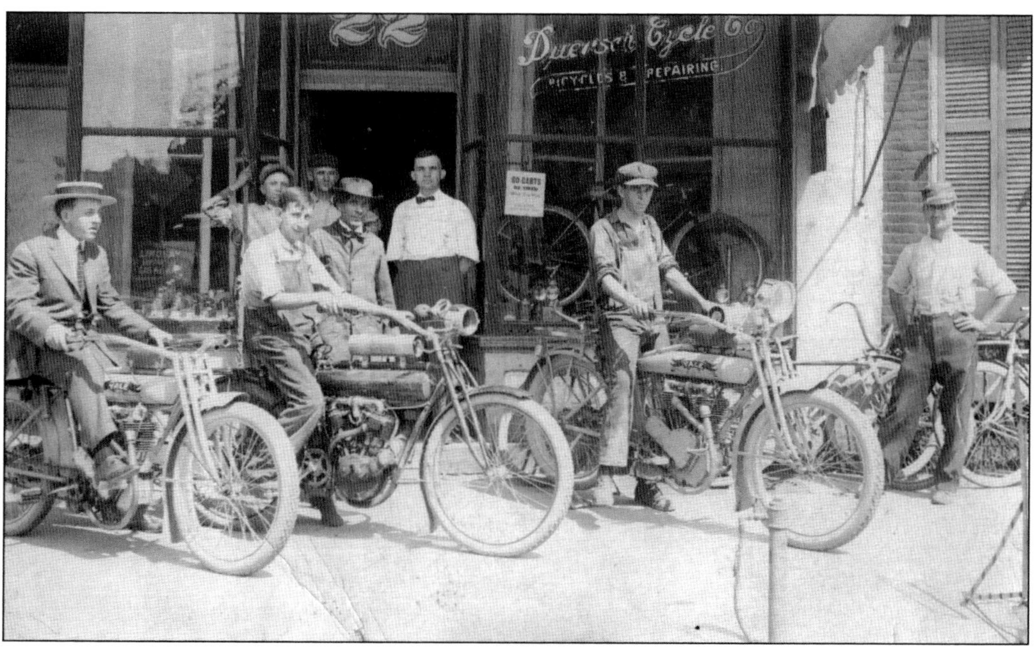

George Duersch (back center) was the proprietor of the Duersch Cycle Company at 22 North Third Street. Aside from selling manual pedal bicycles, electric lamps, and motors and performing miscellaneous electrical wiring work, Duersch also sold motorized bicycles. This real photograph taken sometime around 1913 to 1914 shows two of the hottest motorcycles of the day. The two machines on the ends appear to be 1913 Yale twin-cylinder models. The cycle in the middle looks to be a 1913 Flying Merkel Model 70, manufactured just to the north by the Miami Cycle Company of Middletown, Ohio. Both models had a top speed of approximately 60 miles per hour and retailed for about $260 at the time. The man wearing the wide-brimmed hat and dark buttoned-up coat (front center), according to the card, is the Reverend G.W. Phillips of the First Baptist Church, well-known for his fiery sermons against loose morals. Was he there warning these men of the dangers of fast living, or was he a secret fan of the Merkel?

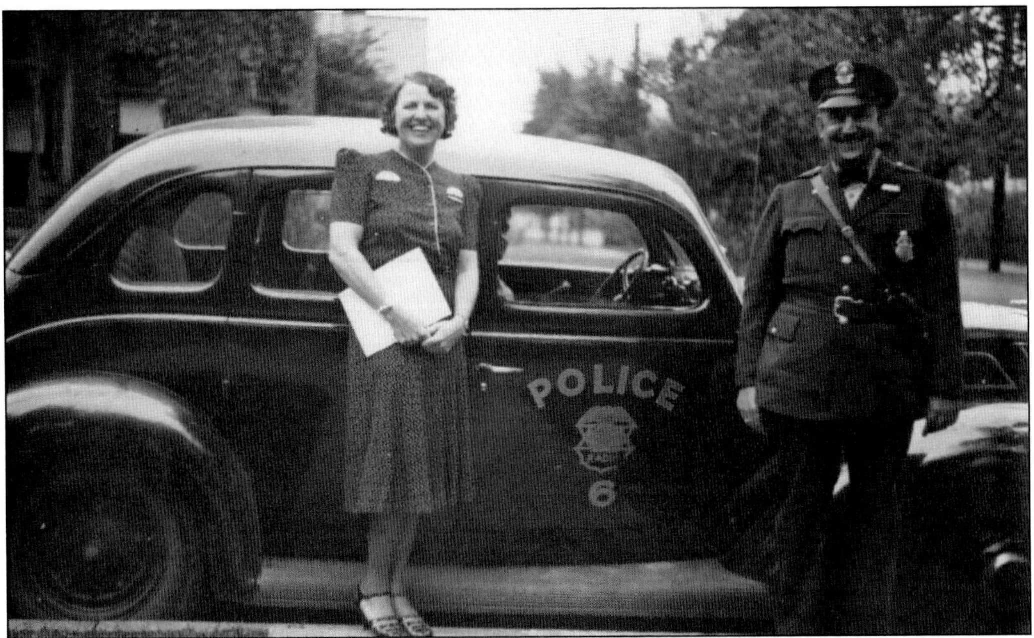

This real-photo postcard was taken in front of the Rentschler home on Seventh and Dayton Streets sometime around the late 1930s. Christine Meyer is shown posing with one of Hamilton's finest of the day, officer Henry "Heinie" Hart. The patrol car in the background appears to be a 1937 Ford and boasts radio dispatch. Two-way-radio police communications were first used in Boston in 1934 and in Hamilton a year later.

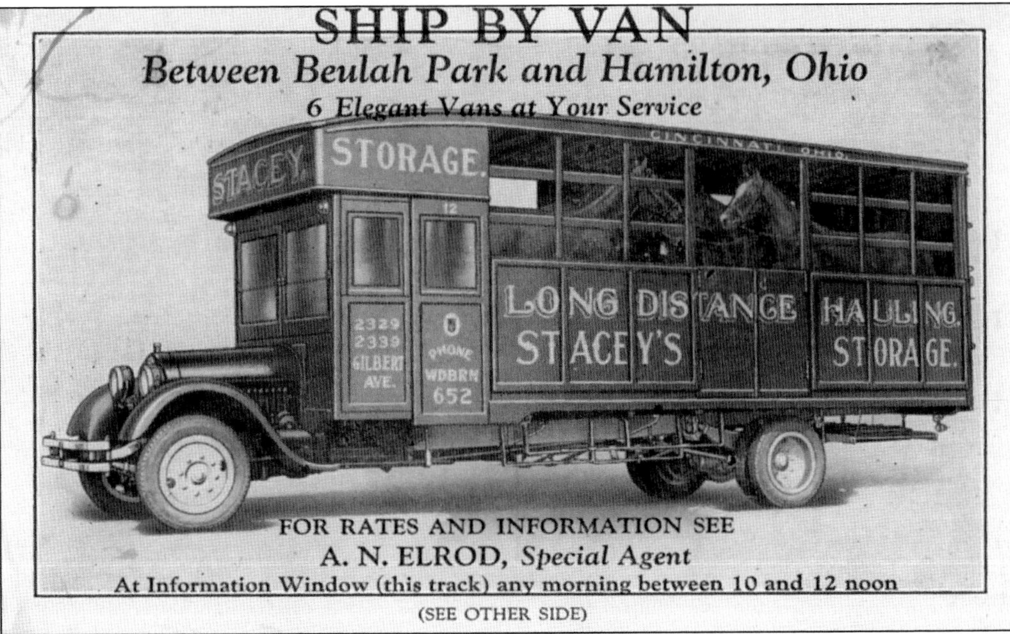

This 1920s card for the William Stacy Storage Co., located on Gilbert Avenue in Cincinnati, advertises hauling services for racehorses between the Butler County Fairgrounds track in Hamilton to Beulah Park in Grove City, Ohio. Beulah Park was the first thoroughbred track in Ohio, opening in 1923.

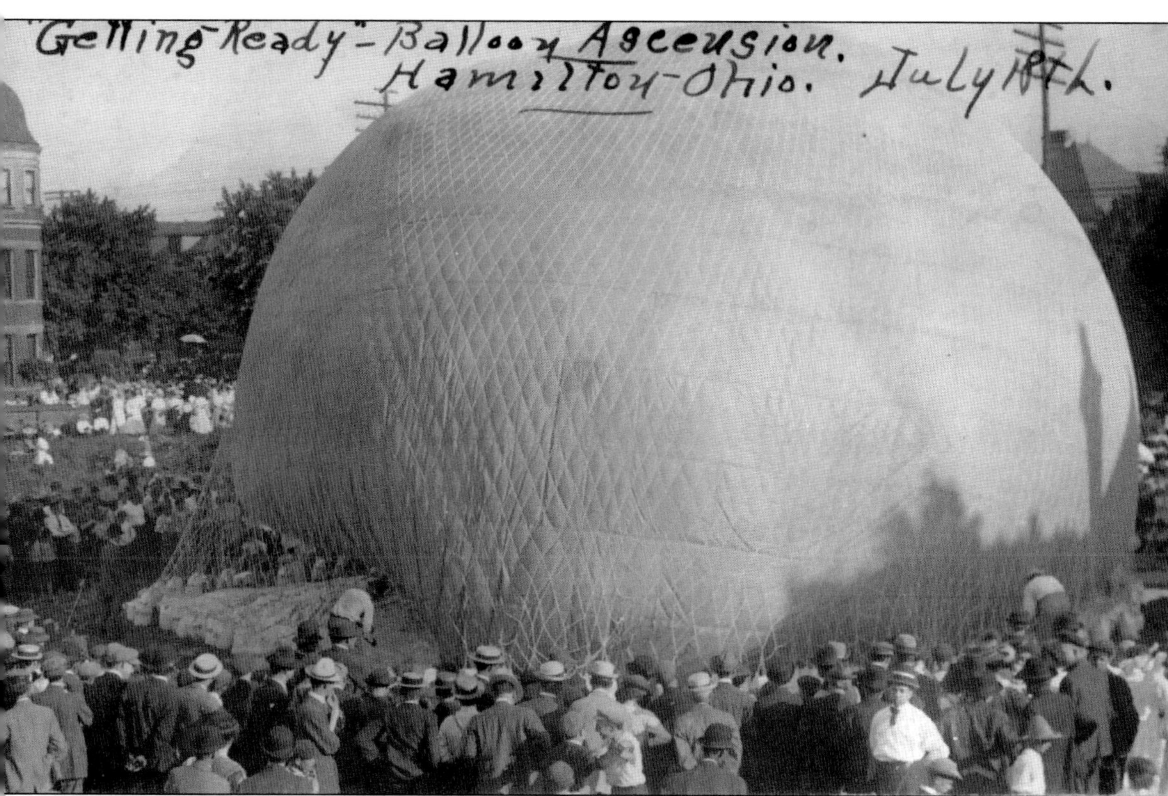

On July 18, 1910, Hamilton nearly made aviation history. Pilots George Howard and Walter Collins of the Holz Balloon Company of Cincinnati selected Hamilton as the starting point in their attempt to break the world balloon endurance record in their balloon *Drifter.* The liftoff point was a vacant lot on the south side of High Street at Sixth Street east of the gas works. A weekend launch was thwarted by high winds, but on Monday the 18th, conditions were ideal. An estimated 10,000 to 15,000 spectators turned out for the launch. At 7:39 p.m., the giant balloon drifted away, but at 6:15 a.m. the following morning, the craft crashed into a cornfield in Mt. Pleasant, Illinois. Both pilots were safe, but the flight of 280 miles was far short of the record. Howard and Collins surmised there must have been a small rupture in the bag. Witnesses reported that a young boy had thrown a rock at the craft as it left the ground; however, this was never proven, and Hamilton's bid for balloon history drifted away.

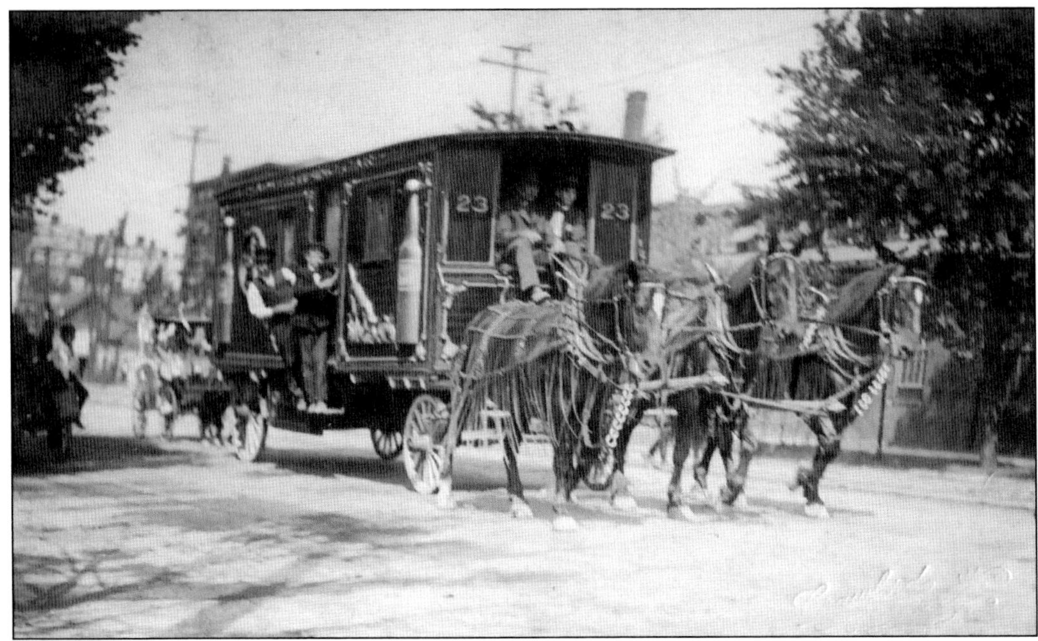

When Peter Schwab took over sole ownership and renamed his brewery the Cincinnati Brewing Company in 1875, the facility was producing 50 barrels of ale a day. By 1890, the number of barrels produced per day had jumped to 400. One key to the brewery's success involved its promotional methods. Advertising cars were used to take the product to the public. Not only were the wagons rolling billboards, they also had the ability to dispense Schwab's beer at public and private events. The above view shows one such event, the 1909 Labor Day parade. Below, a group of employees in 1905, including Peter Schwab Jr. (second from left), who would become brewery president after his father's death in 1913, is seen resting in front of a car. (Below, courtesy of BCHS.)

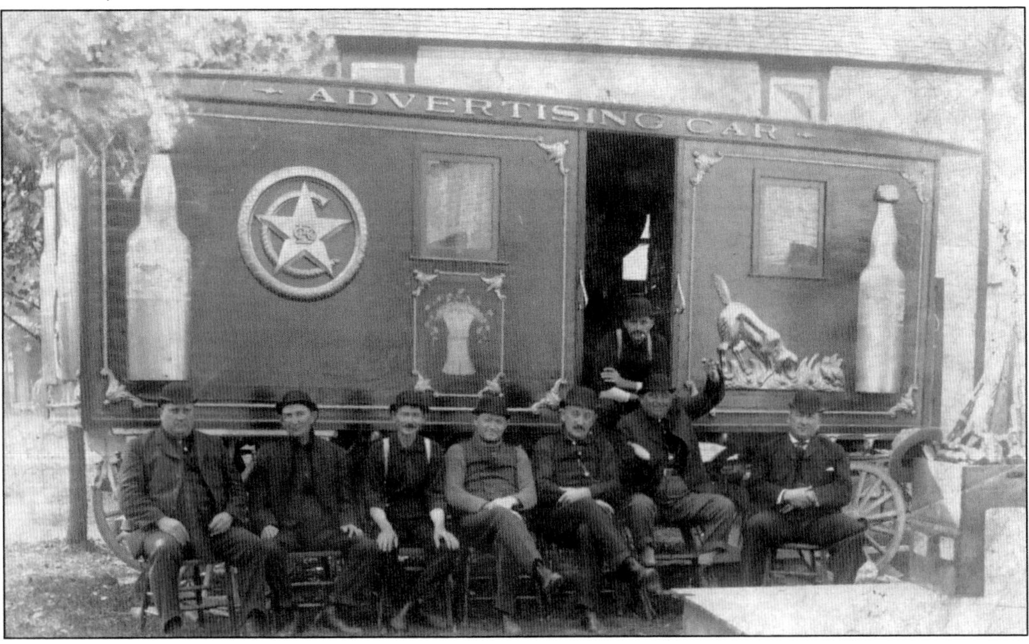

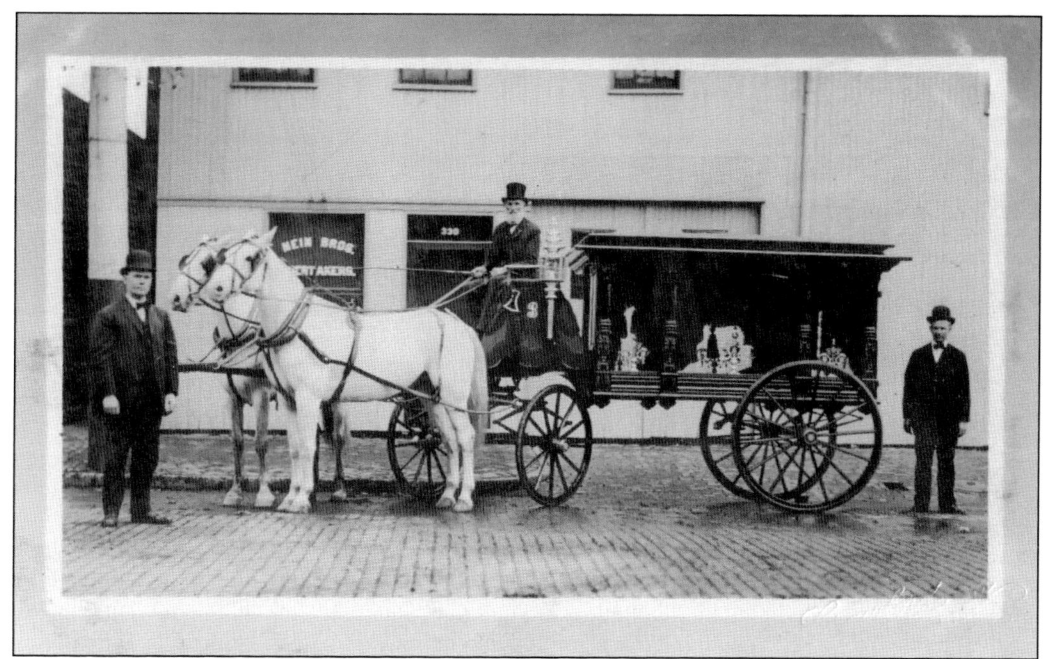

This real-photo postcard from 1905, taken in front of the Nein Brothers Undertakers and Embalmers business at 332 Court Street, shows Frank (far left) and William Nein (far right) posing with their finely crafted hearse. Frank Curry is driving the team. (Courtesy of BCHS.)

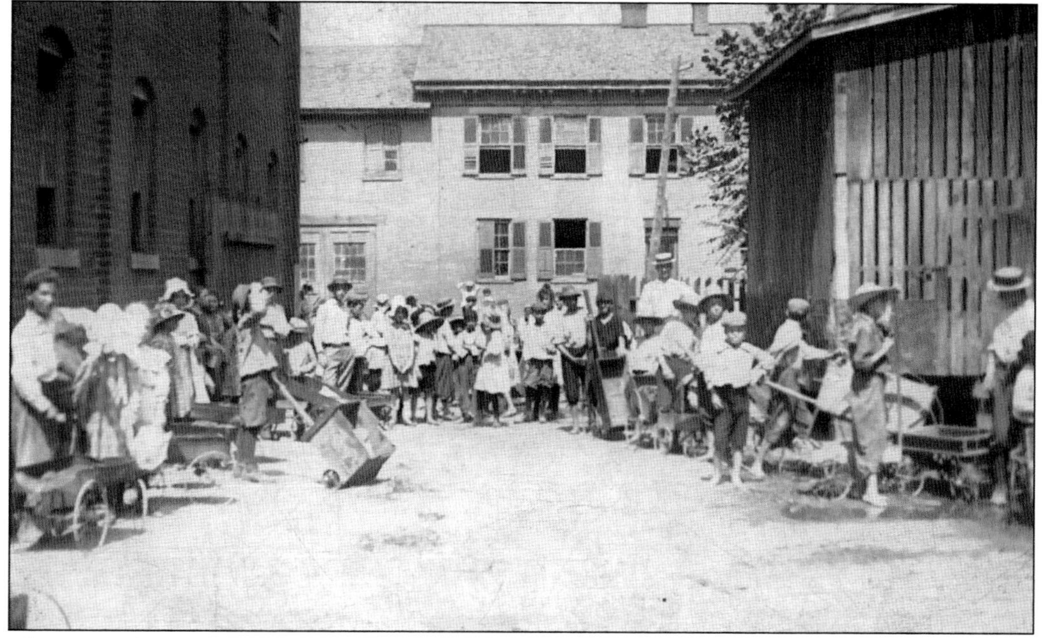

This view shows children lining up for ice at the Cincinnati Brewing Company around 1910. On the west side of South Front Street near the CH&D railroad line, the brewery, owned and operated by Peter Schwab (pronounced Swope), became a regional brewing force during the late 1800s. In June 1913, the brewery played a large role in the ice famine that struck the city, as its ice machines were out of commission during replacement. (Courtesy of BCHS.)

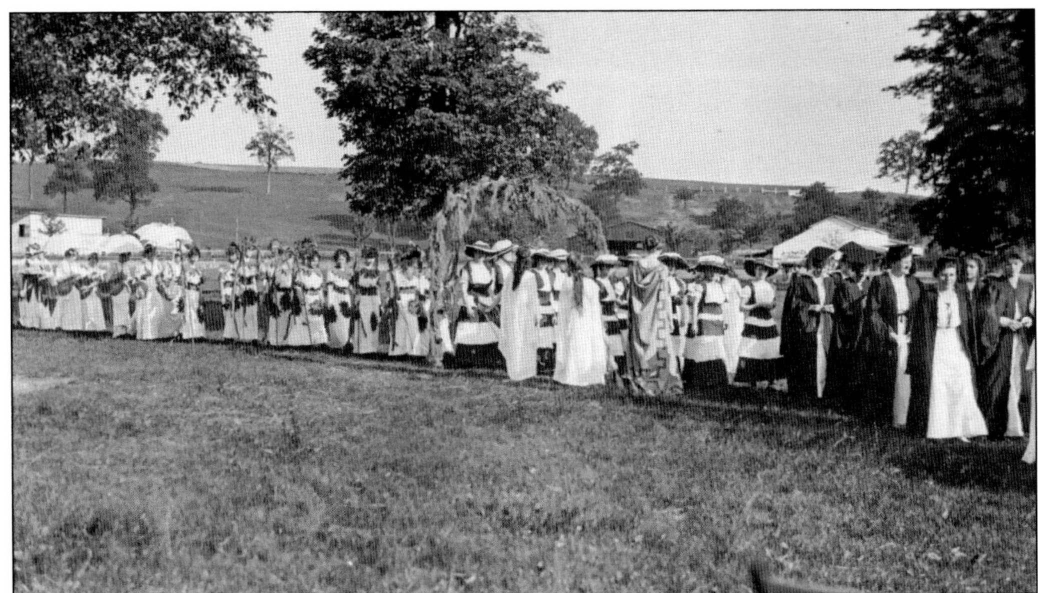

Several hundred Hamilton women and children, and female representatives from Miami University and the Oxford, Glendale, and Western Colleges gathered on June 5, 1915, at the Butler County Fairgrounds to celebrate the YWCA, its members, and their local, national, and global work. The Ministering of the Gift Pageant was reported as quite the spectacle to behold. Brightly colored costumes, music, singing, dancing, and games were the order of the day.

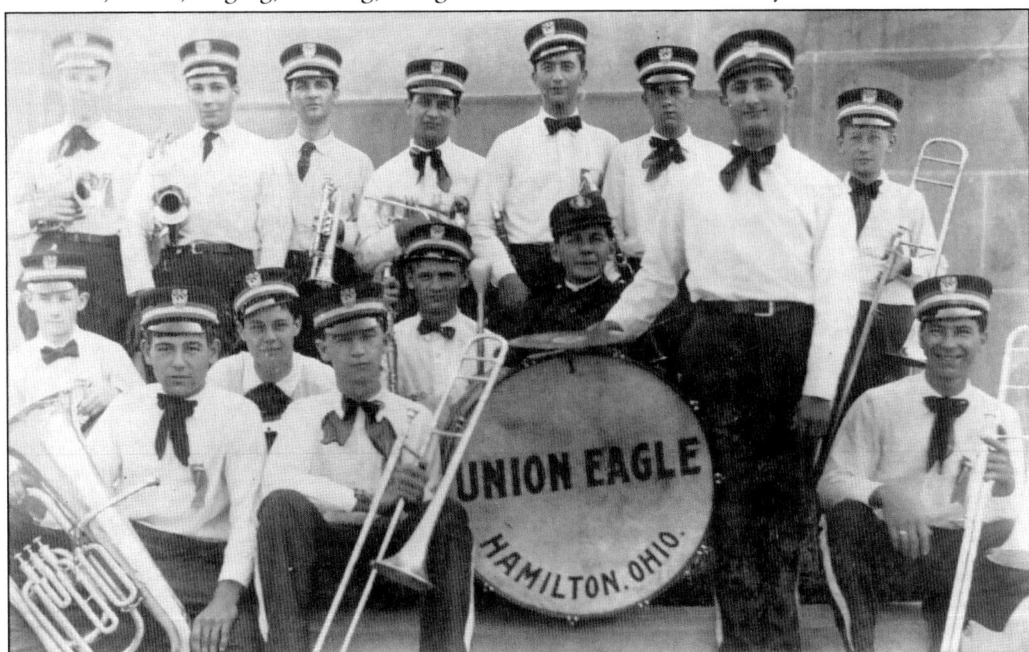

The Union Eagle had originally started out as a drum corps, but by the mid-1900s, the group had become a band. Composed of young businessmen and skilled laborers from throughout the city, the group was headquartered with the Butler County Cycle Club in rooms located in the Frechtling Block on High Street. The band was a staple at local parades but was "glad to play any and all occasions."

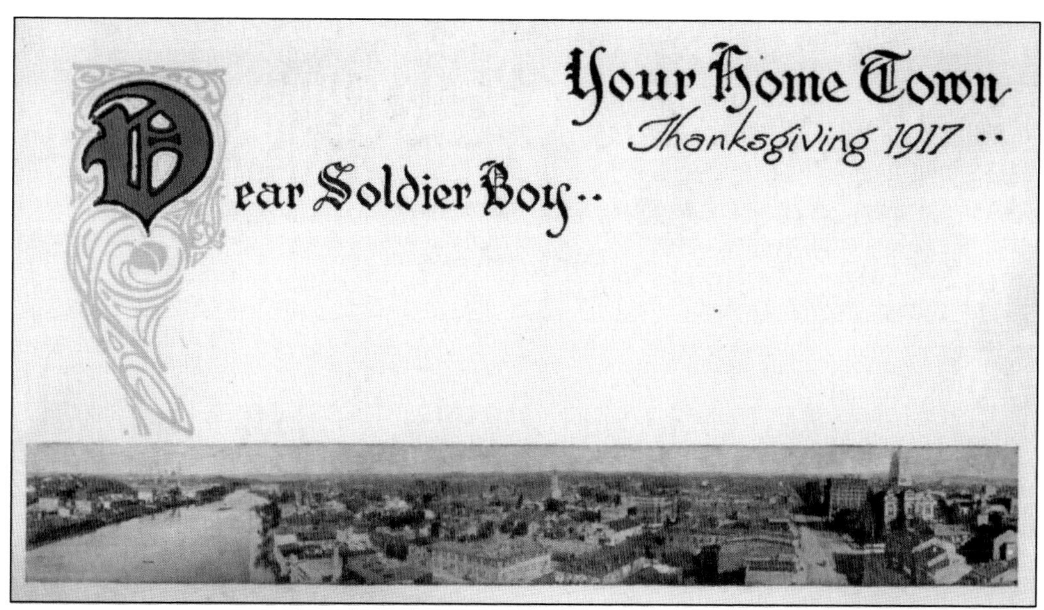

Hamilton sent nearly 1,000 of its young men overseas to fight in World War I, and 65 made the ultimate sacrifice. One such soldier to leave Hamilton and serve was Leroy McNeal of Company E, 330th Infantry. He was the son of Elisabeth McNeal and grew up on Stephens Street east of the J. Rupp & Sons slaughterhouse. McNeal enlisted on May 28, 1917, at the age of 29. Local leaders initiated a morale program, and in November 1917, postcards were sent to hometown boys serving in Europe. The panoramic view at the bottom of the card above appears to have been taken from the top of the Soldiers, Sailors and Pioneers Monument.

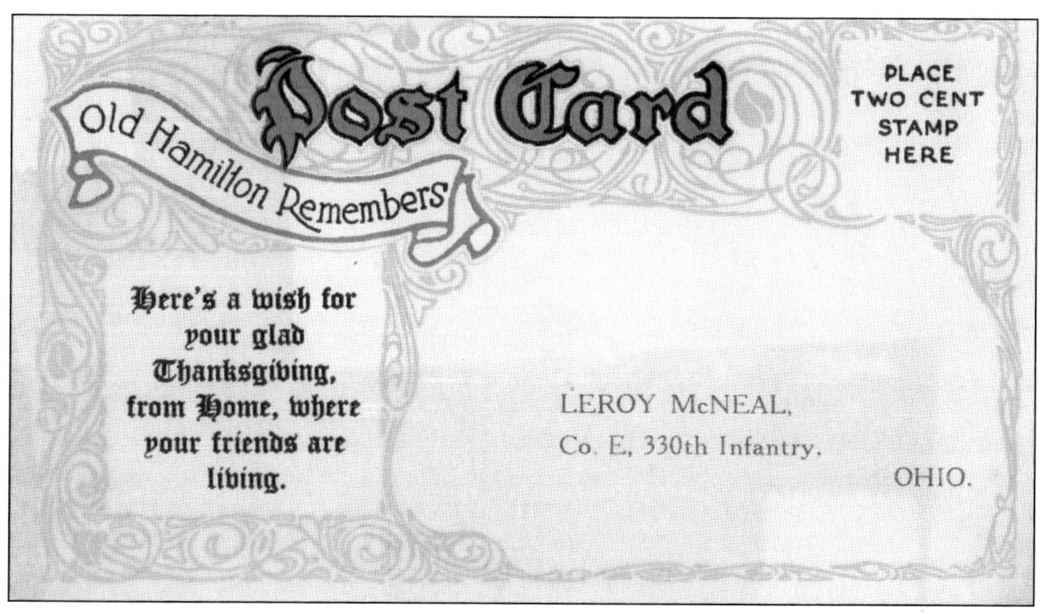

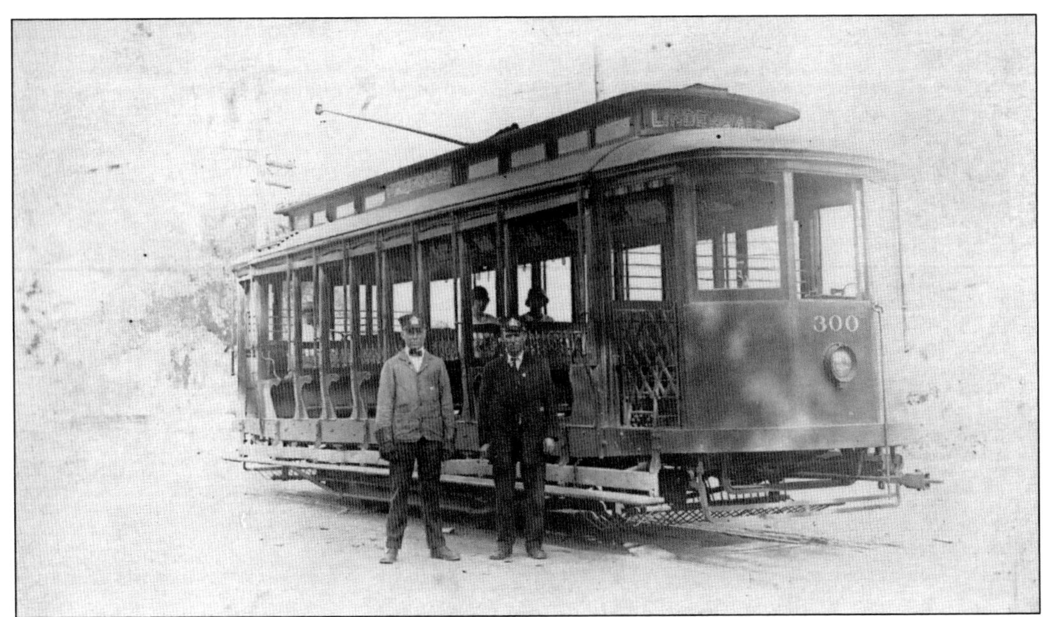

Interurban rail travel appeared in Hamilton in the 1890s, and by 1902, the Cincinnati & Hamilton Street Railway Company ruled the local rails. In 1905, the company reorganized as the Ohio Traction Company, which operated until 1926. In 1907, The Ohio Electric Railway incorporated and absorbed 14 local interurban entities, including the Cincinnati & Hamilton Street Railway Company and the Cincinnati & Miami Valley Traction Company, which ran from Hamilton to Dayton. In 1918, the newly formed Cincinnati & Dayton Traction Company acquired the Cincinnati to Dayton rails and ran them until 1926 until the Cincinnati, Hamilton & Dayton Railway Company was formed, which later was absorbed by the Cincinnati & Lake Erie Railroad. These two views show typical Hamilton traction cars, which serviced the Lindenwald area. By 1939, buses had replaced the streetcars.

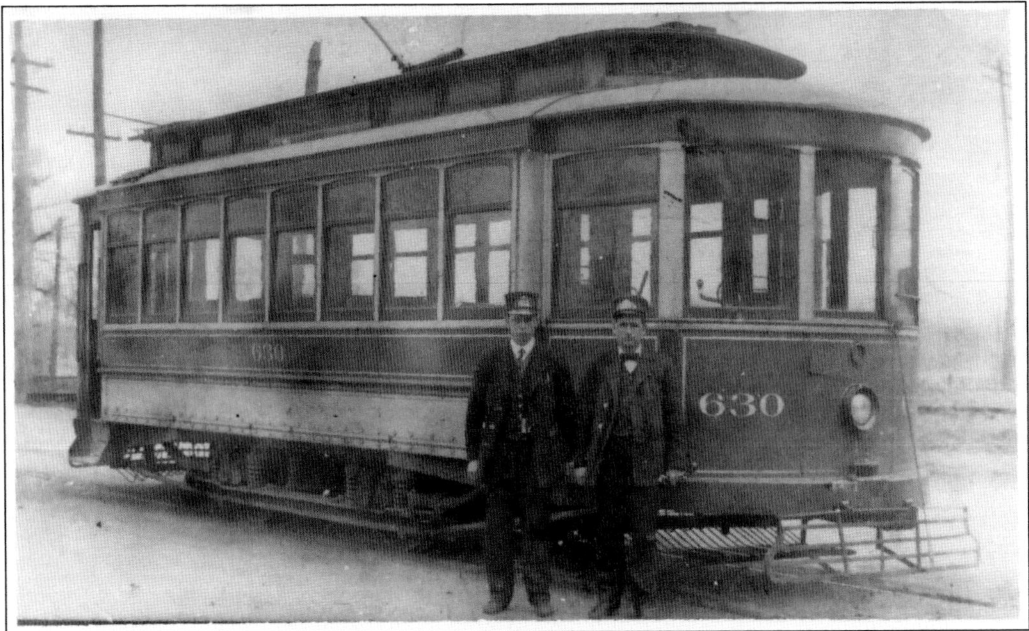

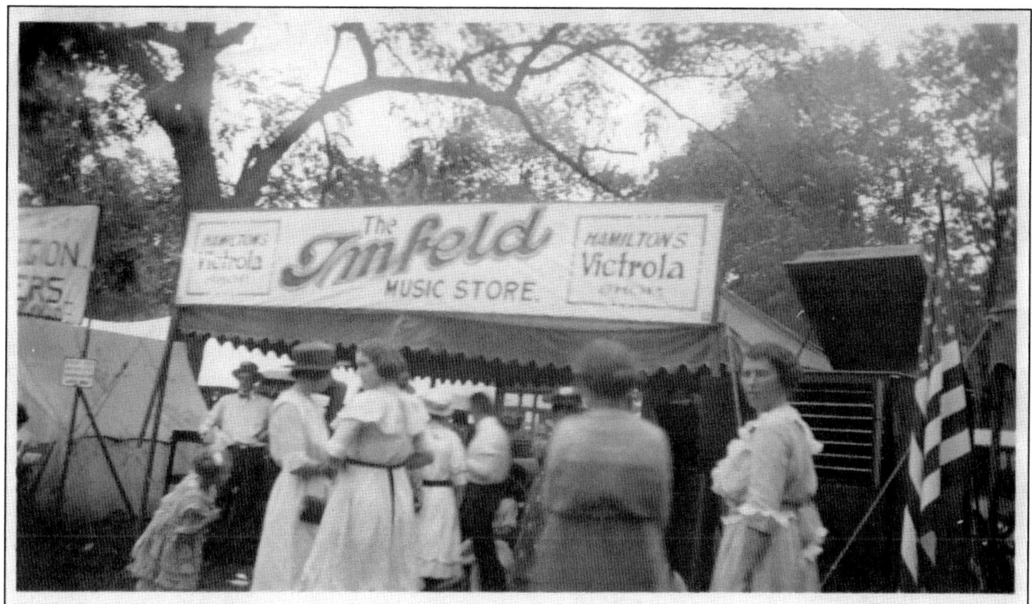

Ferd Imfeld began giving music lessons from his Dayton Street residence in 1901. Soon, his business expanded to include the sale of musical instruments, radios, phonographs, and even appliances. This view shows an Imfeld display tent, possibly at the Butler County Fairgrounds or Lindenwald Park, in the early 1910s. Note the huge Victrola display model (right).

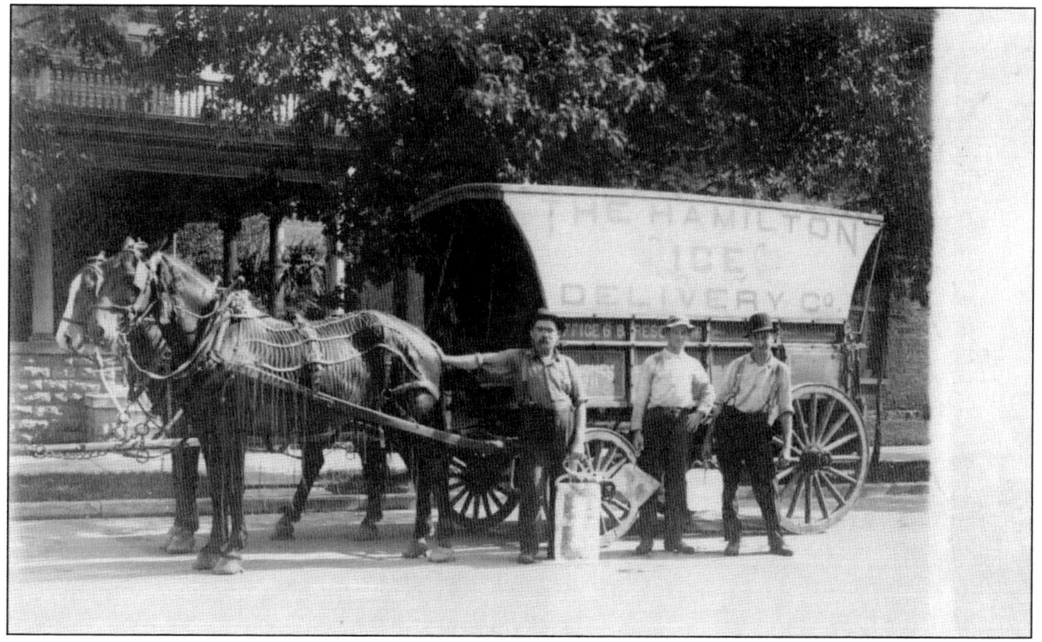

Located on the southwest corner of Sixth Street and Reservoir at the site of the old Campbell icehouses, the Hamilton Ice Delivery Company closed in May 1920. For decades, ice-delivery wagons, as seen here, were a familiar sight on streets throughout Hamilton. This card, taken prior to 1910, shows Charles Kirchner (left) with two unidentified coworkers delivering ice at 30¢ per 100 pounds.

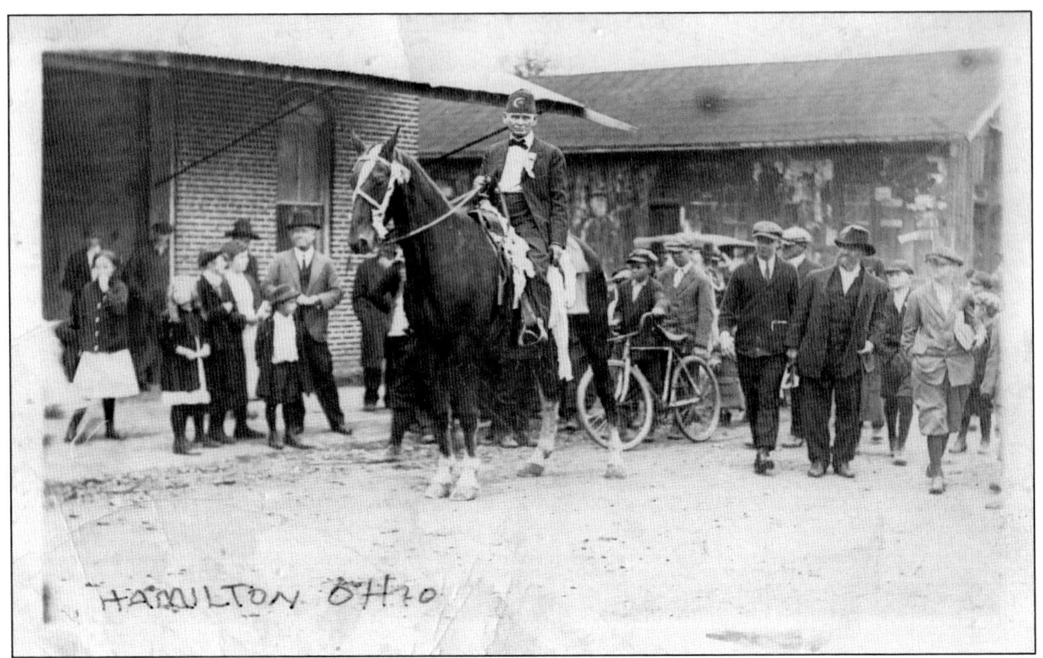

Taken before 1915, this view shows a member of the Dramatic Order of the Knights of Khorassan (DOKK) atop his horse for an unknown parade. The DOKK is an elite branch of the Knights of Pythias, but DOKK meetings, rituals, and initiations are different than typical K of P lodges. There was no DOKK temple in Hamilton, so local members traveled regularly to Cincinnati to participate in meetings and functions.

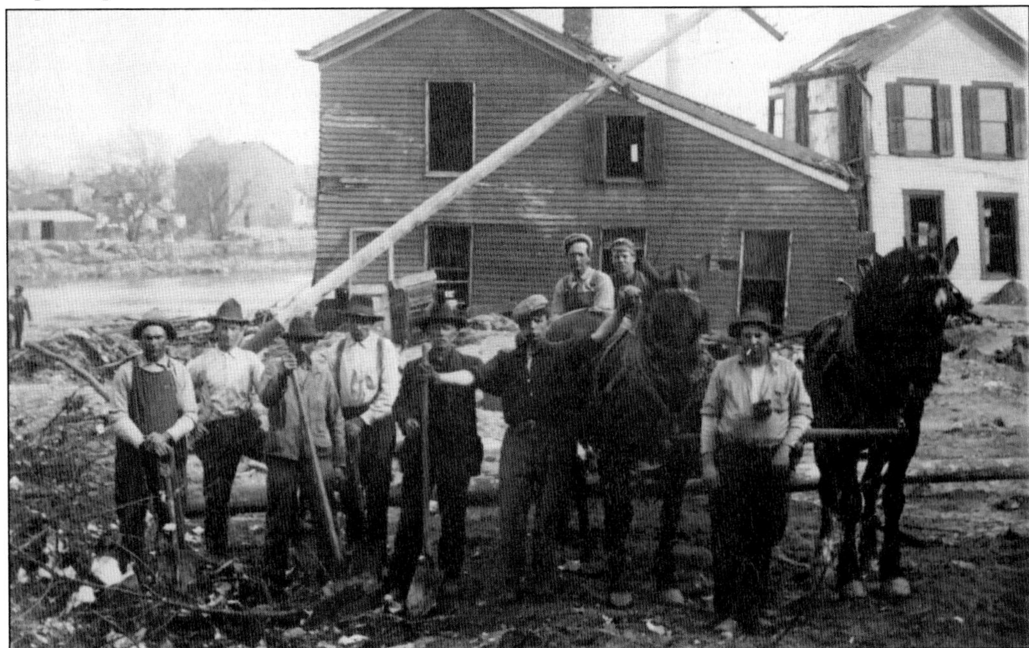

Taken just after the flood in 1913, this real-photo postcard shows a typical street-cleaning gang complete with shovels and a team of horses for the heavy moving. According to the caption on the back, these men are working at the corner of Ross Avenue and South A Street in Rossville.

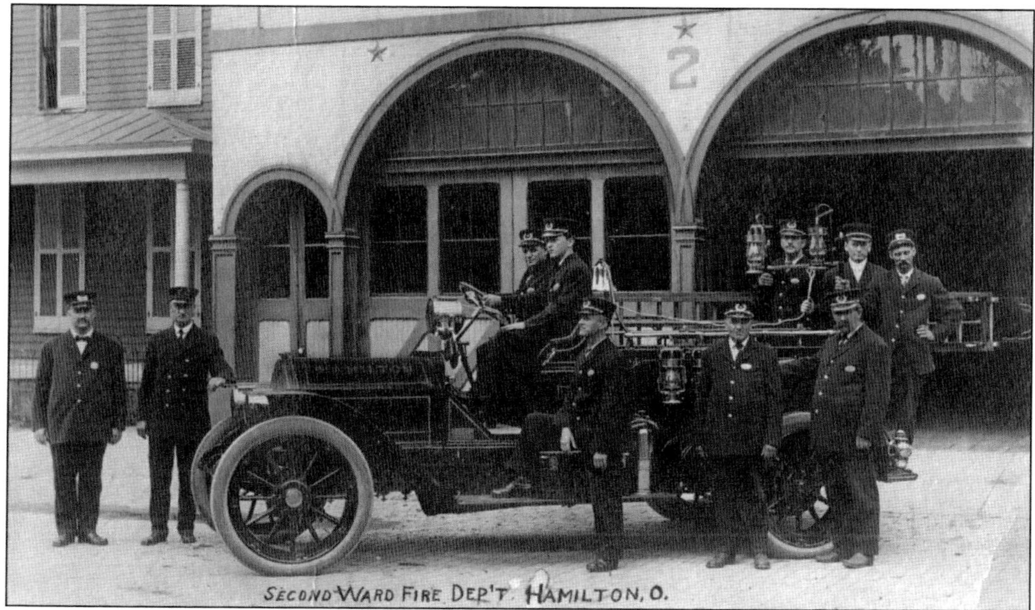

The men of Fire Company No. 2, located in Second Ward on South Third Street, proudly pose with their new motorized fire vehicle. The 1910 American LaFrance Type 5 truck was received by the company on July 26, 1911. Manufactured in Elmira, New York, the Type 5 was a rare vehicle. It was manufactured for one year, with a total of only 48 being produced.

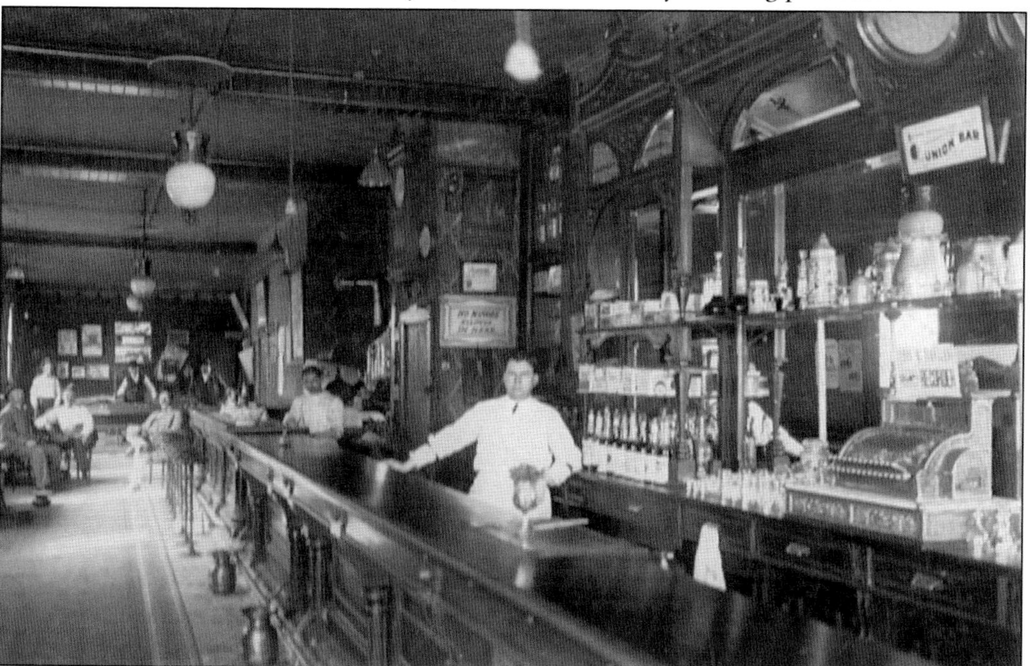

Dated 1905, this view shows the interior of Holzberger's Café, located on the northeast corner of High and Front Streets. The figure seated in the center with his hat on his knee is the proprietor, John A. Holzberger. The bartender (front right) is Lyman Williams, who would later gain fame as the owner of his own saloon, which would be the only Hamilton drinking establishment open on the last legal day before state Prohibition took effect on May 26, 1919.

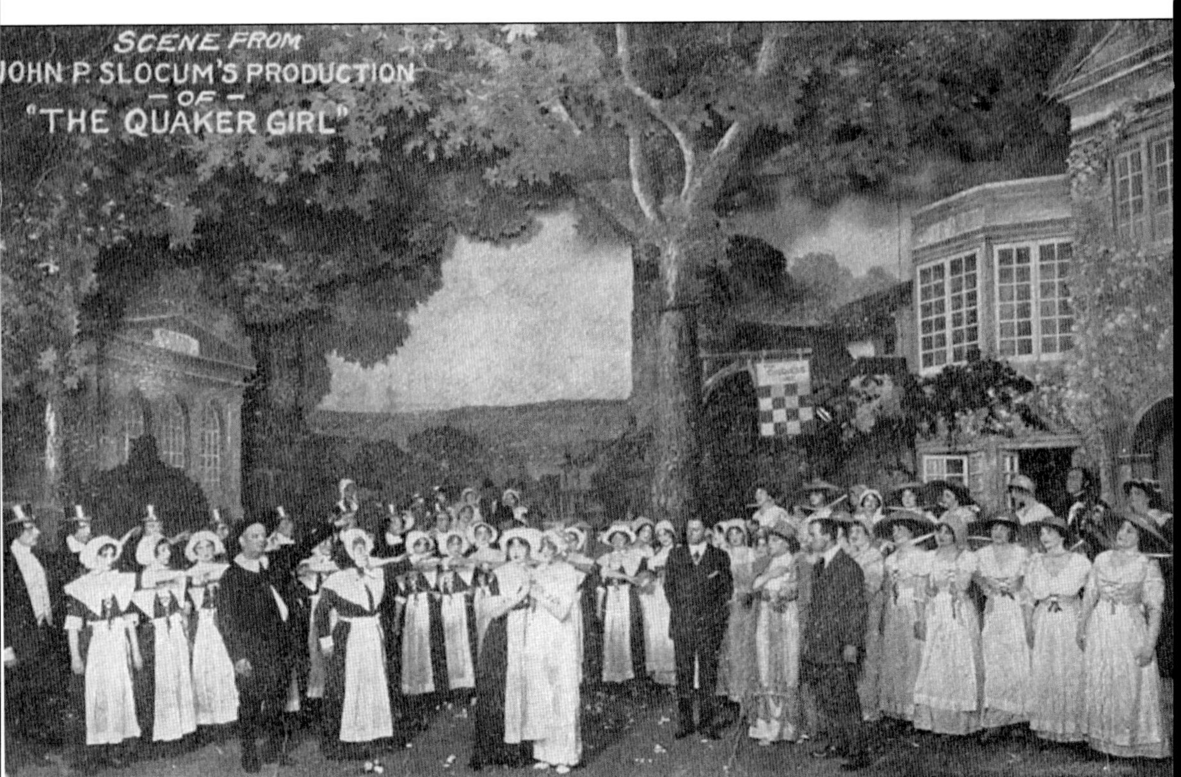

On Sunday, January 10, 1915, the Jefferson Theatre on South Second Street hosted one of the most popular musical comedies of the day. Coming off its popular run in London and on Broadway, *The Quaker Girl* made its way to Hamilton for a one-night-only performance, starring Katherine Murray. Ticket prices ranged from 25¢ to $1.50. A bouquet of roses to throw onto the stage after the performance could be purchased for $2. The following day, newspaper reports said that the play "rocked" the Jefferson with applause and laughter.

Bibliography

Benzing, Esther R. *Historical Gleanings*. Fairfield, OH: self-published, 1976.

Bauer, Cheryl, and Randy McNutt. *Butler County*. Charleston, SC: Arcadia Publishing, 2006.

Blount, Jim. *The 1900s: 100 Years in the History of Butler County*. Hamilton, OH: Past/Present/Press, 2000.

Blount, Jim. *Flood: Butler County's Greatest Weather Disaster – March 1913*. Hamilton, OH: Past/Present/Press, 2002.

Butler County: Atlas and Pictorial Review. Hamilton, OH: Republican Publishing Company, 1914.

County of Butler, Ohio: An Imperial Atlas and Art Folio. Richmond, IN: Rerick Brothers Topographers and Publishers, 1895.

Crout, George C. *Butler County – An Illustrated History*. Woodland Hills, CA: Windsor Publications Inc., 1984.

McClung, D.W. *The Centennial Anniversary of the City of Hamilton, Ohio*. Cincinnati, OH: Lawrence Printing and Publishing Company, 1892.

Memoirs of the Miami Valley, Volume II. Chicago, IL: Robert O. Law Company, 1919.

Piland, Richard N. *Hamilton's Historic Public Schools 1850–2010*. Fairfield, OH: Personalized Research, 2011.

Schwartz, James. *Hamilton, Ohio: Its Architecture and History*. Hamilton, OH: Hamilton City Planning Department, 1986.

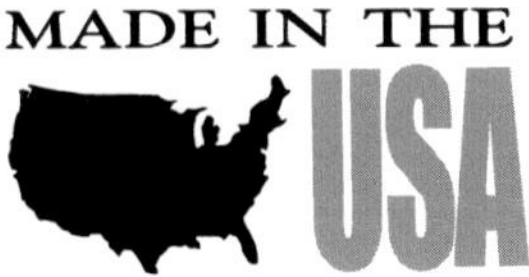

MADE IN THE
USA